Hague Yearbook of International Law
Annuaire de La Haye de droit international

Hague Yearbook of International Law 2019

Editor-in-Chief

Prof. Jure Vidmar

Vice-Editor-in-Chief

Dr. Ruth A. Kok

Editorial Board
Dr. Julian Arato, Dr. Nikos Lavranos, Dr. Daniel Peat, Dr. Daniel Rietiker

Editorial Assistant
Sarah Thin

Email address
hagueyearbook@gmail.com

Advisory Board
Serge Brammertz (*Prosecutor of the International Criminal Tribunal for the Former Yugoslavia (ICTY)*) – Antônio Cançado Trindade (*Judge at the International Court of Justice (ICJ)*) – Jacomijn J. van Haersolte-van Hof (*Advocate (advocaat) at HaersolteHof and arbitrator (The Netherlands)*) – Peter Hilpold (*University Professor at Innsbruck University (Austria)*) – Bruno Simma ((*former*) *Judge at the ICJ*) – Olivia Swaak-Goldman ((*former*) *Head International Relations Task Force, Office of the Prosecutor, International Criminal Court (ICC)*)

The titles published in this series are listed at *brill.com/aaaa*

HAGUE YEARBOOK OF INTERNATIONAL LAW

ANNUAIRE DE LA HAYE DE DROIT INTERNATIONAL

VOLUME 32

2019

Edited by

Jure Vidmar, Ruth Kok *et al.*

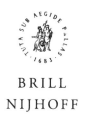

BRILL
NIJHOFF

LEIDEN | BOSTON

Typeface for the Latin, Greek, and Cyrillic scripts: "Brill". See and download: brill.com/brill-typeface.

ISSN 0167-6660
ISBN 978-90-04-50796-8 (hardback)
ISBN 978-90-04-50797-5 (e-book)

Copyright 2021 by Koninklijke Brill NV, Leiden, The Netherlands.
Koninklijke Brill NV incorporates the imprints Brill, Brill Nijhoff, Brill Hotei, Brill Schöningh, Brill Fink, Brill mentis, Vandenhoeck & Ruprecht, Böhlau Verlag and V&R Unipress.
All rights reserved. No part of this publication may be reproduced, translated, stored in a retrieval system, or transmitted in any form or by any means, electronic, mechanical, photocopying, recording or otherwise, without prior written permission from the publisher. Requests for re-use and/or translations must be addressed to Koninklijke Brill NV via brill.com or copyright.com.

This book is printed on acid-free paper and produced in a sustainable manner.

Contents

Editorial   VII
     Jure Vidmar

1 The Structural Crack of the International Legal System: What
Happens with Unattributed Conduct?   1
     Jure Vidmar

2 De Facto Independent Regimes and Overarching Human
Rights Duties   31
     Amrei Müller

3 The 'Unwilling or Unable' Doctrine Unmasked: A Case Study
of ISIL in Syria   69
     Sarah McGibbon

4 Topoi of Ambiguity: WTO Membership without Statehood:
The Case of Separate Customs Territories   103
     Marios C. Iacovides

5 International Courts and Contested Statehood: The ICJ and
ICC in Palestine   135
     Alice Panepinto

6 Greening the Economy of Armed Conflict: Natural Resource
Exploitation by Armed Groups and Their Engagement with
Environmental Protection   175
     Daniëlla Dam-de Jong

7 Armed Groups and Emergent States: Legal and Pragmatic
Approaches to Filling the Gaps in International Law   209
     Tom Hadden

Editorial

This volume is thematically dedicated to international legal obligations of territorial entities without statehood. The term non-state actors is deliberately omitted as it is too broad and too vague for the analytical purposes of this topic. The focus is on those entities that exercise effective territorial control without statehood and/or have acquired a certain non-state territorial legal status under international law. Under the existing rules of public international law, only states can be parties to international treaties and, arguably, it is also only states that are bound by the rules of customary international law. Yet, there is a clear tendency in international politics to impose certain international legal obligations also on certain non-state territorial entities. Sometimes this is done quite formally. Some specialized international legal regimes have emerged that give certain non-states the treaty-making capacity for some functional purposes.

A very good example is the legal regime of the World Trade Organization (WTO) which includes separate customs unions, such as the European Union, Hong Kong, Macao and Taiwan. In some other areas of international law, certain non-state entities have always had a degree of functional legal capacity and thus international legal obligations. A good example are non-state armed groups in non-international armed conflict under international humanitarian law. It thus appears that international law has always accepted that certain non-states can have international legal obligations. The nature and scope of their legal obligations is not general, however. It is functionally determined and depends on the level of international legal capacity of the non-state in question. For example, Hong Kong may have been given a degree of international legal capacity to have international legal obligations under WTO law, but that does not give it general international legal capacity under public international law.

This project was initiated as a subproject of Dr Amrei Müller's Leverhulme Early Career Fellowship (ECF-2016-666) "Healthcare in conflict: Do armed groups have obligations and responsibilities?", embedded at Queen's University Belfast, School of Law, Health & Human Rights Unit. The papers in this volume look at the problem more broadly and set three objectives: (i) analyse the conceptual problems of non-state conduct on the international plane and the gaps in international legal regulation; (ii) investigate how certain specialized international legal regimes have solved this general conceptual problem by giving a degree of functional international legal capacity to certain non-states; and (iii) expose the structural inadequacy of international legal doctrine when international law has to accommodate the consequences of non-state conduct (e.g. an armed attack on a state by a non-state).

The volume starts with a systemic overview by Jure Vidmar who argues that attribution plays a central role in accommodating non-state conduct within the international legal system, yet the concept of attribution is still surrounded by a great deal of uncertainty. Amrei Müller continues with a conceptual analysis of human rights obligations pertaining to non-states that exercise a degree of territorial control and independence. Such entities often adopt international human rights obligations in their own constitutional frameworks. International human rights law may thus remain inapplicable as international law, but it does become a part of domestic law.

Sarah McGibbon analyses the problem of self-defence against non-states which may exercise a degree of territorial control *de facto*, but not in the sense of international law. To address the problem, the concept of 'unwilling or unable' states has been developed which is nothing other than attribution by omission to the territorial state. Marios Iacovides demonstrates on the WTO example that international legal capacity, and thus also international legal obligations, do not need to be state-centric in nature. They can be functionally defined. Daniëlla Dam-de Jong addresses the problem of natural sources exploitation by armed groups and environmental protection in armed conflict. She demonstrates that armed groups as such rarely subscribe themselves to respecting certain environmental standards, but this can be quite different with those groups that establish effective territorial control and aspire to achieving statehood and international recognition. The volume is concluded by Tom Hadden's article which addresses the problems in international legal regulation of armed groups in emergent states. International law appears to protect territorial status quo and the existing state boundaries. Yet, a look at old maps suggests that boundaries do change, and indeed quite frequently and profoundly so. Is there a pragmatic solution to reconcile the law of statehood with (armed) struggles for territorial readjustments and practical reality which suggests that such readjustments are more frequent than international legal doctrine is willing to acknowledge?

Professor Jure Vidmar
Chair of Public International Law, Maastricht University
Member of the Permanent Court of Arbitration, The Hague
Editor-in-Chief, Hague Yearbook of International Law

1 The Structural Crack of the International Legal System

What Happens with Unattributed Conduct?

Jure Vidmar*

Abstract

A great deal of international conduct escapes international legal regulation. This is because international law systematically only regulates relations between states. While other actors may have certain international obligations, these are not general in nature and are limited by the functional purpose of such actors. At the same time, the threshold for attribution of non-state conduct to states remains rather demanding. Non-state conduct that is not attributed to a state in most circumstances cannot constitute an internationally wrongful act. Although international legal doctrine has been reluctant to modify the general attribution test based on the ICJ's *Nicaragua* judgment, state practice indicates that new attribution standards have been silently developed, at least where omissions are concerned. While actions are generally subjected to a high attribution bar, omissions have sometimes been subjected to the concept of strict liability. This leads to a clear imbalance and even lack of legal certainty. It is doctrinally unclear which, if any, international legal obligations even carry strict liability. At present, it seems that such a determination is political rather than legal in nature. This article thus demonstrates that the current attribution theory in international law is in need of systemic change. Otherwise, international law risks a situation where states will increasingly resort to political criteria to determine when conduct is attributable to a certain state.

Keywords

Attribution – state responsibility – non-state groups – international legal capacity – unattributed conduct

---

* Professor of Public International Law, Maastricht University, the Netherlands. Member of the Permanent Court of Arbitration, The Hague.

1   Introduction

What is the international legal capacity of the so-called Islamic State (henceforth: Daesh)? Do states have the right to self-defence against Daesh? Was the downing of MH17 an internationally wrongful act and who is responsible for it? What is the legal status of Kosovo and what is the legal status of Taiwan? Does Serbia need to respect Kosovo's territorial integrity and China that of Taiwan? Whose bilateral investment treaties apply in the territory of Crimea – Ukrainian or Russian? Are non-state armed groups bound by any human rights obligations in non-international armed conflict?

This article argues that international law has a major structural flaw: a limited international legal capacity of non-states and a high threshold for attribution of non-state conduct to states. As a result, a great deal of international conduct either remains unregulated, or does not lead to any legal consequences. This creates problems in the practical application of international law and its ability to deal with a range of concrete challenges in the international community.

Legal scholarship has attempted to address these problems within the substantive subfields of international legal regulation, such as the law on the use of force, the law of statehood, international investment law, international human rights law, and international humanitarian law, among others. Several doctrines have been proposed for these purposes, including: human rights obligations for various non-state actors;[1] self-defence against non-state actors;[2] a degree of statehood for certain *de facto* territorial regimes;[3] the use of force in the territories of the so-called unwilling or unable states;[4] and different effective control tests that have

---

1   For an overview see Jean d'Aspremont, 'Non-State Actors in International Law: Oscillating between Concepts and Dynamics' in Jean d'Aspremont (ed), *Participants in the International Legal System* (Routledge 2011). William Worster, 'Relative International Legal Personality of Non-State Actors' (2016) 42 Brooklyn Journal of International Law 207.

2   For an overview see Kimberley Trapp, 'Can Non-State Actors Mount an Armed Attack?' in Marc Weller (ed), *The Oxford Handbook on the Use of Force* (OUP 2015).

3   See William Worster, 'Functional Statehood in Contemporary International Law' (unpublished 2016), available at <https://papers.ssrn.com/sol3/papers.cfm?abstract_id=2807156>.

4   Elena Chachko and Ashley Deeks, 'Who is on Board with "Unwilling or Unable"?' (*Lawfare*, 10 October 2016) <https://www.lawfareblog.com/who-board-unwilling-or-unable> accessed 25 May 2021.

been developed across the subfields of international legal regulation.[5] But these doctrines have only added more confusion to the international legal system.

The central proposition of this article is that such conceptual shortcomings of international legal regulation do not originate in the substantive subfields of international law. Kosovo and Taiwan are not problems of the law of statehood; self-defence against Daesh is not a problem of the law on the use of force; bilateral investment treaties in Crimea are not a problem of investment law. These are all symptoms of a larger conceptual problem: a lack of theoretical clarity on what international law can and cannot regulate. Doctrinal work has thus far attempted to supress certain symptoms without addressing the causes which, in turn, has led to a range of new problems.

This article seeks to solve the underlying conceptual problem rather than suppress the symptoms. The aim is to outline the theoretical shortcomings of the international legal system and discuss how international law could move toward a more inclusive legal order. This will be done in three steps: (i) international legal capacity of the subjects in the international legal system; (ii) attribution and horizontal obligations between these subjects; and (iii) the issue of vertical relations between the international community and international legal persons.

In his seminal work *The Concept of Law*, HLA Hart argued that international law was a simple set of primary rules without any systemic coherence significant for municipal legal orders.[6] The Report of the Study Group of the United Nations (UN) International Law Commission (ILC) on Fragmentation of International Law came to a similar conclusion: 'The international legal system has never enjoyed the kind of coherence that may have characterized the legal orders of States.'[7]

The lack of systemic coherence can lead to problems in the practical application of the rules of international law. As the Study Group of the ILC further observed:

---

5   See Marko Milanovic, 'Special Rules of Attribution of Conduct in International Law' (2020) 96 International Law Studies 295.

6   HLA Hart, *The Concept of Law* (3rd edn, OUP 2012) chapter 10.

7   See UNGA, 'Report of the Study Group of the International Law Commission on Fragmentation of International Law: Difficulties Arising From the Diversification and Expansion of International Law' (13 April 2006) UN Doc A/CN.4/L.682 ["Fragmentation Report"] para. 493.

> [T]he emergence of conflicting rules and overlapping legal regimes will undoubtedly create problems of coordination at the international level. But ... no homogenous, hierarchical meta-system is realistically available to do away with such problems. International law will need to operate within an area where the demands of coherence and reasonable pluralism will point in different directions.[8]

International legal scholarship has tried to overcome the lack of systemic coherence by introducing certain concepts and principles from municipal legal systems. The project on international constitutionalism has been particularly prominent in this regard. Its proponents have indeed tried to conceptualise international law as a constitutionalised 'homogenous, hierarchical meta-system.'[9] But critics have pointed out that any instances of a hierarchy of norms in international law are merely perceived, while the practical application of legal norms remains non-hierarchical in nature.[10] This line of thought originates in the Hartian description of international law as a *non*-system, and then seeks to achieve at least some systemic coherence through the development of the so-called conflict rules.[11] These are the rules that resolve conflicts between different norms and sub-regimes of the international legal order.

This article challenges the assumption that no homogenous meta-system is available to ensure a systemic coherence of the international legal order. Such a meta-system need not, however, be hierarchical in nature; neither does the overarching systemic framework need to be constitutionalism or constitutional theory. This article demonstrates that international legal order lacks its *own* legal and political theory which would coherently explain how international law operates as a system. International law is in essence a system of private law obligations between states with some very rudimentary systemic public law elements. The nature and function of these elements should not be exaggerated.

---

8   *Ibid.*

9   *Ibid.* Compare also Erika de Wet, 'The International Constitutional Order' (2006) 55 International and Comparative Law Quarterly 51; Jan Klabbers, Anne Peters and Geir Ulfstein, *The Constitutionalization of International Law* (OUP 2009).

10   See Erika de Wet, 'Paradigmen in der internationalen Praxis: Normenhierarchie versus systemische Integration' in Bardo Fassbender (ed), *Paradigmen im internationalen Recht: Implikationen der Weltfinanzkrise für das internationale Recht: mit But Diskussion* (Müller 2012) 81; Nico Krisch, *Beyond Constitutionalism: The Pluralist Structure of Postnational Law* (OUP 2010).

11   See Fragmentation Report (note 7) 249–256.

2 International Legal Capacity and Subjects in the International Legal System

This chapter considers the international legal capacity for law-making and law-breaking. In other words, it asks who creates international legal obligations and who can breach these obligations. It is argued that public international law continues to operate within an eminent private law paradigm.

2.1 Law-making Capacity

International law is a legal system derived from states. This is not to say that actors other than states do not exist in this system.[12] But states are those actors which have full international legal capacity. This also follows from the formal sources of law: it is states which conclude international treaties in the sense of the Vienna Convention of the Law of Treaties (VCLT);[13] and it is state practice, combined with *opinio juris* (again derived from states) which form customary international law.[14]

International treaties can be of various kinds. They can be bilateral, multilateral or indeed so multilateral that they are virtually universal. They can regulate something quite technical and specific, such as construction of a system of locks on a river in the border area between two states,[15] or establish something as complex as the United Nations (UN),[16] or the European Union (EU).[17] Treaties between states can thus create international organisations and other legal creatures with their own organs which can also make autonomous decisions,[18] at least to some extent, and some more than others – depending on what states have agreed to in the underlying treaty. In some instances, we may ask ourselves if states do not sometimes create a Frankenstein over whom they lose control.[19]

---

12 *Ibid.*

13 Vienna Convention on the Law of Treaties (1969) 1155 UNTS 332 ("VCLT") art 1.

14 See *Military and Paramilitary Activities in and against Nicaragua (Nicaragua v United States of America)*, Merits ["*Nicaragua* case"] [1986] ICJ Rep 14, para. 184.

15 See, e.g., the *Case Concerning the Gabčíkovo-Nagymaros Project (Hungary v Slovakia)* [1997] ICJ Rep 7 ["*Gabčíkovo-Nagymaros* case"], para. 15.

16 Charter of the United Nations (1945) 1 UNTS XVI ["UN Charter"].

17 Consolidated Version of the Treaty on the European Union [2008] OJ C115/13 ["TEU"].

18 See, e.g., UN Charter (note 16) arts 39-42 for legally binding measures of UN Security Council; and TEU (*ibid.*) arts 13-22 for the EU institutional arrangement.

19 See Andrew Guzman, 'International Organizations and the Frankenstein Problem' (2013) 24 EJIL 999, 1000, arguing that 'States sometimes create their own form

When the UN Security Council adopts a legally-binding resolution, its binding nature is anchored in Chapter VII of the UN Charter which is an international treaty. Hence, even the law-making powers of the UN can be traced back to states, or more specifically, to the very specific treaty which has been ratified by nearly all states in the world.[20] At the same time, it is a selection of states who vote in the Security Council; this is not an autonomous organ devoid of state influence.[21] The General Assembly resolutions are not legally binding, but they may be relevant for the identification of customary international law.[22] And it is again states who vote in the General Assembly. In a sense, this body may be, *inter alia*, seen as a provider of secretarial services for the identification of international custom. It is always difficult to identify what states believe for the purposes of *opinio juris*, but the General Assembly is probably the most prominent place where states go on the record and do so collectively.

In terms of legal capacity, international law-*making* appears to be a prerogative of states, although sometimes this happens indirectly and through international organisations.[23] How about law-*breaking*? Is this also only a prerogative of states? Here, we come to the question of capacity to commit an internationally wrongful act. In other words, can only an act of state be an internationally wrongful act; and what is an act of state?

2.2   *The Capacity for Law*-breaking

In the *Reparations Advisory Opinion*, the International Court of Justice (ICJ) acknowledged that rights and duties under international law were not only inherent in states but also in international organisations.[24] The Court importantly added that this does not mean that the level of these rights and duties is the same as that of states, but that even international organisations have international legal capacity for the purposes of their

---

of artificial life, the international organization (IO). Dr Frankenstein created his monster in an attempt to improve on a world populated only by humans. States create IOs with the hope of enhancing international cooperation beyond what can be achieved by states alone. Like Frankenstein's monster, IOs created by states may behave differently from the way they are expected to. There is always a risk that an IO will impact the system in ways that harm, rather than help, the interests of states. An IO can become a monster.'

20   For a list of UN member states see: http://www.un.org/en/member-states.

21   UN Charter (note 16) arts 23-32.

22   See the *Nicaragua case* (note 14) para. 188.

23   *Ibid.*

24   *Reparation for Injuries Suffered in the Service of the United Nations (Advisory Opinion)* [1949] ICJ Rep 174.

THE STRUCTURAL CRACK OF THE INTERNATIONAL LEGAL SYSTEM

functioning. The ICJ reasoned: 'The subjects of law in any legal system are not necessarily identical in their nature or in the extent of their rights, and their nature depends upon the needs of the community.'[25] After establishing that the UN had international personality, the Court continued:

> That is not the same thing as saying that it is a State, which it certainly is not, or that its legal personality and rights and duties are the same as those of a State. Still less is it the same thing as saying that it is "a super-State", whatever that expression may mean. It does not even imply that all its rights and duties must be upon the international plane, any more than all the rights and duties of a State must be upon that plane. What it does mean is that it is a subject of international law and capable of possessing international rights and duties, and that it has capacity to maintain its rights by bringing international claims.[26]

The rise of international human rights law also gives international legal subjectivity to individuals,[27] as does international refugee law,[28] while international criminal law sanctions individuals as perpetrators of war crimes and crimes against humanity.[29] But we should not forget that even in these instances we still have in the background treaties concluded by states, as well as customary international law which is shaped and formed by states.[30] Moreover, actors such as international organisations in principle can enter into international treaties and thus create interna-

---

25 *Ibid.* at 8.

26 *Ibid.* at 9.

27 Robert McCorquodale, 'An Inclusive International Legal System' (2004) 17 Leiden Journal of International Law 477.

28 Convention Relation to the Status of Refugees (1951) 189 UNTS 137, art 1.

29 Trial of the Major War Criminals before the International Military Tribunal, vol.1 (Judgment) (Nurnberg 1947) at 223, recognising that '[c]rimes against international law are committed by men, not by abstract entities, and only by punishing individuals who commit such crimes can the provision of international law be enforced.'

30 See the Rome Statute of the International Criminal Court (1998) 2187 UNTS 38544 ["Rome Statute"] which has been ratified by 123 *states*. Article 5 of this international *treaty* defines war crimes, crimes against humanity and genocide as crimes for which the Court can – subject to some other conditions – exercise its jurisdiction over individuals.

tional legal obligations.[31] But their treaty-making capacity is limited by their functional purposes and international organisations are in practice not bound by very many international legal obligations.

Municipal legal systems generally distinguish between human beings and corporations who have legal capacity for different purposes, much in line with what the ICJ pronounced in the *Reparations Advisory Opinion*. But then we certainly have other actors involved, such as animals. A range of legal rules protect them against animal cruelty and regulate hunting. On the other hand, legal rules also regulate liability when animals cause harm.[32] This of course does not mean that a shark would be charged with the crime of murder and go to jail for killing a surfer; or that a bear would be charged with animal cruelty and be liable for damages if it attacks your cattle when looking for food.

Although animals enjoy a level of protection in our human legal systems, their legal capacity is not such that they could be held liable for breaching human laws.[33] In some circumstances it may be, however, that humans or even corporations, who do have such capacity, would be liable for the conduct of animals.[34] Factual harm caused by an animal may well be crime or tort in law.[35] Not that of a shark or bear, of course; we will need to *attribute* that conduct to someone with such level of legal personality to even have the capacity to commit a crime, or be legally liable under tort law.[36] In essence, in every legal system actors exist which are capable of causing *factual* harm and may even be capable of being harmed themselves, but do not have the legal capacity to be legally responsible for their own conduct. In the end their conduct will be wrongful only if an actor with an adequate level of legal capacity can be made liable for it. In other words, a certain conduct – however grave or damaging – will

---

31 See Jose Alvarez, *International Organizations as Law-Makers* (OUP 2006). See also Olivier Corten and Pierre Klein, 'Are Agreements between States and Non-State Entities Rooted in the International Legal Order?' in Enzo Cannizzaro (ed), *The Law of Treaties Beyond the Vienna Convention* (OUP 2011) 3.

32 In many legal systems, different kind of animals underlie the distinction between strict liability and negligence. For example, if your pet tiger causes harm, you will be held liable to matter how much precaution you took that this would not happen. This could be different if such harm were caused by your horse. See, e.g., Walter van Gerven, Jeremy Lever and Pierre Lauroche, *Tort Law* (Oxford, Hart, 2001) chapter 6.

33 *Ibid.*

34 *Ibid.*

35 *Ibid.*

36 See JR Spencer, 'Tortious Liability for Criminal Acts' in Matthew Dyson (ed), *Unravelling Tort and Crime* (CUP 2014) 304, 324.

only be wrongful if it can be *attributed* to a person with the right level of legal capacity to have obligations under the legal system in question.

3 Attribution and the Horizontal Relationship between Subjects

Thus far, it has been argued that the capacity to hold international legal obligations can be, in principle, stretched beyond states, but in practice very few direct non-state obligations exist under treaty or customary international law. In most circumstances, non-state conduct will need to be attributed to a state. This chapter consider how attribution works in international legal doctrine and seeks to untangle the knot of attribution and responsibility. While the attribution theories have been ascribed to the law of responsibility, notably through the inclusion in ARSIWA, the attribution rules can do more than merely determine who is responsible for an internationally wrongful act. Even the question of whether or not there has been an internationally wrongful act can depend on whether or not a certain conduct is attributable to a certain to state, or to any state. In this sense, the law of state responsibility is not only secondary in nature. It does not only regulate the consequences of a breach of a primary rule. It can also determine whether or not there has been a breach.

3.1 State Responsibility and the Primary/Secondary Dichotomy

The law of state responsibility is said to be secondary in nature because it regulates the consequences of a breach of legal obligation, while it does not determine whether or not there has been a breach of the underlying primary norm. As the ICJ has put it in the *Gabčíkovo/Nagymaros* case between Hungary and Slovakia:

> A determination of whether a convention is or is not in force, and whether it has or has not been properly suspended or denounced, is to be made pursuant to the law of treaties. On the other hand, an evaluation of the extent to which the suspension or denunciation of a convention, seen as incompatible with the law of treaties, involves the responsibility of the State which proceeded to it, is to be made under the law of state responsibility.[37]

---

37 The *Gabčíkovo-Nagymaros* case (note 15), para. 47.

This is a two-step approach. Wrongfulness is identified under the primary norm – in this case originating in treaty law – and once this has been established, the law of state responsibility is used to determine the consequences of wrongfulness. The problem is that this approach only works when the conduct can – by definition – only be an act of state. This was precisely the case in the factual circumstances of *Gabčíkovo/ Nagymaros*.

In order to suspend or denounce a treaty, the state needs to act through its organs.[38] It is inherent in the very concept of the act of treaty suspension that such conduct can only come from a state, otherwise this cannot be a treaty suspension. Not all international conduct is so straightforward. States do not only act through their organs in a sense of Article 4 of the Articles on Responsibility of States for Internationally Wrongful Acts (ARSIWA) which reads: '*The conduct* of *any State organ* shall be considered an *act of that State* under international law, whether the organ exercises legislative, executive, judicial or any other functions.'[39]

In a number of other situations, a certain conduct may or may not be an act of state, depending on the circumstances. Contrast Article 4 with Article 8 of ARSIWA: '*The conduct* of a *person or group* of persons shall be considered an *act of a State* under international law *if the person or group* of persons is in fact *acting on the instructions* of, *or under the direction or control* of, that State in carrying out the conduct.'[40]

This is much more complicated. Unlike in the *Gabčíkovo/Nagymaros* types of situations, in an Article 8 ARSIWA situation, we do not start with the assumption that the conduct at stake even was an act of state. We have conduct which is capable of being internationally wrongful when it can be attributable to a state. There is no internationally wrongful act until it can be proven that the actor responsible for it had the legal capacity to violate international law in general, and that it was bound by the particular rule in question.

In the much criticized *Tadić* judgment, the International Criminal Tribunal for the former Yugoslavia (ICTY) used the attribution rules from

---

38   International Law Commission, 'Articles on Responsibility of States for Internationally Wrongful Acts, with commentaries' (2001) ["ARSIWA"], published in International Law Commission, 'Report of the International Law Commission on the work of its fifty-third session' (23 April–1 June and 2 July–10 August 2001) UN Doc A/56/10; adopted by the UN General Assembly in UNGA Res 56/83 (28 January 2002) UN Doc A/RES/56/83, commentary to Article 2 para. 2.

39   *Ibid.* art 4 (emphases added).

40   *Ibid.* art 8 (emphases added).

THE STRUCTURAL CRACK OF THE INTERNATIONAL LEGAL SYSTEM 11

the law of state responsibility to determine whether the armed conflict in Bosnia-Herzegovina, which was *prima facie* of a non-international nature, had been internationalized by the involvement of a foreign state.[41] This distinction is crucial as quite different rules apply in different types of armed conflict: non-international armed conflict (NIAC) as opposed to international armed conflict (IAC).[42] To put it simply, the identification of the primary legal rules of armed conflict depended on whether or not certain acts of Bosnian Serbs could be attributed to what was then the Federal Republic of Yugoslavia (FRY).

As this was an ICTY case, it was about the international criminal responsibility of an individual. However, it was first necessary to establish what the applicable rules even were in that situation. In order to do so, the ICTY resorted to the attribution rules.[43] Criticism of this approach is based on a dogmatic distinction between the primary and secondary rules. The critics say that the secondary attribution rules should not have been applied before wrongfulness was determined under the primary rules[44] and also that state responsibility should have had no place in a case concerned with individual criminal responsibility.[45]

As Antonio Cassese subsequently argued: 'The ICTY admittedly had to establish in *Tadić* whether the armed conflict in Bosnia was internal or international. However, as no rules of international humanitarian law were of assistance for such determination, the Tribunal explicitly decided to rely upon international rules on state responsibility.'[46] Indeed, how else could the Tribunal determine whether or not a foreign state was involved enough that an internal conflict had become an international one to which quite different rules apply? One can believe that the attribution rules are secondary in nature, but if one interprets that secondary nature as sequential order, how exactly does one then identify the actors in a certain conduct and thus determine the applicable law – NIAC or IAC?

---

41   *Prosecutor v Duško Tadić* (Judgement) ICTY, IT-94-1-A, Appeals Chamber (15 July 1999) ["*Tadić* case"] para. 83-87.

42   *Ibid.* para. 83.

43   *Ibid.* paras. 99-114.

44   See, e.g., Marco Sassoli, 'The legal qualification of the conflict in the former Yugoslavia: double standards or new horizons for international humanitarian law?' in Sienho Yee and Wang Tieya (eds), *International law in the Post-Cold War World: Essays in Memory of Li Haopei* (Routledge 2001) 325.

45   Marko Milanovic, 'State Responsibility for Genocide' (2006) 17 EJIL 553, 585.

46   Antonio Cassese, 'The Nicaragua and Tadić Tests Revisited in Light of the ICJ Judgment on Genocide in Bosnia' (2007) 17 EJIL 649, 649.

The second alleged problem in *Tadić* is that state responsibility was conflated with individual criminal responsibility.[47] But a conflation of this kind in reality did not happen. Even with international criminal responsibility we still have states in the background, as individual crimes are derived from violations of international humanitarian law (IHL) – and in IHL, the identity of the actors determines the applicable law. If we start from the general principle of criminal law *nullum crimen nulla poena sine lege*; we indeed first need to know the applicable law; we need to identify *lex* before we can determine *crimen* and *poena*. How could the ICTY identify *lex* in *Tadić* without resorting to the rules of attribution? The attribution rules helped identify the type of armed conflict and thus the applicable law, and only then did it become clear which international crimes Duško Tadić could have committed. There is no conflation of individual criminal responsibility and state responsibility at stake in this case. It is simply that the attribution rules, which are attached to the law of state responsibility, identify the actors and thus also determine the applicable law. Only once this was clarified under general international law was the ICTY able to proceed with determining individual criminal responsibility.

In international law, we always end up coming back to states. States A and B may be parties to treaty X, states A and C may be parties to treaty Y and states B and C may be parties to treaty Z. In this system, the scope of legal obligations between states A and B is different than between states A and C, which is again different than that between states B and C. If conduct 1 is contrary to the obligations arising under treaty X, the question of whether or not there actually was a breach of international

---

47 See *Application of the Convention on the Prevention and Punishment of the Crime of Genocide (Bosnia and Herzegovina v Serbia and Montenegro)* (Judgment) [2007] ICJ Rep 43 , para. 403. Especially consider the following argument: '[T]he Court observes that the ICTY was not called upon in the *Tadić* case, nor is it in general called upon, to rule on questions of State responsibility, since its jurisdiction is criminal and extends over persons only. Thus, in that Judgment the Tribunal addressed an issue which was not indispensable for the exercise of its jurisdiction. As stated above, the Court attaches the utmost importance to the factual and legal findings made by the ICTY in ruling on the criminal liability of the accused before it and, in the present case, the Court takes fullest account of the ICTY's trial and appellate judgments dealing with the events underlying the dispute. The situation is not the same for positions adopted by the ICTY on issues of general international law which do not lie within the specific purview of its jurisdiction and, moreover, the resolution of which is not always necessary for deciding the criminal cases before it.'

legal obligation will crucially depend on the identity of the actors involved. If the conduct is attributable to state C, there will be no breach. Even if the conduct were in principle attributable to state A, there will still be no breach where relations between states A and C are concerned.

Determining the identity of the actor – which happens via attribution – is thus again of primary importance, as only then does it become clear which rules were applicable – and could be breached – in the first place. It is true, however, that sometimes this first step is already implied by the nature of the act. This happens where an act is by definition legal in nature and it is presupposed that the new legal situation could only be created by an act of state in the sense of Article 4 ARSIWA (e.g., treaty suspension).[48] This is quite different where legal consequences need to be attached subsequently to a factual occurrence.

The distinction between primary and secondary rules of international law should not be taken too far. There is no gap between the two sets. These rules help us determine whether or not there was an internationally wrongful act and who is responsible for it. Importantly, the attribution rules do not attribute responsibility; they attribute conduct. Attribution of conduct can, however, determine whether the conduct in question was an internationally wrongful act in the first place, not only who is responsible for it.

3.2   *The Problem of Attribution in the International Legal Order*

It has been established that international law can only be breached if the conduct is attributable to a legal person with the right level of international legal capacity to bear legal obligations in a particular situation. But how does the concept of attribution work in international law?

In the *Nicaragua* case, the ICJ had to consider whether the conduct of the Nicaraguan contras was attributable to the United States.[49] The ICJ established a very demanding threshold by holding that, for the United States to incur responsibility, 'it would in principle have to be proved that that State had effective control of the military or paramilitary operations in the course of which the alleged violations were committed.'[50] Where a state does not have full and generalised territorial control, it does not incur responsibility if it is 'merely' financing, training, supplying and other-

---

48   See note 39.
49   The *Nicaragua case* (note 14) paras. 115 and 116.
50   *Ibid.* para. 115.

wise supporting rebels in a foreign state.[51] It needs to be proven that the foreign state had *effective control* of the operation in which the alleged violations happened. This may be quite difficult to prove. International responsibility effectively becomes a question of evidence which may often be unavailable to anyone other than the state trying to escape responsibility. In the *Nicaragua* case, the ICJ referred to responsibility, but the high *Nicaragua* threshold creates a gap not only in responsibility. It can also mean that the entire conduct was not internationally wrongful.

On 17 July 2014, MH17 was downed over the territory of Ukraine, in an area over which that state does not exercise effective control.[52] It is believed that the plane was shot down by insurgents fighting against the government of Ukraine, but they are not a state.[53] Common knowledge tells us that the insurgents are backed by Russia,[54] but do we have enough evidence to conclude that the rather demanding *Nicaragua* threshold test for attribution to a foreign state has been met?[55]

If the conduct cannot be attributed to either state involved in the situation – Ukraine or Russia – does this mean that they escape *responsibility*, or indeed that this was not an internationally wrongful act in the first place? Pursuant to Article 2 of the ILC Articles on Responsibility of States for Internationally Wrongful Acts (ARSIWA), the latter is correct. The Article reads: 'There is an internationally wrongful act of a State when conduct consisting of an action or omission: (a) is *attributable* to the State under international law; *and* (b) constitutes a *breach of an international obligation* of the State.'[56] Article 2 of ARSIWA thus refers us to the rules of attribution which are, however, also a part of the secondary rules on state responsibility. Moreover, it follows from this formulation that until the conduct can be attributed to a state, wrongfulness remains purely notional and as such it is not an internationally wrongful act. While the MH17 situation was an arbitrary deprivation of human lives in factual terms, it was not necessarily a violation of the right to life under international human rights law.

---

51 *Ibid.* para. 292.

52 See 'MH17 Malaysia plane crash: What we know', *BBC News* (London, 14 October 2015) <http://www.bbc.com/news/world-europe-28357880> accessed 26 May 2021.

53 *Ibid.*

54 See Mark Gibney, 'The Downing of MH17: Russian Responsibility?' (2015) 15 Human Rights Law Review 169, 170.

55 *Ibid.* at 170-171.

56 ARSIWA (note 38) art 2 (emphasis added).

The attribution threshold applied in the *Nicaragua case* made the contras analogous to a wild animal in tort law: it can cause harm in fact, but no one will be liable for it in law. The animal itself does not have a sufficient level of legal capacity, and if no humans were involved, no one will be legally liable for the factually harmful act of a wild bear. In tort law, human involvement in the life of an otherwise wild animal could lead to strict liability. For example, if I choose to have a pet tiger, I will be liable for its actions no matter what and regardless of any fault on my part. If my tiger escapes and causes harm, I will be liable even if I built a very strong cage and the animal escaped without any negligence on my part.

In international law, the ICJ came close to applying strict liability in the *Corfu Channel case*. The Court established Albania's responsibility merely because this state knew or ought to have known that there were mines in its territorial waters.[57] The ICJ did not require any fault on the part of Albania for laying mines but, arguably, applied an equivalent of strict liability known in municipal tort law. Applying this doctrine to the case of MH17, is Ukraine responsible for the downing of the plane if it knew or ought to have known that the rebels had access to advanced missile launchers? An imbalance is perceivable: when states *act* through proxy, they easily fall below the demanding *Nicaragua* threshold, yet when states fail to prevent another actor from causing harm, they may incur responsibility via the *Corfu Channel* strict liability test. In the case of MH17, it is then unclear which legal obligation Ukraine actually violated by omission. If it is the right to life, is it the negative obligation not to deprive somebody of life, or the positive obligation to ensure that nobody is put at risk of being deprived of life? It is unclear how attribution by omission relates to the multiplicity of legal obligations that can arise under the same treaty provision, such as Article 6 of the International Convention on Civil and Political Rights (ICCPR).[58]

The concept of attribution in international law is theoretically unclear and confusing, and operates together with the concept of effective control which also remains insufficiently defined. Yet, attribution is of central importance as it links the actor, the conduct, and the legal obligation. Unexplained in the international legal system remains a theory of attribution and its role in identifying and determining a breach of an international legal obligation. It appears that some concepts have

---

57   *The Corfu Channel Case (United Kingdom v Albania)* [1947] ICJ Rep 2, at 22.
58   The International Covenant on Civil and Political Rights (ICCPR) (1966) 999 UNTS 171, art 6.

been brought to international law from municipal private law attribution theories. Indeed, the law of international responsibility is modelled on principles of tortious liability known in municipal legal systems. Yet, international law seems to lack systemic coherence and borrows municipal concepts sporadically and without any pre-determined certainty.

3.3 'The International Community as a Whole': From Private to Public Law?

International law-making is reminiscent of the concept of creation of legal obligations in municipal private law (e.g. the analogy between domestic contract law and international treaty law). Indeed, some languages do not even employ separate terms for contracts and treaties, and it is understood that treaties are international contracts between states. Despite these private law foundations of international law, certain public law concepts have nevertheless been introduced into the international legal order, but it remains ever-elusive how these concepts operate. In the *Barcelona Traction* case, the ICJ stated that certain obligations are 'the concern of all States. In view of the importance of the rights involved, all States can be held to have a legal interest in their protection; they are obligations erga omnes.'[59] Following this logic, when certain norms are breached, it is not a single state but the international community as a whole who is injured. This is well-illustrated also in the position of the Study Group of the International Law Commission on Fragmentation of International Law: 'If a State is responsible for torturing its own citizens, no single State suffers any direct harm ... such action violates some values or interests of all, or ... [of] the international community as a whole.'[60]

At least theoretically, international legal doctrine has established a distinction between horizontal legal relations between states, and vertical legal relations between the state and the international community. This is similar to the methodological divide between private law and public law known in municipal legal systems. Private law governs the horizontal legal relations between different persons of law (contract and torts), while public law regulates vertical relations between the community (the state) and the subjects of law, as well as the relations between

---

59   *Barcelona Traction, Light and Power Company, Limited (Belgium v. Spain)* [1970] ICJ Rep 3, para. 33.

60   Fragmentation Report (note 7) para. 393.

THE STRUCTURAL CRACK OF THE INTERNATIONAL LEGAL SYSTEM 17

the organs of this public community (constitutional law, administrative law, criminal law).

In international law, the distinction between private and public international law means something quite different. Public international law has traditionally developed as a system of rules governing obligations between states which are for the most part reminiscent of contracts and torts domestically. Private international law has developed as a system of rules governing the relationship between the individual and foreign law/foreign states (e.g. marriage concluded by nationals of different states). The divide between public and private international law is therefore conceptualised on the basis of the identity and nature of actors in a *municipal* legal system. To put it simply, where the rules govern relations between states, they are called public and where they regulate relations between individuals (e.g. application of foreign law), they are called private.

A theoretical divide between private law and public law akin to the one known in municipal legal systems also exists within the normative framework of the international legal order. In other words, the public/private law divide exists even within the set of rules traditionally – and somewhat misleadingly – termed as public international law. Yet, this divide has never been methodologically constructed in international legal theory, in part to avoid terminological confusion.

4 The Relationship between the 'International Community' and its Subjects

Thus far, it has been established that public international law operates within a private law paradigm. States make treaties and states can breach those treaties. An individual state can only breach a treaty to which it is a party. We are essentially operating within a contractual logic. Meanwhile, multilateral treaties, the concept of customary international law and some other concepts, such as *jus cogens* and obligations *erga omnes*, have introduced certain elements of public law or at least a public law mindset within this private law paradigm. This chapter considers where the limits of the public law paradigm are in public international law and where the international legal system operates beyond the strict contractual logic.

4.1 The Public Law Concepts in the International Legal Order

The use of phrases such as 'the international community as a whole' may be seen as a silent adoption of the idea of public law within the international legal order. Such phrasings introduce a sense of a community, but does this have any implications for how international law operates? The debate seems to be trapped between two somewhat difficult concepts: obligations *erga omnes* and norms of *jus cogens*.[61] The norms most commonly associated with these two concepts are the prohibitions of torture, slavery, racial discrimination, aggression, genocide and the right of self-determination (or rather prohibition of colonialism).[62] Instead of looking for hierarchical – or even constitutional – superiority of these concepts,[63] international legal theory needs to identify their theoretical foundations and asks what these foundations tell us about the idea of public law which is lingering in the background.

In one explanation, all non-bilateral obligations have an *erga omnes* character.[64] This view is problematic as it ignores the ICJ's reference to the 'importance of the rights involved', contained in the *Barcelona Traction* dictum. The 'importance' is a substantive issue and can only be defined by the special character of the obligations at stake. Maurizio Ragazzi argues that the obligations of this character have two components: "the moral content" and the "required degree of support by the international community."[65]

The concept of obligations *erga omnes* thus reflects the notion of a value-loaded international community interest. However, when establishing importance for the international community as a whole, the ICJ has only given circular references and rather generally invoked norms and principles of international law. In *East Timor*, the Court accepted the *erga omnes* character of the right of self-determination by arguing that self-determination was 'one of the essential principles of contemporary international law'.[66] *East Timor* thus defines the 'importance' identified

---

61 See Erika de Wet, '"Jus Cogens" and "Obligations Erga Omnes"', in Dinah Shelton (ed), *The Oxford Handbook of International Human Rights Law* (OUP 2013) 541.

62 ARSIWA (note 38) commentary to Article 26.

63 Compare Erika de Wet and Jure Vidmar (eds), *Hierarchy in International Law: The Place of Human Rights* (OUP 2012).

64 Claudia Annacker, 'The Legal Regime of Erga Omnes Obligations in International Law' (1993) 46 Österreichische Zeitschrift für öffentliches Recht und Völkerrecht 131, 136.

65 Maurizio Ragazzi, *The Concept of International Obligations Erga Omnes* (Clarendon 1997) 163.

66 *East Timor (Portugal v Australia)* [1995] ICJ Rep 90, para. 29.

THE STRUCTURAL CRACK OF THE INTERNATIONAL LEGAL SYSTEM   19

in *Barcelona Traction* as something which is 'essential'. Such circularities are of little help when one needs to explain which norms are the concern of the 'international community as a whole', why that is so, and how is that manifested in the international legal *system*.

The ICJ has also been unable to identify obligations *erga omnes*, their content and underpinnings, on the basis of the formal sources of law alone. As Maurizio Ragazzi has put it, obligations *erga omnes* reflect 'an exceptionless [sic] moral norm (or moral absolute) prohibiting an act which, in moral terms, is intrinsically evil (*malum in se*)'.[67] According to Ragazzi, obligations *erga omnes* are binding not only because states agree that they are, but even more importantly, 'because nobody can claim exceptions from moral absolutes.'[68] The second claim, that 'moral absolute' operates as a direct source of international law, remains debatable. It is nevertheless undisputed that the concept of obligations *erga omnes* nevertheless has its underpinnings in strong moral values and it is these underpinnings that shape international law making.

Although the concept of obligations *erga omnes* is value-loaded, it is not seen as a hierarchically superior international law. The Report of the Study Group of the International Law Commission on Fragmentation of International Law defines the concept along the following lines:

> A norm which is creative of obligations erga omnes is owed to the 'international community as a whole' and all States – irrespective of their particular interest in the matter – are entitled to invoke State responsibility in case of breach. The erga omnes nature of an obligation, however, indicates no clear superiority of that obligation over other obligations. Although in practice norms recognized as having an erga omnes validity set up undoubtedly important obligations, this importance does not translate into a hierarchical superiority...[69]

Obligations *erga omnes* may thus be seen as a legal manifestation of certain shared community values in the international community, or of an international public order. While the concept may encompass 'moral absolutes', it does not take any hierarchical precedence over other norms of international law. The legal effects of these obligations remain unclear.

---

67   Ragazzi (note 65) 183.
68   *Ibid.*
69   Fragmentation Report (note 7) para. 380.

It thus also remains unclear how these shared community values (the international public order) are accommodated within the international legal system.

A strong sense of an international community is also inherent in the concept of *jus cogens*. For a long time, the ICJ had been reluctant to employ the term *jus cogens* and was referring to an *erga omnes* character as virtually a synonym for *jus cogens*.[70] It is now somewhat difficult to separate the two concepts. The ICJ has not explored the content of obligations *erga omnes* beyond the overlap with *jus cogens*, which is itself a somewhat mysterious concept.[71]

It is in the nature of *jus cogens* norms that they have an *erga omnes* effect.[72] Indeed, we are talking about jus cogens *norms* and erga omnes *obligations*. Arguably, *jus cogens* violations trigger *erga omnes* obligations – for the international community as a whole. Yet not all obligations *erga omnes* are to be found on the flipside of *jus cogens*.[73] Which obligations have an *erga omnes* but not *jus cogens* character remains unclear. Christian Tams concludes that '[e]*rga omnes* outside *jus cogens* is likely to remain uncharted territory until States begin to invoke the concept more commonly in formalised proceedings.'[74] Obligations *erga omnes* may be seen as a legal manifestation of the international community interest. To the extent of their overlap with norms of *jus cogens*, they may also be seen as an enforcement mechanism of the latter. It is wrong, however, to see obligations *erga omnes* as hierarchically superior law. What implications does this have for the idea of an international public order?

---

70   For more on the relationship between *jus cogens* and obligations *erga omnes* see Christian Tams, *Enforcing Obligations Erga Omnes in International Law* (CUP 2005) 157; Erika de Wet, 'The International Constitutional Order' (2006) 55 International and Comparative Law Quarterly 51, 57; Stefan Kadelbach, 'Jus Cogens, Obligations *Erga Omnes* and other Rules – The Identification of Fundamental Norms' in Christian Tomuschat and JM Thouvenin (eds), *The Fundamental Norms of the International Legal Order: Jus Cogens and Obligations Erga Omnes* (Nijhoff 2006) at 21–26; Michael Byers, 'Conceptualising the Relationship Between Jus Cogens and Erga Omnes Rules' (1997) 66 Nordic Journal of International Law 211, at 213–19.

71   For a survey of obligations for which the ICJ has established that they are of *erga omnes* character see Christian Tams, *Enforcing Obligations Erga Omnes in International Law* (CUP 2005) 117–18.

72   See De Wet (note 70) 61.

73   *Ibid.*

74   Tams (note 70) 157.

4.2 *International Community Values beyond Limitations on the 'Freedom of Contract'?*

In the 1969 Vienna Convention on the Law of Treaties (VCLT), the concept of *jus cogens* was for the first time unequivocally mentioned in international treaty law.[75] However, even in this instance it was only given a rather narrow power to void treaties. The Convention also remained silent on the content of the concept. Article 53 of the VCLT, *inter alia*, provides that 'a peremptory norm of general international law is a norm accepted and recognized by the international community of States as a whole'.[76] The concept of peremptory norms thus also rests on the presumption of the existence of an international community of states with a shared interest. It is notable, however, that the VCLT qualified the notion of the international community with states, while the ICJ a year later, with regard to obligations *erga omnes*, only referred to the international community. The Court known for its conservative approach to international law certainly did not omit 'states' accidentally.

In the Article 53 definition, a peremptory norm is subject to acceptance – by the international community of states as a whole – of the normative content as well as its peremptory character. Does this mean that *jus cogens* is an inherently treaty law concept? The concept indeed predates the 1969 VCLT and was invoked by writers even in the pre-Second World War era.[77] At the time, it was unclear whether or not it was a concept generally operating in international law. This has now been generally accepted.[78] Even the VCLT reference to 'general international law' suggests that *jus cogens* is a concept of customary international law.

Any norm of customary international law requires its acceptance by states through state practice and *opinio juris*. However, the acceptance of the special peremptory character, not only normative content, by 'the international community of states as a whole' points to the strong ethi-

---

75 VCLT (note 13) art 53.

76 *Ibid.*

77 For a detailed account on the early writings on *jus cogens* see Dinah Shelton, 'Normative Hierarchy in International Law' (2006) 100 American Journal of International Law 291, 297–99.

78 There are currently 111 state parties to the Vienna Convention. Many of its provisions are nevertheless binding on non-parties to the Convention via customary international law. Although some states have refrained from ratification precisely because of Article 53, there is little doubt that the article has customary international law status. Indeed, the status of permanent objector to *jus cogens* has not been accepted by the international community of states.

cal underpinning of these norms.[79] Sandesh Sivakumaran argues that *jus cogens* represents a minimum threshold of the international value system.[80] The strong community-oriented ethical underpinning of *jus cogens* norms has implications for the law-making. International law is, in principle, a consensus-based legal system. States create treaty obligations for themselves and at free will. It is *state* practice and *opinio juris* which leads to the emergence of customary norms of international law, from which states again have an escape route through the concept of a persistent objector. In principle, it is only new states which become automatically bound by pre-existing customary law and even automatically accede to certain treaties previously governing their territory (e.g. human rights treaties).[81] Yet the peremptory status of certain norms, encompassing the minimum threshold of the international value system, also overrides some fundamental tenets of a consensus-based international law making.

The ethical underpinning of the peremptory norms can compensate for deficiencies in universal acceptance of these norms. In this context three examples appear to be particularly instructive: (1) the right to the freedom from torture is supported by very strong *opinio juris*, yet state practice is rather weak. There is nevertheless little doubt that the freedom from torture has a *jus cogens* status.[82] (2) Apartheid South Africa claimed that it was a persistent objector to the prohibition of racial discrimination. This claim was universally rejected on the basis that unlike ordinary customary law, peremptory law does not allow for the persistent objector's status.[83] (3) France used to claim that it had never consented to the concept of *jus cogens* as such.[84] This argument was rejected and now

---

79 De Wet (note 70) at 57.

80 Sandesh Sivakumaran, 'Impact on the Structure of International Obligations' in Martin Scheinin and Menno Kamminga (eds), *The Impact of Human Rights Law on General International Law* (OUP 2009) 146.

81 See Akbar Rasulov, 'Revisiting State Succession to Humanitarian Treaties: Is There a Case for Automaticity?' (2003) 14 EJIL 141.

82 See Richard Garnett, 'The Defence of State Immunity for Acts of Torture' (1997) 18 Australian Yearbook of International Law 97, making the following argument: 'It may be argued ... that the absolute nature of the conventional prohibitions, when coupled with the near universal *opinion juris* amongst states as to the illegality of the practice, may be a sufficient basis for concluding that torture is prohibited as a peremptory norm.'

83 Byers (note 70) at 222.

84 *Ibid.* at 229. See also Shelton (note 77) at 166.

THE STRUCTURAL CRACK OF THE INTERNATIONAL LEGAL SYSTEM 23

even France has accepted the binding nature of these norms in terms of both content and character.[85]

These examples reveal that with regard to peremptory norms, international law-making may work differently. As Robert McCorquodale argues, 'some human rights create legal obligations on a state irrespective of whether it has ratified a particular treaty, either because the human right is part of customary international law and so binding on all states or by virtue of a rule of *jus cogens*, which no state can derogate from or evade by contrary practice'.[86] Moreover, in *Furundzija*, the International Criminal Tribunal for the former Yugoslavia (ICTY) reasoned: 'Because of the importance of the values [which the prohibition of torture] protects, this principle has evolved into a peremptory norm of *jus cogens*, that is a norm that enjoys a higher rank in the international hierarchy than treaty law and even "ordinary" customary rules.'[87]

Despite this judicial pronouncement, hierarchical superiority of *jus cogens* remains a contested issue, particularly so after the ICJ's *Germany v Italy* decision on jurisdictional immunities.[88] Nevertheless, the concept of *jus cogens* does appear to reflect community values which override state centrism and certain classical tenets of international law-making. The concept changes the traditional paradigm of international law as voluntary law and introduces a set of norms which can be legally binding on states even in the absence of their consent. It thus manifests a strong sense of the international community interest which prevails over the will of individual states. However, they have not been given any effects

---

85   See Alain Pellet, 'Comments in Response to Christine Chinkin and in Defense of Jus Cogens as the Best Bastion against the Excesses of Fragmentation' (2006) 27 Finnish Yearbook of International Law 83, 85.

86   McCorquodale (note 27) at 486.

87   *Prosecutor v Anto Furundžija* (Judgment) IT-95–17/1, T Ch II (10 December 1998) at 260, para. 153.

88   *Jurisdictional Immunities of the State (Germany v. Italy)* [2012] ICJ Rep 99 ["*Jurisdictional Immunities* case"] Consider para. 93, where the ICJ provided the following reasoning with regard to the question of whether *jus cogens* takes precedence over immunities because of its special character. The ICJ noted that '[t]his argument ... depends upon the existence of a conflict between a rule, or rules, of jus cogens, and the rule of customary law which requires one State to accord immunity to another." The ICJ found that "no such conflict exists.' This is so because '[t]he two sets of rules address different matters. The rules of State immunity are procedural in character and are confined to determining whether or not the courts of one State may exercise jurisdiction in respect of another State. They do not bear upon the question whether or not the conduct in respect of which the proceedings are brought was lawful or unlawful.'

of hierarchical superiority in international judicial practice. When *jus cogens* norms are breached, the concept does not create remedies that would trump other international legal obligations.[89]

International legal doctrine has thus introduced certain concepts that imply the presence of a 'hierarchical meta system',[90] but it appears that Dino Krtitsiotis is right when he concludes that international law does not know how to accommodate these concepts. He argues: 'Our "international community" is "deep" enough to have conceived of the idea of *jus cogens* but not deep enough to know what to do with it. It is caught in the perennial mire of something called *erga omnes* (or obligations owed to the "community" as a whole), and continues to inch toward so-called crimes and offences against the "international order".'[91] The problem is that all these concepts envisage a strong sense of community and its values. While such a community sense may well limit the treaty-making capacity of states (Article 53 VCLT), it is questionable whether these public law principles can be accommodated within the international legal system which is essentially of a private law nature. It appears that the value-loaded concepts of *jus cogens* and *erga omnes* serve a similar purpose as limitations on the freedom of contract in municipal law.

It remains to be explored whether these legal manifestations of the 'fundamental values of the international community' have any public law effects that reach further than posing certain limitations on the 'freedom of contract'? Does the concept of *jus cogens* operate beyond its contractual-like (private law) context of Article 53 VCLT? Are there any other instances of public law effects in the international legal order (e.g. self-defence against non-state actors, as there exists no bilateral horizontal obligation between two parties)? How does international law systemically accommodate the public law notion of the international community as a whole?[92] Which legal relations in the international community are neither bilateral nor multilateral, but concern vertical relations between the international community as a whole and a person of international law?

---

89   See the *Jurisdictional Immunities* case, *ibid*.

90   Cf Fragmentation Report (note 7) para. 493.

91   Dino Kritsiotis, 'Imagining the International Community' (2002) 13 EJIL 961, 990.

92   Compare Nico Krisch, 'The Decay of Consent: International Law in an Age of Global Public Goods' (2014) 108 American Journal of International Law 1.

4.3 Towards a Political Theory of the Law of the International Community

In municipal settings, public law and political theorists have been investigating the relationships between (i) institutions of the state; and (ii) the state and the individual. This is necessarily different in international law where the actors involved differ from those at domestic level. Arguably, the relationship between the institutions of the international community have been addressed by the studies on fragmentation of international law.[93] These studies have addressed the problem of the relationship between the different regimes of international law built around different institutions (e.g. WTO law, international criminal law, international human rights law, international investment law), and have proposed a robust system of conflict rules to regulate the relationship between these regimes. At the same time, the vertical relationship between the state and the individual has remained either understudied or overtly influenced by municipal theories that are not always readily transposable to the international level.

Inspired by the rise of international human rights law and international criminal law after the Second World War, some scholars have started to place the individual in the centre of the international legal system and have conceptualised a domestic-like vertical relationship between the individual and the international community.[94] But international human rights and international criminal law are still derived from the law-making powers of states. The scope of these legal regimes depends on whether or not a particular state is a party to a certain treaty, whether it has filed reservations to that treaty, and sometimes also on how states have voted in the UN Security Council. In other words, the position of the individual in international law is not regulated by a 'public law of the international community', but by a private law system of treaty-created obligations between states.

If a 'public law of the international community' exists, the vertical relationship in this system is the one between the international community and the state. On the international plane, it is the state which takes the position of the individual in a municipal public order. International human rights and international criminal law may well play an important role in the political theory governing the vertical

---

93 See Fragmentation Report (note 7) para. 493.
94 See McCorquodale (note 27) at 486. See also Anne Peters, 'Humanity as the A and Ω of Sovereignty' (2009) 20 EJIL 513.

relationship between the international community and the state, but this is because the protection of human rights and punishing international crimes belong to the fundamental values of the international community as a whole.

International human rights and international criminal law in this public law model do not operate from the level of an individual, but from the overarching level of the community vis-à-vis the state. It needs to be asked whether the notion of 'the international community as a whole' can be conceptualised as a legal fiction to represent an international sovereign authority and develops a political theory of international law which defines the vertical relationship between the fictitious international sovereign – the international community as a whole – and the state.

5 Conclusions

Public international law operates in a private law paradigm. In its essence, this is a system of contract-like and tort-like relations between states. The word public in public international law is a misnomer. A comprehensive public law umbrella is absent in this system. In order for the system to function, however, some rudimentary elements of public law have been introduced to help regulate the private law relations between states. The concept of *jus cogens* is probably nothing different than an international analogy to public law limitations on the freedom of contract. Obligations *erga omnes* presume the existence of an international community or international society and create a vertical (public law type) relationship between states and the community. This relationship, however, is rudimentary and not underpinned by a comprehensive political and constitutional theory the way this is ordinarily done in municipal settings. The most visible effect of obligations *erga omnes* appears to be that states have to withhold recognition where a new state seeks to emerge in violation of a peremptory norm. States are under this obligation even where they are not directly wronged in bilateral relations. The obligation to withhold recognition is also significant because the statehood-seeking entity is at that stage a non-state actor, it is only trying to become a state. *Jus cogens* thus prevents a certain new legal situation from being realised, and an obligation *erga omnes* is generated so as to prevent other states from helping consolidate the illegal situation.

THE STRUCTURAL CRACK OF THE INTERNATIONAL LEGAL SYSTEM   27

Apart from that, international law operates within an inherently contractual paradigm. A great deal of conduct can happen on the international plane that is harmful in fact, but it will not necessarily be wrongful in law. If this conduct is not attributed to a state with a relevant international legal obligation, it will fall outside of the purview of international legal regulation. This does not only mean that state responsibility would not be engaged; it can also mean that there would be no illegality. The conduct in question will not amount to an internationally wrongful act.

The rules of state responsibility are often said to be the secondary rules that do not regulate whether or not a certain conduct is lawful.[95] But the primary/secondary rules distinction can be arbitrary. For example, the circumstances precluding wrongfulness in many instances deal exactly with what the title suggests – regulate whether or not a certain conduct was wrongful, they do not only regulate responsibility for wrongfulness. Similarly, the attribution rules can determine whether or not a certain conduct was wrongful. Several possibilities exist. Certain conduct can be an internationally wrongful act if it is attributable to state A, but not if it is attributable to state B. This is because the conduct may be unlawful under treaty T to which state A is a party, but state B is not. Furthermore, if certain conduct is in principle unlawful under a treaty or customary international law, but came from a non-state actor, it will not be an internationally wrongful act if it is not attributed to a state party to a treaty or bound by the relevant customary rule. This means that there would be no internationally wrongful act if the conduct is not attributable to a state.

While the law of international responsibility is broader than state responsibility, other actors do not tend to have very many international legal obligations. International organisations have a treaty making capacity for their functional purposes, but they are not party to very many treaties. The nexus of their international legal obligations is therefore rather limited. Individuals can incur international criminal responsibility, but this is restricted to a rather narrow list of international crimes.[96] Finally, non-state armed groups have certain rights and duties under international humanitarian law pertaining to non-international armed conflict.[97] Again,

---

95   The *Gabčíkovo/Nagymaros case* (note 15) para. 47.
96   See the Rome Statue (note 30) art 5 which defines war crimes, crimes against humanity and genocide as crimes for which the Court can – subject to some other conditions – exercise its jurisdiction over individuals.
97   *Tadić* case (note 41) paras. 83-87.

however, these rules are rather restricted and functionally limited to situations of non-international armed conflict.

The nexus of international legal obligations for the most part applies to states. Therefore, if conduct is not attributable to a state, it cannot be internationally wrongful. Furthermore, the ICJ has established a very high threshold requirement for attribution of conduct to a state where conduct does not originate directly from a state organ. This threshold was elaborated on in the cases of *Nicaragua* and *Bosnian Genocide* and is reflected in Article 8 ARSIWA. Where states act by proxy, for example in armed conflict, they will escape international responsibility relatively easily as the attribution threshold is high and evidence often in the hands of the implicated state itself. When the attribution threshold in such circumstances is not reached, the conduct in question remains unattributed. This does not mean that nobody was responsible for an unlawful conduct. It actually means that the conduct was not unlawful. If conduct was authored by a non-state armed group, for example, yet is not attributable to a state, it cannot be unlawful, because a non-state armed group conceptually does not have the level of international legal capacity inherent in states, and therefore does not and cannot have state-like international legal obligations.

This is the major structural flaw of international law: a limited international legal capacity of non-state actors and a high attribution threshold to attribute non-state conduct to states. As a result, a great deal of international conduct, especially where states act by proxy, remains unregulated. However, when identifying this structural deficiency of international law, one must also keep in mind what international law is for; what it can and what in cannot regulate. International law is not there to regulate or even punish all harm that happens in the world. International law is, conceptually speaking, quite simply a system of torts and contracts between states with some rudimentary public law elements which make this private law system work.

One way forward would be to simply stick to this point and acknowledge that the reach of international law is rather limited and that most non-state conduct, even if supported or at least tolerated by states, falls outside of the purview of international law. Another possibility would be to reach a new international understanding on the attribution threshold and move beyond *Nicaragua*, *Bosnian Genocide* and their reflections in ARSIWA. This would mean that more non-state conduct could be attributable to states. It appears that state practice is already going in that direction where omissions rather than actions are concerned. Indeed, at least in some situations, states have been deemed to be strictly liable. The theoretical foundations of this move to strict liability are unclear and even politicised. In the interest of legal certainty and doctrinal clarity, the international legal system would need to rethink the whole concept of attribution.

2 De Facto Independent Regimes and Overarching Human Rights Duties

Amrei Müller *

Abstract

By analysing relevant practice and statements of four de facto independent regimes – the Republic of Abkhazia, the Nagorno-Karabakh Republic, the Pridnestrovian Moldavian Republic, and the Republic of Somaliland – this Article first establishes that these regimes are able to comply with overarching human rights obligations as a matter of fact. Overarching human rights obligations are obligations that do not arise from one specific human right protected in regional or global human rights law, but general obligations that enable duty-bearers to implement all other specific human rights obligations, among them obligations related to (democratic) institution building and to reiterative domestic law-making processes. In a second step, the Article evaluates this finding. It argues that these and other de facto independent regimes with the same coercive and normative capabilities to comply with these overarching obligations should be recognised as full human rights duty-bearers alongside states, even though this is not the case to date. Discussing the wider legal, practical and normative implications of this submission, it concludes with suggesting that all *other* de facto independent regimes and other armed non-state actors with influence or control over populations should rather become bound by selected rules of the law of occupation or so-called 'responsibilities for human rights' to close existing regulatory gaps in international humanitarian law (IHL) of non-international armed conflicts (NIACs) in a practice-informed and normatively convincing way.

---

* Lecturer/Assistant Professor (Ad Astra Fellow) at University College Dublin Sutherland School of Law.

32   2 – MÜLLER

Keywords

Overarching human rights obligations – human rights duty-bearers – Abkhazia – Nagorno-Karabakh Republic – Pridnestrovian Moldavian Republic – Somaliland

1   Introduction

This contribution analyses first whether selected de facto independent regimes[1] are able to comply with overarching human rights obligations as a matter of fact. Second, having established that this is the case, it explores whether it is reasonable to call for the extension of the binding force of international human rights law to some of these entities, thereby contributing to the closing of gaps in international humanitarian law (IHL) applicable to situations of non-international armed conflict (NIAC).[2]

Overarching human rights obligations/duties[3] are obligations that do not arise from one specific human right enshrined in domestic and/or international (regional or global)[4] human rights law, but general obliga-

---

1   De facto independent regimes are defined here as non-state collective entities, i.e. entities distinct from its members that exercise short- or long-term quasi-governmental authority in a defined territory, and that may or may not be engaged in an armed conflict and that may or may not have all the characteristics of states. The non-state character of the entities implies entities whose conduct cannot be attributed to states under Articles 4-10 Draft Articles on Responsibility of States for Internationally Wrongful Acts (ARSIWA), but it could include entities that receive support from a state or share a (patron) state's objective, as long as their acts are not attributable to that state. See International Law Commission, 'Articles on Responsibility of States for Internationally Wrongful Acts, with commentaries' (2001), published in International Law Commission, 'Report of the International Law Commission on the work of its fifty-third session' (23 April–1 June and 2 July– 10 August 2001) UN Doc A/56/10; adopted by the UN General Assembly in UNGA Res 56/83 (28 January 2002) UN Doc A/RES/56/83.
2   Gaps exist when no NIAC exists and IHL of NIACs thus does not apply, and in situations not regulated by IHL of NIACs, i.e. all situations involving acts and omissions of NSAGs that are not directly associated with the armed conflict. For more details on the scope of application of IHL of NIACs, see Sivakumaran, *The Law of Non-International Armed Conflict* (OUP, 2012) 164-79 and 236-52.
3   The terms 'obligation' and 'duty' are used interchangeably in this contribution.
4   *Global* human rights law means human rights law set out in global UN human rights treaties, such as the ICCPR, ICESCR and CRC and interpreted by UN treaty bodies. *Regional* human rights law means human rights law set out in regional human rights treaties, such as the ECHR and interpreted by regional human rights

tions that enable duty-bearers (usually states) to implement all other specific human rights obligations. Examples of such overarching obligations are first and foremost obligations to build (democratic or democratising) institutions that allow duty-bearers to 'secure',[5] to 'respect and to ensure'[6] or to 'achiev[e…] progressively the full realisation of'[7] the human rights of all individuals on the basis of equality[8] of rights-holders. Further examples are the duties to adopt domestic legislation necessary for the implementation of human rights that complies with the legality standard developed in international human rights law, [9] and obligations to create an 'enabling environment'[10] conducive to the protection of human rights in a pluralist democratic society.

There are four reasons for this focus. First, these overarching obligations are particular (if not unique) to human rights law, primarily because they reveal the normative grounding of this body of law in the instrumental relationship between equality, human rights and democracy exceptionally well. Overarching obligations are thus different in character from obligations that flow from IHL – a body of law built on a differ-

---

    courts. *International* human rights law comprises both global and regional human rights law.

5   European Convention on Human Rights (ECHR) (entered into force 3 September 1953) ETS 005, art 1.

6   International Covenant on Civil and Political Rights (ICCPR) (entered into force 23 March 1976) 999 UNTS 171, art 2(1).

7   International Covenant on Economic, Social and Cultural Rights (ICESCR) (entered into force 3 January 1976) 993 UNTS 3, art 2(1).

8   This is clear from the numerous non-discrimination / equality clauses in international human rights treaties, eg ECHR art 14; ICCPR arts 2(1), 14(1), 26; ICESCR arts 2(2), 3; UN Human Rights Committee (HRC), General Comment 18 – Non-discrimination (10 November 1989) UN Doc HRI/GEN/1/Rev.1; UN Committee on Economic, Social and Cultural Rights (CESCR) General Comment 20 – Non-discrimination in Economic, Social and Cultural Rights (2 July 2009) UN Doc E/C.12/GC/20.

9   See eg HRC, General Comment 31 – The Nature of the General Legal Obligation Imposed on States Parties to the Covenant (29 March 2004) UN Doc CCPR/C/21/Rev.1/Add 13 [7]-[8], [13]; CESCR, General Comment 9 – The Domestic Application of the Covenant (3 December 1998) UN Doc E/C.12/1998/24 [2]-[3] and General Comment 3 – The Nature of States Parties' Obligations (14 December 1990) UN Doc E/1991/23 [3]; for an analysis of the obligations to adopt 'appropriate safeguards' in domestic law to protect ECHR rights, see Müller, 'Obligations to 'Secure' the Rights of the Convention in an 'Effective Political Democracy': How Should Parliaments and Domestic Courts Interact?' in Saul et al (eds), *The International Human Rights Judiciary and National Parliaments* (CUP 2017) 167, 171-79. See also n 25.

10   See section 2.2 below; and n 50.

ent humanitarian, top-down or more technocratic normative logic.[11] Analysing whether selected de facto independent entities can comply with these particular human rights duties will therefore ensure that de facto compliance with *human rights* obligations is analysed, rather than compliance with possibly overlapping substantive obligations under IHL.[12] Second, these overarching obligations relate to some of the fundamental coercive capacities and, importantly, normative characteristics that any entity claiming or aspiring to become a human rights duty-bearer should arguably display in order to be able to comply with numerous other human rights obligations flowing from specific rights, even if only with minimum core obligations. The implementation of minimum core obligations is a priority under human rights law and will therefore frequently be the primary focus in crisis situations involving independent de facto regimes.[13] In other words, the compliance with these overarching obligations is often a precondition for, or at least highly conducive to, the implementation of all other human rights duties. Third and relatedly, the focus on de facto compliance with overarching obligations will help to develop a narrowed-down understanding of what *type* of de facto independent regime has the capacity to, in fact, comply with human rights law more broadly, and might therefore gradually be recognised as full human rights duty-bearers in international human rights law in addition to states. Last but not least, there are normative reasons for the focus on overarching obligations: it will show particularly well that any entity that is poten-

---

11   Unlike human *rights* law the detailed content of which and corresponding duties are primarily defined and specified in domestic law through institutionalised participative processes in 'democratic societies' respecting the political equality of its members (bottom-up) in light of international human rights treaties, IHL defines relatively strict *duties* binding states and NSAGs in times of NIAC, aiming to protect basic humanitarian interests of people affected by armed conflict (top-down).

12   There is such overlap, at least on the surface, in areas concerning the protection of basic human survival needs. This is the case even though in fact, all human rights obligations are related to the underlying normative logic of human rights law, and all IHL obligations are related to the normative logic of IHL, and thus differ to some extent. However, in many cases, this nonetheless leads to similar substantive obligations flowing from both IHL and human rights law in relation to the protection of basic human survival needs of most (but not all – i.e. IHL excludes combatants from some protections) human beings.

13   See eg CESCR, General Comment 3 (n 9) [10]; CESCR General Comment 14 – The Right to the Highest Attainable Standard of Health (11 August 2000) UN Doc E/C.12/2000/4 [6], [47]; and General Comment 19 – The Right to Social Security (23 November 2007) UN Doc E/C.12/GC/19 [60], [65].

tially recognised as a full human rights duty-bearer will not only obtain human rights duties, but inevitably also considerable public privileges or rights that assume the exercise of democratically legitimised public authority by this entity over individuals. After all, it is a fundamental aim of human rights law that any (usually state) authority is exercised in a legitimate fashion, with legitimacy understood in the context of human rights law as grounded in respect for and protection of (political) equality, human rights and thus democracy. This, of course, directly challenges governmental authority, and, in some cases, state borders, in a way that would not occur should de facto independent regimes rather become bound by additional norms of IHL, including potentially the law of occupation. The broader implications of this recognition for the desirable development of international law binding de facto independent regimes and other collective armed non-state actors are explored in the concluding section of this contribution.

Section 2 introduces overarching human rights obligations and highlights how they express human rights law's normative logic. Section 3 reviews the human rights 'practice' of selected de facto independent regimes – their interpretation and application of human rights in their 'domestic' laws and policies (reception) – to evaluate whether some of them might, as a matter of fact, be capable of complying with overarching human rights duties. Section 4 concludes with a brief evaluation of the findings, discussing their broader implications for the possible development of international law binding de facto independent regimes, non-state armed groups (NSAGs) and other non-state actors that control or influence individuals.

2   Overarching Human Rights Duties

As their overarching duty under international human rights law, states are required to adopt 'all appropriate means'[14] or 'measures',[15] including in particular legislative measures,[16] to 'secure',[17] to 'respect and to ensure'[18] or to 'achiev[e...] progressively the full realisation of'[19] the rights

---

14   ICESCR art 2(1).

15   ICCPR art 2(2); see also HRC, General Comment 31 (n 9) [7].

16   See (ns 9, 25).

17   ECHR art 1.

18   ICCPR art 2(1).

19   ICESCR art 2(1).

that are set out in the respective treaties. Whilst this process must be guided by the rights and principles stated in these treaties and developed in international practice, it gives states reasonable flexibility when deciding what the most suitable legal, policy- and other measures are to protect the human rights within their particular domestic economic, social, cultural, historical and political context.[20] It also permits taking account of domestic resource constraints,[21] and calls for constant adaption and refinement in light of changing circumstances.[22] It thus both obliges and permits (empowers) domestic authorities to specify and consolidate, in domestic laws and policies, the content of human rights and corresponding duties that are abstractly defined in treaties and international jurisprudence and, in case of conflicting rights or conflicts between human rights and public interests, to ensure that they are fairly balanced[23] in domestic law and policies.

As is clear from numerous equality and non-discrimination clauses[24] in international human rights treaties, these specification and balancing processes in national law and policies must respect the equality of the human rights of all individuals who are affected by them. This implies that these processes must constantly and repeatedly be justified and thus legitimised through participative and even democratic processes, as it is only such processes that can take account of the equality of rights of the individuals who find themselves under a particular states' jurisdiction and who will be affected by these laws and policies. This influences both the legality standard with which domestic laws that concretise limitations to rights and measures taken to discharge 'positive' human rights obligations have to comply, as well as the shape of the institutional structure and ultimately, the political regime, that protects human rights at the domestic level. It also underlies the obligations to create an 'enabling environment' for the realisation of human rights, as well as to 'progressively realise' human rights whilst prioritising the implementation of

---

20   As, for example, captured in the ECtHR's margin of appreciation doctrine.

21   ICESCR art 2(1); CESCR, General Comment 19 (n 13) [4], [14], [30], [40]-[42]; CESCR, Statement on an Evaluation of the Obligations to Take Steps to the "Maximum Available Resources" Under an Optional Protocol to the Covenant (21 September 2007) UN Doc E/C.12/2007/1.

22   See also below section 2.3.

23   As foreseen in the limitation clauses of international human rights treaties, eg ECHR arts 8(2)-11(2); ICCPR arts 12(3), 18(2), 19(3), 21 and 22(2); ICESCR arts 4 and 8(1)(a), (c).

24   See (n 8).

DE FACTO INDEPENDENT REGIMES AND OVERARCHING HR DUTIES   37

minimum core rights. More light shall be shed on these elements of overarching human rights duties in the following.

2.1   *Adopting Domestic Law in Line with Human Rights Legality Standard*

Concerning the legality standard, it is clear from the ECtHR's and UN
treaty bodies' interpretation of the 'determined by law'/'protected/pre-
scribed by law'/'lawful'[25] and 'necessary in a democratic society'[26] requirements that most domestic laws shall be adopted with the (at least
indirect) involvement of an elected legislature.[27] This is further confirmed by (equal) political participation rights;[28] more general calls on
states to ensure 'the participation of the population'[29] in domestic deci-

---

25   See eg ECHR arts 2, 5(1), (2), (4), 6(1), 8(2)-11(2); ICCPR arts 6(1), 8(c)(i), (ii), 9(1),
      12(1), (3), 13, 14(1), 15 (concerning criminal law), 17(1),(2), 18(3), 19(3), 20, 21, 22(2);
      ICESCR arts 4, 8(1)(a), (c). On the legality standard see also Harris et al (eds), *The
      Law of the ECHR* (OUP, 2018) 20-22; and HRC, General Comment 36 – The Right
      to Life (30 October 2018) CCPR/C/CG/36, with numerous examples of legislative
      measures that states should adopt to protect the right to life.

26   ECHR arts 8(2)-11(2); ICCPR arts 14(1), 21 and 22(2); ICESCR arts 4 and 8(1)(a) and
      (c).

27   In line also with Protocol 1 to the European Convention for the Protection of
      Human Rights and Fundamental Freedoms (ECHR Protocol 1) (entered into
      force 18 May 1954), ETS 009 art 3; and art 25 ICCPR. See Harris *et al* (n 25) 20; for
      more details, also see Lavrysen, 'Protection by the Law: The Positive Obligation
      to Develop a Legal Framework to Adequately Protect ECHR Rights' in Brems and
      Haeck (eds), *Human Rights and Civil Liberties in the 21st Century* (Springer 2014)
      69-129; and Müller, (n 9)172-73.

28   Eg ICCPR art 25; Universal Declaration Human Rights (adopted 31 January 1948)
      UNGA Res 217 A(III) (UDHR) art 21; Convention on the Rights of the Child (entered
      into force 2 September 1990) 1577 UNTS 3, art 15; Convention on the Rights of
      Persons with Disabilities (entered into force 3 May 2008) 2515 UNTS 3, arts 4 (3), 29,
      33 (3); ECHR Protocol 1 art 3; HRC, General Comment 25 – The Right to Participate
      in Public Affairs, Voting Rights and the Right of Equal Access to Public Service (12
      July 1996) UN Doc CCPR/C/21/Rev.1/Add.7 [5]-[6].

29   Eg CESCR, General Comment 14 (n 13) [11]; CESCR, General Comment 18 – The
      Right to Work (6 February 2006) UN Doc E/C.12/GC/18 [42]; HRC, General
      Comment 25 (n 28) [6], [8], on equal participation other than through elections.
      The participatory element is also emphasised by the Committee on Rights of the
      Child, see eg Committee on Rights of the Child, General Comment 19 – On Public
      Budgeting for the Realization of Children's Rights (20 July 2016) UN Doc CRC/C/
      GC/19 [33]; and by UN special procedures mandate holders eg Report of the UN
      Special Rapporteur on Extreme Poverty and Human Rights (11 August 2009) UN
      Doc A/64/279 [71]-[72]; and Report of the Independent Expert on the Promotion
      of a Democratic and Equitable International Order (14 July 2015) UN Doc A/
      HRC/30/44 [36]-[37].

sion-making, planning and law-making processes related to the domestic implementation of (international) human rights; and UN treaty bodies' announcements that, when evaluating states' compliance with international human rights treaties, they 'look [...] at whether implementation [...] complies with democratic principles'.[30] Other elements of the legality standard for domestic law developed by the ECtHR and UN treaty bodies – among them accessibility, precision, generality and foreseeability[31] and non-discrimination[32] – also aim to limit the power of executive authorities and the judiciary to restrict equal human rights. They limit the executive's and judiciary's discretion in this regard,[33] and ensure that the law is applied and enforced in a non-discriminatory fashion, thus respecting political equality.

2.2 Democratic/Democratising Institutional Structures and an Enabling Environment for Political Participation

When it comes to the overarching obligation under human rights law to set up the domestic institutional structure required for the protection of human rights, the ECtHR and UN treaty bodies have emphasised that this structure shall have democratic or democratising features. For example, the CESCR has confirmed that the ICESCR 'neither requires nor precludes any particular form of government or economic system being used as the vehicle for the steps [to be taken to implement socio-economic rights] ..., provided only that it is democratic,'[34] while the ECtHR has long held that 'democracy is the only political model contemplated by

---

30 CESCR, General Comment 19 (n 13) [63].

31 E.g. HRC, General Comment No 16 – The Right to Respect of Privacy, Family, Home and Correspondence, and Protection of Honour and Reputation (8 April 1988) UN Doc HRI/GEN/1/Rev.9 (Vol. I) [8], [10]; HRC, *Pinkey v Canada* Communication 27/1978 (29 October 1981) UN Doc CCPR/C/14/D/27/1977 [34]. On relevant the ECtHR's jurisprudence, see Lautenbach, *The Concept of the Rule of Law and the European Court of Human Rights* (OUP, 2013) ch 3.

32 *Ünal Tekeli v Turkey* App no 29865/96 (ECtHR, 16 November 2004) [61]; *Konstantin Markin v Russia* App no 30078/06 (ECtHR, 7 October 2010) [66]-[67].

33 See eg *Roman Zakharov v Russia* App no 47143/06 (ECtHR, 5 Dec 2015) [246]; *Kennedy v UK* App no 26839/05 (ECtHR, 18 May 2010) [155].

34 CESCR, General Comment 3 (n 9) [8] (my emphasis); HRC, General Comment 25 (n 28) [1]. This does not imply that only democratic states can ratify human rights treaties. Rather, state parties are under an obligation to (progressively) democratise, i.e. to set up democratic institutions that enable them to progressively secure the equal rights of the people under their jurisdiction.

DE FACTO INDEPENDENT REGIMES AND OVERARCHING HR DUTIES 39

the Convention and, accordingly, the only one compatible with it.'[35] They have further specified that this implies the existence of a comprehensive unitary institutional framework consisting of an elected legislature[36] and an independent judiciary,[37] and that democratic systems are further incorporating various principles, such as the separation of powers,[38] political parties,[39] free elections,[40] political pluralism[41] and judicial review.[42]

Of course, these principles and the functioning of a democratic system based on the principles of political equality and popular control are also furthered by the protection of rights to freedom of expression, of assembly and association,[43] and political participation rights, including the right to vote and to stand for election.[44] The right to freedom of expression and information is particularly important for the development of an independent and pluralistic media landscape, exercising its 'public watchdog' function[45] by exposing actions or omissions of government to

---

35 Eg Ždanoka v Latvia App no 58278/00 (ECtHR, 16 March 2006) [98]; *Refah Partisi (the Welfare Party) and Others v Turkey* App nos 41340/98 and others (ECtHR, 13 February 2003) [86]; more recently, *Navalnyy v Russia* App no 29580/12 (ECtHR, 15 Nov 2018) [175]. Similarly, *Yatama v Nicaragua*, judgment (Preliminary Objections, Merits, Reparations and Costs) Inter-American Court of Human Rights Series C No 127 (23 June 2005) [195-201], referring *inter alia* to the Inter-American Democratic Charter, adopted by the General Assembly of the Organization of American States, AG/RES 1838 (XXXI-O/01), 11 September 2001.

36 ECHR Protocol 1 art 3; ICCPR art 2(3)(b).

37 ECHR arts 6(1) and 10(2); ICCPR arts2(3) and 14(1).

38 *Van de Hurk v the Netherlands* App no 16034/90 (ECtHR, 19 April 1994) [44-55]; *Animal Defenders International v UK* App no 48876/08 (ECtHR, 22 April 2013); Kosar, 'Policing the Separation of Powers: A New Role for the European Court of Human Rights?' (2012) 8 *European Constitutional Law Review* 33.

39 ICCPR art 25(b), alluded to also in HRC, General Comment 25 (n 28) [17], [25]-[26]. *United Communist Party of Turkey v Turkey* App no 19392/92 (ECtHR, 30 January 1998) [25], [42]-[45]; *Refah Partisi* (n 35) [88].

40 ICCPR art 25(b); HRC, General Comment 25 (n 28) [7], [10]-[12], [19], [21]. ECHR Protocol 1 art 3, and Harris et al (n 25) 914-42, for an overview of ECtHR jurisprudence concerning the right to vote and free elections.

41 HRC, General Comment 25 (n 28) [25]; *Refah Partisi* (n 35) [89].

42 ICCPR art 2(3); HRC, General Comment 31 (n 9) [15]; HRC General Comment 25 (n 28) [20]; ECHR arts 6, 13.

43 HRC, General Comment 25 (n 28) [8],[12],[26].

44 ICCPR art 25; UDHR art 21; ECHR Protocol 1 art 3; see also HRC, General Comment 25 (n 28) [10]-[12], [25]; and HRC, General Comment 31 (n 9) [13] ,[20].

45 See eg *Jersild v Denmark* App no 15890/89 (ECtHR, 23 September 1994) [35]; *Financial Times Ltd and Others v UK*, 821/03 (ECtHR, 15 December 2009) [95]; HRC, General Comment 34 – Freedom of Opinion and Expression (12 September 2011) UN Doc CCPR/C/GC/34 [13].

public scrutiny,[46] thereby enabling citizens' meaningful political participation in decision-making processes in a democratic system. Civil society organisations[47] can fulfil a similar 'public watchdog' function when benefitting from the protection of the rights to freedom of expression and association,[48] but can also contribute to creating a more inclusive, and thus more equality-respecting environment for minorities or structurally disadvantaged groups, facilitating their equal partaking in political decision-making processes.[49] Protecting and facilitating press freedom and ensuring that civil society organisations can operate without undue restrictions is thus part of a broader obligation under human rights law to create an 'enabling environment'[50] for equal political participation of rights-holders in a 'democratic society', as well as a space for pluralistic open debate.

An 'effective political democracy' also includes an independent judiciary which can *inter alia* offer an effective remedy to those whose human rights have been violated. Under human rights law, an independent judiciary comprises 'competent' courts 'established by law'.[51] This means that they shall be set up based on legislation emanating from an elected, and

---

46   *Özgür Radyo-Ses Radyo Televizyon Yayin Yapim Ve Tanitim AS v Turkey* App nos 64178/00, 64179/00, 64181/00, 64183/00, 64184/00 (ECtHR, 20 March 2006) [78].

47   This includes NGOs and so-called human rights defenders whose important functions in a democratic society are recognised in the 1998 UN Declaration on the Right and Responsibility of Individuals, Groups and Organs of Society to Promote and Protect Universally Recognized Human Rights and Fundamental Freedoms (often referred to as 'UN Declaration on Human Rights Defenders') UNGA Res 53/144 (8 March 1999) UN Doc A/RES/53/144. See also CESCR, Statement on Human Rights Defenders and Economic, Social and Cultural Rights (29 March 2017) UN Doc E/C.12/2016/2,

48   See eg *Vides Aizsardzibas Klubs v Latvia* App no 57829/00 (ECtHR, 27 May 2004) [42]; and UN Declaration on Human Rights Defenders (n 47), [1], [3] (referring *inter alia* to civil society's monitoring role).

49   HRC, General Comment 25 (n 28) [25]; UN Declaration on Human Rights Defenders (n 47) [1] and [3].

50   The UN Special Rapporteur on the Situation of Human Rights Defenders regularly refers to obligations to create a 'safe and enabling environment' for human rights defenders, see in particular: Report of the UN Special Rapporteur on the Situation of Human Rights Defenders (23 December 2013) UN Doc A/HRC/25/55; and Report of the UN Special Rapporteur on the Situation of Human Rights Defenders (15 January 2019) UN Doc A/HRC/40/60/Add.3 [28] and [70].

51   ICCPR art 14(1); ECHR art 6(1); HRC, General Comment 32 – Right to Equality before Courts and Tribunals and to Fair Trial (23 August 2007) UN Doc CCPR/C/GC/32 [3], [18].

thus democratically controlled, legislature.[52] Furthermore, the judiciary's independence from the executive (and legislature) is ensured by its ability to make legally binding decisions[53] that shall not be set aside by any non-judicial body,[54] and the requirement that they must be executed.[55] The independence of individual judges shall furthermore be guaranteed by appropriate appointment procedures, ensuring that the selected individuals are 'of integrity and ability with appropriate training or qualifications in law',[56] by adequate remuneration and service conditions,[57] and by 'guaranteed tenure until a mandatory retirement age or the expiry of their term of office.'[58]

2.3 Progressive Realisation and Prioritisation of Minimum Core Rights

Other overarching obligations flowing from human rights law relate to the obligation to 'progressively realise' these rights whilst prioritising the implementation of so-called minimum core rights. The obligation to 'progressively realise' human rights recognises that it is rarely the case that state duty-bearers can immediately comply with the numerous duties that human rights law poses on them. Resource constraints are only

---

52 Nowak, *UN Covenant on Civil and Political Rights: CCPR Commentary* (NP Engel, 2005) 319; see also relevant ECtHR jurisprudence, *Zand v Austria* App no 7360/76 (ECtHR, 16 May 1977) [69]; *Coëme v Belgium* App no 23492/96 (ECtHR, 22 June 2000) [89]-[99].

53 HRC, General Comment 32 (n 51) [18]; see also eg *Bentham v the Netherlands* App no 8848/80 (ECtHR, 23 October 1985) [40], [43]; *Leander v Sweden* App no 9248/81 (ECtHR, 26 March 1987) [82]; *Chahal v UK* App no 2241/93 (ECtHR 15 November 1996) [154].

54 This reflects the principle of the finality of court judgments. See eg *Cooper v UK*, App no 48843/99 (ECtHR, 16 December 2003) [129]-[133]; *Assenov v Bulgaria* App no 24760/94 (ECtHR, 28 October 1998) [148]. See also, Basic Principles on the Independence of the Judiciary, adopted by the Seventh United Nations Congress on the Prevention of Crime and the Treatment of Offenders held at Milan from 26 August to 6 September 1985 and endorsed by UNGA Res 40/32 (29 November 1985) UN Doc A/RES/40/32 and UNGA Res 40/146 (13 December 1985) UN Doc A/RES/40/146 [4].

55 Eg *Van de Hurk* (n 38) [52]; *Öneryildiz v Turkey* App no 48939/99 (ECtHR, 30 November 2004) [152].

56 UN Basic Principles on the Independence of the Judiciary (n 54) [10]; and HRC, General Comment 32 (n 51) [19].

57 UN Basic Principles on the Independence of the Judiciary (n 54) [11]; HRC, General Comment 32 (n 51) [19].

58 UN Basic Principles on the Independence of the Judiciary (n 54) [12]; HRC, General Comment 32 (n 51) [19].

one of the considerations that underlie this notion. Other constraints can come for example in form of lack of knowledge of common threats to human rights or an external source of threats that states of jurisdiction are unable to address effectively,[59] or lack of expertise.[60] 'Progressive realisation' requires and allows states to plan the incremental implementation of human rights towards their full realisation, involving sequencing and priority setting in light of local circumstances.

In this context, it can, however, also be noted that the obligations to secure human rights through democratic institutions can themselves be subject to progressive realisation. In other words, if a state's existing institutional framework is inadequate and/or if institutions rely on authoritarian or (top-down) technocratic approaches to devise the measures to implement human rights, the principle of progressive realisation requires that steps are taken to build effective administrative, executive, legislative and judicial institutions and to democratise them over time.[61] The notion of progressive realisation is moreover closely related to the idea of 'dynamic interpretation' and application (and broader implementation) of human rights law: an obligation to constantly adapt the legislative and other measures for the realisation of human rights in light of 'present-day conditions',[62] taking account of new threats to human rights as well as changing circumstances, manifesting themselves in form of cultural, social, religious, scientific, economic and other developments. Ideally, such a process is facilitated through democratic institutions that implement human rights in light of the developing collective preferences of rights-holders.

---

59   Eg when policies promoted by other states or international organisations undermine the protection of human rights in a particular country, see eg CESCR, General Comment 8 – The Relationship between Sanctions and Respect for Economic, Social and Cultural Rights (12 December 1997) UN Doc E/C.12/1997/8.

60   In such cases, the CESCR often recommends cooperation with other states or specialised UN agencies, see eg CESCR, General Comment 12 – The Right to Adequate Food (12 May 1999) UN Doc E/C.12/1999/5 [40]; CESCR, General Comment 13 – The Right to Education (8 December 1999) UN Doc E/C.12/1999/10 [60]; CESCR, General Comment 14 (n 13) [64]; CESCR, General Comment 17 – The Right of Everyone to Benefit from the Protection of the Moral and Material Interests Resulting from any Scientific, Literary or Artistic Production of Which He or She is the Author (12 January 2006) UN Doc E/C.12/GC/17 [57].

61   The long-term unsustainability of implementing human rights through autocratic or technocratic regimes is convincingly established in Shue, *Basic Rights: Subsistence, Affluence and U.S. Foreign Policy* (Princeton University Press, 2nd edn, 1996) 71-78.

62   See eg *Tyrer v UK* App no 5856/72 (ECtHR, 25 March 1978) [31].

At the same time, human rights law imposes minimum core obligations on all states that are to be realised as a matter of priority.[63] The minimum core content of each human right corresponds to particularly urgent human interests – such as the interest to survive.[64] Due to their importance, minimum core rights cannot be limited as this would extinguish them as rights.[65] This includes that they cannot be limited through democratic decisions, including democratic decisions about resource allocations, and they thus put egalitarian (counter-majoritarian) limits to democracy.[66] Moreover, it is questionable whether it is ever necessary[67] to derogate from minimum core rights temporarily 'in times of emergency threatening the life of the nation' to an extent this is 'strictly required by the exigencies of the situation'.[68] UN treaty bodies and the ECtHR have defined the minimum core content of numerous human rights, with the CESCR leading the way in this area.[69]

3 De Facto Independent Regimes as Potential de Facto Human Rights Duty-bearers

The analysis now turns to examine the statements and practice of selected de facto independent regimes to assess whether some of them in fact assume overarching human rights obligations introduced above. The de facto independent regimes chosen for closer analysis here are relatively strong, have been exercising control over territory for a considerable period of time, and are able to engage in significant institution building and reiterative law-making processes. The focus will be on developments in the Republic of Abkhazia (RoA or Abkhazia), the Nagorno-Karabakh Republic (NKR), the Pridnestrovian Moldavian Republic (Transnistria), and the Republic of Somaliland (Somaliland). The focus on these four entities

---

63 CESCR General Comment 3 (n 9) [10]; General Comment 19 (n 13) [60]; General Comment 14 (n 13) [47].

64 Bilchitz, *Poverty and Fundamental Rights: The Justification and Enforcement of Socio-Economic Rights* (OUP, 2007) 222-24.

65 For details, see Müller, 'Limitations to and Derogations from Economic, Social and Cultural Rights' (2009) 9 *Human Rights Law Review* 557, 579-83.

66 Besson, 'Human Rights and Democracy in a Global Context: Decoupling and Recoupling' (2011) 4 *Ethics & Global Politics* 19.

67 See Müller (n 65) 591-99.

68 ICCPR art 4(1); ECHR art 15(1); ACHR art 27.

69 Eg CESCR, General Comment 19 (n 13) [59]-[61]; General Comment 14 (n 13) [43].

also originates from the high likelihood that they exercise de facto (human rights) jurisdiction – the threshold criterion under human rights law that triggers a human rights duty-bearer's concrete human rights duties towards concrete individual rights-holders in the first place.[70]

Before we immerse ourselves in the exploration of these de facto independent regimes' statements and practice, one caveat is in order. The often politically controversial nature of de facto independent regimes' activities – in particular their exercise of public powers in de facto compliance with the aforementioned overarching human rights obligations that by definition increases their legitimacy through effective human rights protection – leads to a situation in which there is limited international engagement with or monitoring of these entities' 'practice'. It is therefore often difficult to find objective information about the undertakings of de facto independent regimes in this area. Depending on political outlook, some sources will not tire in stressing the harmfulness and illegitimacy of the de facto independent regimes' activities, whereas others will emphasise a particular regime's (or other armed non-state actor's) mass popularity as well as their sophistication in protecting human rights, including through setting up relevant public (democratic or democratising) institutions. To mitigate these difficulties, the following analysis relies on an array of sources, with a preference for academic literature, UN-, NGO- and news-reports that promise neutral reporting and balanced analysis. However, 'official' websites of Abkhazian, NKR-, Transnistrian and Somaliland authorities have also been consulted, not least to find out about these entities' interpretation and application of human rights in their respective domestic laws and policies.

3.1 De Facto Independent Regimes' Constitutions Indicating Intentions to Secure Human Rights in a Democratic System

The constitutions of the RoA, the NKR, Somaliland and Transnistria suggest that these entities wish to set up democratic or democratising regimes protecting equal human rights of all individuals who come un-

---

70 ICCPR art 2(1); ECHR art 1; CRC art 2(1); Optional Protocol to the International Covenant on Economic, Social and Cultural Rights (entered into force 5 May 2013) UN Doc A/RES/63/117 (OP-ICESCR), art 2. The present author has analysed the possibility of some de facto independent regimes and armed non-state actors exercising de facto human rights jurisdiction elsewhere, see Müller, 'Can Armed Non-State Actors Exercise Jurisdiction and Thus Become Human Rights Duty-Bearers?' (2020) 20(2) Human Rights Law Review 269. This piece builds on this analysis.

der their de facto jurisdiction. For example, the Somaliland Constitution of 2000 proclaims that 'the political system of the Republic of Somaliland shall be based on peace, cooperation, democracy and plurality of political parties',[71] establishing an executive power headed by a directly elected president;[72] a two-chamber legislature, the lower house of which is 'directly elected by secret ballot in a free general election';[73] and an independent judiciary,[74] thus adhering to the separation of powers doctrine.[75] It also asserts the equality of all Somaliland citizens and prohibits discrimination,[76] and contains an extensive fundamental rights chapter,[77] reiterating that the latter shall be interpreted in light of international human rights law.[78] Somaliland has furthermore announced that it considers itself bound by international human rights treaties, in particular the ICCPR, the ICESCR and the CRC.[79] Similar pronouncements are made in the 1994 RoA,[80] the 2017 (2nd) NKR[81] and the 1996 Transnistrian consti-

---

71   Somaliland Constitution art 9 (*Somalilandlaw 2010*) Translated by Ibrahim Hashi Jama <//www.somalilandlaw.com/Somaliland_Constitution_Text_only_Eng_IJSLL .pdf> accessed 29 March 2021.

72   Somaliland Constitution arts 80-81, and chapter III.

73   Somaliland Constitution art 40, and chapter II.

74   Somaliland Constitution art 79(2), and chapter IV.

75   Somaliland Constitution art 37(2).

76   Somaliland Constitution art 8.

77   Somaliland Constitution arts 8, 21-36.

78   Somaliland Constitution art 10(2); Jama, 'The Somaliland Constitution: Experience to Date and Future Developments', *Discussion Paper*, June 2008, <www .somalilandlaw.com/SL_CONSTITUTION_paper_0608.pdf> accessed 29 March 2021, 16.

79   Somaliland Constitution arts 10(1)-(2) and 21(2); see also an overview provided at: Somalilandlaw.com/Jama, 'Somaliland Human Rights Law' <www.somalilandlaw .com/somaliland_human_rights_law.html> accessed 29 March 2021

80   Constitution of Abkhazia (RoA) (26 November 1994) <https://unpo.org/ article/697> accessed 3 December 2020 arts 1 and 2 (RoA as a 'democratic state'); art 7 (separation of powers); fundamental rights (ch 3, arts 11-13); directly elected legislature (arts 36, 37); directly elected president (art 49); independent judiciary (ch 5, arts 68, 77); equality and non-discrimination (art 12).

81   Constitution of the Nagorno-Karabakh Republic (20 February 2017) <http:// president.nkr.am/en/constitution/> accessed 29 March 2021: NKR as a democratic state (art 1); fundamental rights (arts 3 and 23-80); separation of powers (art 4); equality and non-discrimination (arts 28-30); elected president (arts 88-90); elected legislature (arts 106-109); independent judiciary (arts 135,137).

tutions.[82] These entities have also pledged to comply with international human rights treaties.[83]

In the next step, the (domestic) law and practice of these de facto independent regimes is examined in more detail for potential de facto compliance with the overarching human rights duties that were introduced in section 2.

3.2 Elected Legislative and Executive Authorities and Their Law-making

The RoA, NKR, Transnistria and Somaliland have made and continue to make efforts to set up a representative legislature by recognising a right to vote[84] and organising elections[85] and, albeit in varying degrees, by taking steps to develop multi-party systems.

The RoA has, for example, held regular parliamentary and direct presidential elections since 1991 and 1999 respectively which have been described as 'pluralistic and competitive'.[86] Following some political turmoil, as a result of which the Abkhazian Supreme Court overturned the result of the second round of the presidential elections of September

---

82   Constitution of the Pridnestrovian Moldavian Republic (adopted during the 24 December 1995 national referendum and signed by the President of the Pridnestrovskaia Moldavskaia Respublica (Transnistria) (on 17 January 1996) <http://mfa-pmr.org/en/bht> accessed 29 March 2021: art 1 (Transnistria as democratic state); arts 6 and 55 (separation of powers); fundamental rights (arts 16-52); equality and non-discrimination (art 17); elected legislature (art 59); directly elected president (art 68); independent judiciary (arts 80(4)-84).

83   RoA Constitution (n 80) art 11 (referring to the UDHR, ICCPR and ICESCR); NKR Constitution (n 81) art 3(4) (establishing that the a general duty to 'ensure the protection of fundamental human and civil rights in conformity with the common principles and norms of the international law') and art 61(2) (establishing a right to 'apply to international bodies for the protection of human rights and freedoms').

84   RoA Constitution (n 80), art 38; NKR Constitution (n 81) arts 2(2), 7 and 48; Transnistrian Constitution (n 82) arts 1 and 31; Somaliland Constitution (n 71) art 22(2).

85   All four entities have adopted laws regulating parliamentary and presidential elections, see eg закон о выборах Президента Республики Абхазия, № 911-с-XIV (7 June 2004); Избирательный кодекс Приднестровской Молдавской Республики, № 332-3 (9 August 2000); Избирательный кодекс НКР, (29 October 2014) <//www.nankr.am/hy/1327> accessed 28 March 2021; and for an overview of Somaliland election laws, see <http://www.somalilandlaw.com/electoral_laws.html> accessed 28 March 2021.

86   Ó Beacháin, 'The Dynamics of Electoral Politics in Abkhazia' (2012) 45 *Communist and Post-Communist Studies* 165, 165.

DE FACTO INDEPENDENT REGIMES AND OVERARCHING HR DUTIES 47

2019 in which no candidate got more than 50% of the vote,[87] new competitive presidential elections were held in March 2020, in which 57% of the Abkhazian voters elected Aslan Bzhaniya as president.[88] Overall, power has been transferred relatively peacefully between the government and opposition several times over the past two decades in the RoA – a feature indicating that Abkhazia may have 'achieved a greater level of democratic practice than many other post-Soviet systems including other unrecognised ... states'.[89]

The NKR also regularly held multi-party[90] parliamentary elections since 1991, and (it seems, reasonably competitive) presidential elections since 1994.[91] However, since the NKR lost substantive parts of its territory in November 2020, the democratic future of the NKR seems uncertain.[92]

The Transnistrian regime, by contrast, has been described as 'hybrid', 'meaning that it is based on a combination of democratic and authoritarian features'.[93] Parliamentary elections taking place since 1990 have been described as 'relatively free and fair',[94] resulting in a considerable turnover of elected members in the Transnistrian unicameral parliament (the Supreme Soviet)[95] and a cautious but gradual development of a multi-

---

87   'Supreme Court of Abkhazia Orders Rerun of Presidential Election' (*Open Caucasus Media*, 10 January 2020) <https://oc-media.org/supreme-court-of-abkhazia-orders -rerun-of-presidential-election/> accessed 28 March 2021. In the September 2019 elections, the two candidates received 47% (Khadzhimba) and 46% (Kvitsiniya) of the vote respectively, while the remainder voted 'against all', an option on the ballots.

88   'Aslan Bzhania Elected President of Abkhazia' (*Open Caucasus Media*, 23 March 2020) <https://oc-media.org/aslan-bzhaniya-elected-president-of-abkhazia/> accessed 28 March 2021.

89   Ó Beacháin (n 86) 166.

90   On the multi-party system in the NKR, see Kolstø and Blakkisrud, '*De facto* States and Democracy: The Case of Nagorno-Karabakh' (2012) 45 *Communist and Post-Communist Studies* 141, 145-46.

91   *Ibid.*, 149; and concerning the most recent parliamentary and presidential elections in spring 2020, see Istrate, 'Four Take Aways from Nagorno Karabakhs Elections' (*Emerging Europe*, 2 April 2020) <https://emerging-europe.com/news/four -takeaways-from-nagorno-karabakhs-elections/> accessed 28 March 2021.

92   Mejlumyan, 'Nagorno-Karabakh Shuffles Top-Officials, Plans New Elections' (*Eurasianet,* 2 January 2021) <https://eurasianet.org/nagorno-karabakh-shuffles -top-officials-plans-new-elections> accessed 28 March 2021.

93   Protsyk, 'Secession and Hybrid Regime Politics in Transnistria' (2012) 45 *Communist and Post-Communist Studies* 175, 181.

94   *Ibid.* 181.

95   *Ibid.* 178; Protsyk, 'Representation and Democracy in Eurasia's Unrecognized States: The Case of Transnistria' (2009) *Post-Soviet Affairs* 25.

party system.[96] However, most recent parliamentary elections of November 2020 indicate a decrease in election competitiveness due to abolishing the 25% turnout threshold for parliamentary elections, the reduction of the size of the Supreme Soviet from 43 to 33 members, and the 'concentration of power in the hands of big business [the Sheriff Holding]' that 'led to a monopolisation of the political space'.[97] Sheriff Holding controls the predominant Transnistrian political party 'Renewal', which currently not only has an absolute majority in the Supreme Soviet, but also won the Presidency in 2016. When it comes to presidential elections, Transnistrian president Igor Smirnov stayed in power from 1990-2011[98] without facing serious electoral competition. Competitive presidential elections have been held in 2011, leading to a transfer of power in that same year[99] and again as a result of the 2016 presidential elections.[100]

Somaliland held two multi-party parliamentary election in 2005 and, after numerous postponements and rescheduling, in May 2021; and several presidential elections since 2003. In the peaceful and open 2021 parliamentary elections, the two opposition parties won a majority. [101] The most recent presidential election of November 2017 has been described by local and international observers as 'peaceful and credible',[102] involv-

---

96 Protsyk (n 93) 180.

97 Dirun, 'How Big Business Attempts to Hijack the Popular Vote to the Supreme Council of Transnistria in 2020' (*De Facto States Research Unit*, 23 November 2020) <https://defactostates.ut.ee/blog/how-big-business-attempts-hijack-popular-vote -supreme-council-transnistria-2020> accessed 28 March 2021; and Ernst, 'Breakaway Transnistria fully under Sheriff's Control as Obnovlenie Party Sweeps Board in Parliamentary Election' (*bne Intellinews*, 3 December 2020) <www.intellinews. com/breakaway-transnistria-fully-under-sheriff-s-control-as-obnovlenie-party-sweeps-board-in-parliament-election-198054/> accessed 29 March 2021.

98 Protsyk (n 93) 177.

99 The 2011 presidential elections resulted in a surprise win for the opposition candidate *ibid.* 181.

100 Leşanu, 'Transnistria's Presidential Elections: A Hard-fought Contest with no Punches Pulled, as Russia Diverts its Attention from the Unrecognised State' (*EUROPP/LSE blog*, 23 December 2016) <http://bit.ly/2hwzSua> accessed 29 March 2021.

101 'Somaliland Elections: Opposition Parties Win Majority of Seats' (*Aljazeera news*, 6 June 2021) <https://www.aljazeera.com/news/2021/6/6/somaliland-opposition -wins-first-parliamentary-polls-since> accessed 20 June 2021.

102 Omaar and Muse Ali, 'A Negotiated Democracy: Factors that Influenced Somaliland's 2017 Elections', (*The Elephant*, 19 April 2018) <www.theelephant.info/topic/ somaliland/?print=pdf-search> accessed 29 March 2021; see also International Election Observation Mission, 'The Limits of Consensus? Report on the Somaliland Presidential Elections, 13th November 2017', <https://www.ucl.ac.uk/bartlett/

DE FACTO INDEPENDENT REGIMES AND OVERARCHING HR DUTIES   49

ing inter alia the first ever televised debate of the three presidential candidates.[103]

This is not to say that elections held in the RoA, the NKR, Transnistria and Somaliland are without flaws, or that the elected legislatures clearly represent all stratums of the electorate or are immune from undue executive intervention. To name but a few of the shortcomings in addition to the ones mentioned above, it can be recalled that Somaliland's presidential[104] and, in particular, parliamentary elections have been postponed time and again.[105] Moreover, the Somaliland constitution hampers the development of a multi-party system by limiting the number of political parties allowed to compete in elections to three,[106] and relatedly does not permit independent candidates to run in parliamentary or presidential elections.[107] Since 2014, the RoA has been criticised for increasingly excluding ethnic Georgians living in Abkhazia from participating in elections.[108] In Transnistria, at least until 2011, the electoral commission showed a strong bias towards the incumbent president,[109] and since the 2020 parliamentary elections the political space appears to be in full control of the Sheriff Holding.[110] In the NKR, the limited power of the parliament (National Assembly) in relation to the presidency has been deplored,[111] and after the lost war against Azerbaijan and Turkey in No-

---

development/sites/bartlett/files/somaliland_election_report_final_draft.pdf> accessed 30 March 2021.

103   *Ibid.*

104   Presidential elections have also been postponed numerous times before they were finally held in November 2017, see eg Report of the UN Independent Expert on the Situation of Human Rights in Somalia' (28 October 2015) UN Doc A/HRC/30/57 [9],[15].

105   See eg Report of the Independent Expert on the Situation of Human Rights in Somalia (16 September 2019) UN Doc A/HRC/42/62 [82], [113]. However, parliamentary elections were finally held in May 2021, see (n 101).

106   Somaliland Constitution (n 71) art 9(2).

107   For a critical analysis, see Jama (n 78) 14-15.

108   OHCHR, 'Report on Cooperation with Georgia' (15 August 2018) UN Doc A/HRC/39/44 [61]-[63]; Hammarberg and Grono 'Human Rights in Abkhazia Today' (Palmecenter July 2017) 17, 52-54 <www.palmecenter.se/wp-content/uploads/2017/07/Human-Rights-in-Abkhazia-Today-report-by-Thomas-Hammarberg-and-Magdalena-Grono.pdf> accessed 28 March 2021

109   Association Promo-LEX, 'Human Rights in the Transnistrian Region of Moldova' (2007) <https://promolex.md/wp-content/uploads/2017/06/eng_doc_1233068241.pdf> accessed 28 March 2021 43-44.

110   Dirun (n 97); and Ernst (n 97).

111   Kolstø and Blakkisrud (n 90) 146.

vember 2020, most governance functions has been concentrated in the NKR executive.[112]

However, the elected parliaments in these four de facto independent regimes are involved in genuine law-making processes and have adopted numerous laws enhancing the protection of human rights in their respective 'jurisdictions' that also seem to be in line with the human rights legality standard.[113] Laws adopted by all four parliaments are proclaimed and published in *Official Gazettes*[114] and/or on the internet,[115] complying with the accessibility criterion.

The Abkhaz parliament (People's Assembly) appears to lead the way in proactive law-making. It has been described as being 'heavily involved in the law-making process', a process that is widely perceived as 'overall authentic' by those contributing to it and affected by it.[116] Among the examples of laws that seem to be well in line with the human rights legality standard is the Abkhaz Criminal Code.[117] The Code has been judged to positively incorporate human rights principles like clarity and foreseeability, non-discrimination and fair trial rights.[118] Though there has been criticism of the Abkhaz parliament drawing heavily on legislation of the Russian Federation, there appear to be numerous examples of pieces of legislation that 'introduced [...or] retained' important distinctions, or 'go well beyond the legislation in the Russian Federation today',[119] for ex-

---

112   Mejlumyan (n 92).

113   This is facilitated by constitutional provisions, establishing eg that 'when restricting basic rights and freedoms, laws must define the grounds and extent of restrictions, be sufficiently certain to enable the holders and addressees of these rights and freedoms to display appropriate conduct' (NKR Constitution (n 81) art 79); see also Somaliland Constitution (n 71) arts 23(3) and (4), 30, 31(3) and 32(1) and (2); RoA Constitution (n 83) art 35; Transnistrian Constitution (n 82) art 40(4), 78.

114   As foreseen eg in Somaliland Constitution (n 71) art 75.

115   Somaliland Official Gazette (since 2012, in Somali) <http://garyaqaankaguud.com/somaliland-official-gazette/; Abkhaz laws (in Russian) are available at: http://presidentofabkhazia.org/doc/const/ and <http://presidentofabkhazia.org/doc/codecs/>; Transnistrian laws (in Russian only) are available on a searchable database: <https://pravopmr.ru>; Karabakhian laws are available on the website of the NKR parliament: <http://www.nankr.am/ru/7/tab/40> (primarily in Armenian, some also in Russian), all accessed 29 March 2021.

116   Hammarberg/Grono Abkhazia report 2017 (n 108) 17.

117   Уголовный кодекс Республики Абхазия (The Criminal Code of the Republic of Abkhazia), № 1555-c-XIV (10 January 2007).

118   Hammarberg/Grono Abkhazia report 2017 (n 108) 15-16. However, the Abkhaz Criminal Code still permits the use of the death penalty in exceptional circumstances (art 54), with a formal moratorium in place since 2007.

119   *Ibid.* 17.

ample in the area of equality and non-discrimination.[120] The Abkhazian Commissioner for Human Rights has also made concrete suggestions as to how different pieces of Abkhazian legislation can be improved to enhance the protection of human rights.[121]

Judged by their outputs,[122] the Transnistrian and NKR parliaments are also involved in numerous law-making processes. As positive developments in Transnistria, changes to the Criminal Code and the Code of Criminal Procedures of 2012 have brought them closer into line with human rights law can be highlighted (notably with regard to the severity of punishment for crimes), as well as the Law on Public Associations[123] and a Law on Freedom of Conscience and Religious Associations[124] that contain many formulations that are 'consistent with international [human rights] norms.'[125] Some provisions seem, however, too vague or are used too inconsistently to fulfil the clarity and foreseeability standards,[126] and some more recent pieces of legislation, in particular those regulating the activities of civil society organisations and religious organisations, have been judged non-compliant with 'international standards on democracy, the rule of law and human rights'.[127]

---

120   E.g. concerning gender equality, see Закон об обеспечении равных прав и возможностей для мужчин и женщин в Республике Абхазия (Law on Ensuring Equal Rights and Possibilities for Men and Women) № 2253-с-IV (29 December 2008). For further examples, see Report by Hammarberg/Grono Abkhazia report 2017 (n 108) 17.

121   Ежегодный доклад о деятельности Уполномоченного по правам человека в Республике Абхазия за 2018-2019 (Annual report on the activities of the Commissioner for Human Rights in the Republic of Abkhazia 2018-2019) <https:// ombudsmanra.org/upload/iblock/158/1588f1a7fe9ccbb552c204a002daccb2.pdf> accessed 29 March 2021

122   See the long list of NKR laws at <http://www.nankr.am/ru/7/tab/40>accessed 29 March 2021; and Transistrian laws at https://pravopmr.ru> accessed 29 March 2021.

123   Закон «Об общественных объединениях» (Law on Public Associations) № 528-3-IV (04 August 2008).

124   Закон «О свободе совести и религиозных объединениях» (On freedom of conscience and religious association) № 668-3-IV (19 February 2009).

125   Report on Human Rights in the Transnistrian Region of the Republic of Moldova, by Senior UN Expert Thomas Hammarberg (14 February 2013) 13 <https://www.undp.org/content/dam/unct/moldova/docs/pub/Senior_Expert_Hammarberg_Report_TN_Human_Rights.pdf> accessed 31 March 2021.

126   *Ibid.* 13.

127   On civil society organisations, see Report of the UN Special Rapporteur on the Situation of Human Rights Defenders (15 January 2019) UN Doc A/HRC/40/60/Add.3 [91] and [73]; on religious organisations, see Report of UN Special Rapporteur on

The Somaliland parliament has also been actively involved in the legislative process, approaching the formidable task of bringing the Somaliland legal system that has been described by the UN Special Rapporteur on the Situation of Human Rights in Somalia in 2000 as a 'combination of shariah, English, Egyptian and Siad Barre era traditions' and that, 'owing to the multiplicity of references, ... is extremely confusing and considered archaic.'[128] Among the laws adopted to improve the protection of human rights in Somaliland that appear to be largely in line with the human rights legality standard are the Rape and Sexual Offences Law,[129] increasing the protection of women's rights, and a Juvenile Justice Act.[130] However, the UN Special Rapporteur has also criticised some pieces of Somaliland legislation that remain incompatible with human rights law, such as criminal legislation on defamation and libel[131] and prison administration legislation.[132] The Special Rapporteur has also called for the urgent adoption of further legislation to improve the protection of women's rights, e.g., by clearly prohibiting all types of FGM that continue to affect the vast majority of Somaliland women.[133]

3.3   Independent Judiciary and Effective Remedies for Alleged Human Rights Violations

Another building block of the (democratic) institutional system that human rights duty-bearers must establish to protect all human rights is an independent judiciary that can inter alia offer an effective remedy for alleged violations of human rights, as well as fair criminal and civil trials. The RoA, NKR, Transnistria and Somaliland have all taken considerable steps to set up independent judiciaries as devised in their respective constitutions,[134] and their modes of operation have been specified

---

Freedom of Religion and Belief (27 January 2012) UN Doc A/HRC/19/60/Add.2 [19], [59] and [87].

128   Report of UN Special Rapporteur on the Situation of Human Rights in Somalia (26 January 2000) UN Doc E/CN.4/2000/110 [83].

129   Report UNSR Somalia 2019 (n 105) [88] and [113].

130   *Ibid.* [83].

131   Report of UN Independent Expert on the Situation of Human Rights in Somalia' (29 August 2011) UN Doc A/HRC/18/48 [48].

132   Report of UN Independent Expert on the Situation of Human Rights in Somalia (22 August 2012) UN Doc A/HRC/21/61 [30].

133   Report UNSR Somalia 2011 (n 131) [50]; Report UNSR Somalia 2019 (n 105) [113].

134   See ns 74, 80-82.

in numerous domestic laws adopted by their respective parliaments.[135] Courts in the four entities thereby fulfil one important criterion under international human rights law: they are 'established by law'[136] where, in a democratic system, the 'law' is to be understood as parliamentary statute.[137] Concerning Transnistrian courts, even the ECtHR has alluded to the fact that Transnistrian courts might indeed fulfil the 'established by law' condition 'provided that [... such courts] form part of a judicial system operating on a 'constitutional and legal basis' reflecting a judicial tradition compatible with the Convention'.[138] The latter will comprise the 'effective political democracy' contemplated in the ECHR.[139]

The judiciaries in the four de facto independent regimes also comply with other requirements of human rights law aimed to ensure their independence. In the RoA, appointment procedures of judges involving the Abkhaz president and parliament, their tenure, salary and training seem adequate to ensure judges' independence, leading analysts to the conclusion that courts 'work generally well' in Abkhazia.[140] Though problems with the enforcement of their judgments persist, Abkhaz courts have demonstrated their independence, in particular by upholding the property rights of returning ethnic Georgians who were forced to flee Abkhazia during the armed conflict in 1992-93 – decisions that are highly politically charged in a Republic keen to protect 'ethnic Abkhaz identity'.[141]

---

135 Somaliland Organisation of the Judiciary Law (2003), Law No 24/2003. On the Transnistrian judiciary, see eg, Конституционный закон «О судебной системе в Приднестровской Молдавской Республике» (Constitutional Law "On the Judicial System") № 620-КЗ-III (9 August 2005); Конституционный закон «О статусе судей в Приднестровской Молдавской Республике» (Constitutional Law "On the Status of Judges in the Pridnestrovian Moldavian Republic") № 621-КЗ-III (9 August 2005); Конституционный закон «О Верховном суде Приднестровской Молдавской Республики» (Constitutional Law "On the Supreme Court"), № 260-КЗ-III (3 April 2003); Конституционный закон «О Конституционном суде Приднестровской Молдавской Республики» (Constitutional Law "On the Constitutional Court") № 205-КЗ-III (25 November 2002). On the Abkhaz judiciary: Конституционный закон Республики Абхазия «О судебной власти», (Constitutional Law of the Republic of Abkhazia "On Judicial Power") № 3784-с-V (15 June 2015).

136 ICCPR art 14(1); ECHR art 6(1).

137 See n 52.

138 *Ilascu and others v Moldova and Russia* App no 4877/99 (ECtHR, 8 July 2004) [455]-[464].

139 ECHR, preamble.

140 Hammarberg/Grono Abkhazia report 2017 (n 108) 21.

141 *Ibid.* 22 and 40.

This also shows that Abkhaz courts are able to offer at least some remedies for violations of the right to property enshrined in the Abkhaz constitution.[142]

The independence of the Transnistrian judiciary was strengthened in 2012 with the reorganisation of the Office of the General Prosecutor, ending the Office's supervision of courts, including its power to overrule decisions made by judges.[143] However, reports also indicate deficits, for example that judges are appointed and dismissed primarily by the Transnistrian president albeit upon recommendation of a council of senior judges,[144] that defence lawyers are passive and work on the 'presumption of guilt',[145] partly due to pressure from the executive,[146] and that judges and lawyers lack appropriate training[147] and are prone to accept bribes,[148] due to low salaries among other factors. Similar criticism has been voiced concerning the NKR judiciary.[149]

Concerning Somaliland, UN reports indicate that courts have been operating since the early 1990s, contributing to the relative peace and stability in Somaliland compared to other parts of Somalia.[150] Whilst the training of judges and lawyers has improved over the years[151] and the adoption of Code of Conduct and Disciplinary Rule for Judges and Prosecutors of 2012 has helped to limit arbitrary dismissals of Somali-

---

142   RoA Constitution (n 80) art 13.

143   Hammarberg Report on Human Rights in Transnistria 2013 (n 125) 17.

144   *Ibid.* 18; and Promo-Lex Association, 'Report on Human Rights in the Transnistrian Region of Moldova / 2012 Retrospective' (2012) 32 <https://issuu.com/promo-lex/docs/human_rights_transnistria_2010/6> accessed 3 April 2021.

145   International Federation for Human Rights (FIDH) 'Assessing Human Rights Protection in Eastern European Conflict and Disputed Entities' (September 2014) (FIDH report) 23; Hammarberg Report on Human Rights in Transnistria 2013 (n 125) 18 and 19.

146   Promo-Lex Association, 'Report on Human Rights in the Transnistrian Region of Moldova / 2011 Retrospective' (2011) 12 <https://issuu.com/promo-lex/docs/human_rights_transnistria> accessed 3 April 2021.

147   Hammarberg Report on Human Rights in Transnistria 2013 (n 125) 17 and 19.

148   *Ibid.* 18-19; FIDH report (n 145) 22-23.

149   FIDH (n 145) 22-23.

150   See eg Report of the Independent Expert of the UN Commission on Human Rights on the Situation of Human Rights in Somalia (3 March 1997) UN Doc E/CN.4/1997/88 [79]-[84].

151   See eg Report of the UN Independent Expert on the situation of Human Rights in Somalia (17 September 2009) UN Doc A/HRC/12/44 [20]; the College of Law at Hargeisa University offers a comprehensive four year law programme since 2002, see <http://www.uoh-edu.net/college-of-law/> accessed 3 April 2021.

land judges in lower courts and increase their accountability,[152] the independence of the Somaliland judiciary remains under threat by the powers of the Somaliland president who can appoint and dismiss all the justices of the Somaliland Supreme Court at will, except for the Chief Justice.[153] Independence is also undermined by severe underfunding of the judiciary and the complete budgetary dependence of courts on the Ministry of Justice.[154] On a positive note, so-called 'security committees' which had the power to detain and sentence anyone 'seen as a menace to public order',[155] undermining access to courts and fair trial guarantees, were abolished in 2011.[156] Moreover, Somaliland courts have over time increased their jurisdiction in cases involving violence against women which had often been (and continue to be) taken out of the formal legal process and adjudicated through the parallel customary system.[157] This, together with the recruitment and training of more female police officers and prosecutors,[158] has in turn increased the judiciary's capacities to offer at least some remedies for serious violations of women's human rights, including rape and FGM.

The RoA, NKR, Transnistria and Somaliland have also created Human Rights Commissions or Ombudsinstitutions after their parliaments adopted the respective legal basis for these institutions. In the RoA, the 2016 Law on the Commissioner for Human Rights set up the Office of the Commissioner for Human Rights in the RoA which, after some de-

---

152 Mohumed, 'The Principle of Judicial Independence and Somaliland Courts' (*SomalilandLaw*, December 2014) 10, 16 <www.somalilandlaw.com/Independence_of_the_Judiciary_by_Abdishakur.pdf> accessed 29 March 2021.

153 Somaliland Constitution (n 71) art 105. For critique, see Mohumed (n 152) 8, 12-13.

154 Mohumed (n 152) 6, 11-12; Jama (n 78) 14; see also Report of the UN Independent Expert of the UN Commission on Human Rights on Assistance to Somalia in the Field of Human Rights (31 December 2002) UN Doc E/CN.4/2003/115.

155 Report of UN Independent Expert on the Situation of Human Rights in Somalia (23 March 2010) UN Doc A/HRC/13/65; see also Kaplan, 'The Remarkable Story of Somaliland' (2008) 19 *Journal of Democracy* 143, 151.

156 Report UNSR Somalia 2012 (n 132). The campaigns of civil society organisations contributed to the removal of this considerable obstacle to the effective protection of human rights in Somaliland. For more details, see <www.somalilandlaw.com/somaliland_security_committees.html> accessed 28 March 2021.

157 Report UNSR Somalia 2011(n 131); Report of UN Independent Expert on the Situation of Human Rights in Somalia' (4 September 2014) UN Doc A/HRC/27/71 [42].

158 Report UNSR Somalia 2019 (n 105) [90]-[91].

lay due to lack of resources, became operative in November 2018.[159] It has a strong mandate and can receive complaints from everyone living in the RoA (including 'non-citizens') against the actions by any 'state' body or local authority, except for complaints against decisions adopted by the Abkhaz parliament.[160] Judged by her activities that so far include her intervention in cases of death in detention and a push for legislative changes to increase the protection against torture and for mandatory video recording of interrogations,[161] as well as issuing a scathing report on human rights in Abkhazia in 2018-19 containing numerous recommendations of how to address the shortcomings,[162] the Abkhaz Human Rights Commissioner and her Office seem determined to improve the human rights situation in the RoA.[163]

The Human Rights Defender of the Republic of Nagorno-Karabakh works on the basis of the Law of the NKR on the Human Rights Defender adopted in 2005,[164] and, similar to its Abkhaz counterpart, can receive individual complaints and monitor the human rights situation in any public institution or organisation.[165] There is, however, very little information available about the work of the Defender.

The Office of the Ombudsperson for Human Rights in Transnistria has worked since 2006 on the basis of a law adopted in 2005.[166] It also has powers to receive individual complaints and to monitor the human rights

---

159   Hammarberg/Grono Abkhazia Report 2017 (n 108) 26; and Шария, 'В Абхазии открылся долгожданный офис омбудсмена' (Эхо Кавказа, 01/11/2018) <www.ekhokavkaza.com/a/29577621.html> accessed 28 March 2021.

160   Hammarberg/Grono Abkhazia Report 2017 (n 108) 26; see also the informative website of the Abkhazian Human Rights Commissioner: <https://ombudsmanra.org> accessed 28 March 2021.

161   Ekelove-Slydal *et al* 'Human Rights behind Unsettled Borders' (*The Foreign Policy Centre*, 26 September 2019).

162   Ежегодный доклад о деятельности Уполномоченного по правам человека в Республике Абхазия за 2018 –2019 гг., <https://ombudsmanra.org/upload/iblock/158/1588f1a7fe9ccbb552c204a002daccb2.pdf>

163   See also 'Abkhazian Human Rights Commissioner Condemns Torture, Ethnic Discrimination and Domestic Violence', (*Open Caucasus Media*, 30 June 2020) <https://oc-media.org/abkhazian-hr-commissioner-condemns-torture-ethnic-discrimination-and-domestic-violence/> accessed 28 March 2021

164   Law of NKR on the Human Rights Defender (09 February 2005) <www.ombudsnkr.am/en/law_human_rights.html> accessed 28 March 2021.

165   See the website of the Human Rights Defender of the Republic of Nagorno Karabakh <www.ombudsnkr.am/en/useful_info.html> accessed 28 March 2021.

166   Constitutional Law on the Ombudsperson for Human Rights in Transnistria (03/11/2005), <www.ombudsmanpmr.org/konstitutionniy_zacon.htm> accessed 28 March 2021.

situation in prisons and other institutions run by the 'state'.[167] However, a 2013 report of a UN expert on 'Human Rights in the Transnistrian Region of the Republic of Moldova' indicated that the Ombudsperson's Office had a relatively limited outreach.[168]

Somaliland has had a National Human Rights Commission since 2011, the legal basis (a parliamentary act)[169] of which 'meets basic international standards'[170] and UN reports have noted that though it was 'not fully compliant, [the Commission] was close to the spirit of the Paris Principles' in its operations.[171] According to the website of the Commission, it can receive individual complaints, monitor human rights in prisons and other places of detention, and takes on various advisory functions in the area of human rights.[172] Among other things, it has been promoting women's rights through running campaigns about the health implications of FGM and has advocated for the better integration of minorities in the Somaliland political processes.[173]

3.4 Creating an Enabling Environment for (Equal) Political Participation and the Protection of Human Rights

Another overarching human rights obligation that state and non-state de facto human rights duty-bearers shall comply with to allow for the implementation of all human rights is the obligation to create an enabling environment for equal political participation and the protection of human rights, or, in other words, an environment in which a pluralistic 'democratic society' (political community) can thrive and protect the human rights of every member on an equal basis. Beyond holding elections as discussed above, creating such an environment includes the protection of the rights of freedom of expression, assembly and association from which civil society organisations and a free press shall benefit. Moreover, it encompasses various measures to involve structurally disadvantaged groups and individuals in political processes,

---

167   See <www.ombudsmanpmr.org/apparat-upolomochennogo.htm> accessed 28 March 2021.

168   Hammarberg Report on Human Rights in Transnistria 2013 (n 125) 41.

169   Somaliland Human Rights Commission Law (26 December 2010), Law No 39/2010.

170   Report UNSR Somalia 2011 (n 131) [46].

171   Report UNSR Somalia 2012 (n 132) [28].

172   Mandate and Functions of the Somaliland National Human Rights Commission, <http://somalilandhumanrights.org/mandate-and-functions-of-the-slnhrc/> accessed 28 March 2021.

173   Report UNSR Somalia 2019 (n 105) [92] and [97].

including in decision-making processes regarding the steps to be taken to (progressively) realise specific human rights.

All four de facto independent regimes under consideration here have, albeit to varying degrees, a pluralistic and (relatively) free media landscape and an active civil society, including in the area of human rights monitoring and policy-making, benefitting from the rights to freedom of expression and association protected in the respective constitutions of these entities.[174]

A report prepared for the European Union's Special Representative for the South Caucasus and the Crisis in Georgia on 'Human Rights in Abkhazia Today' of July 2017 found that 'civil society organisations (CSOs) and groups are active and vocal in Abkhazia', and have, over the years, 'played an essential role in promoting human rights and pluralism, and advocating for accountable and inclusive governance'.[175] Organisations have pushed for important social reforms, resulting in the establishment of publicly funded institutions like homes for the elderly and a rehabilitation centre for disabled children; have engaged in election monitoring; provided free legal aid, including in the politically-charged cases relating to property rights of ethnic Georgians mentioned above; are advocating for abolishing policies that would deny 'citizenship' to non-ethnic Abkhazians; and have called for measures to address corruption.[176] The relationship between CSOs and the Abkhaz authorities has also been described as 'constructive',[177] with no unreasonably restrictive legislation in place.[178] When it comes to Abkhazia's media landscape, it has been qualified as 'fairly independent', in particular the print media;[179] and Ab-

---

174   Somaliland Constitution (n 71) art 32 (freedom of expression and assembly); RoA Constitution (n 80) art 14 (freedom of speech) art 17 (freedom of association); NKR Constitution (n 81) art 42 (Freedom of expression), art 44 (freedom of assembly), art 45 (freedom of association); Transnistrian Constitution (n 82) art 27 (freedom of expression) art 29 (freedom of association).

175   Hammarberg/Grono Abkhazia Report 2017 (n 108) 30; OHCHR, Report on Cooperation with Georgia (20 August 2019) UN Doc A/HRC/42/34 [44] and [77].

176   *Ibid.* 31; Shvedov, 'Election Season for the Civil Society in the Unrecognised Republics of Caucasus' (*Caucasian Knot,* 26 September 2019) <https://fpc.org.uk/election-season-for-the-civil-society-in-the-unrecognised-republics-of-caucasus/> accessed 28 March 2021

177   *Ibid.*

178   Hammarberg/Grono Abkhazia Report 2017 (n 108) 31-32.

179   *Ibid.* 28-29.

khaz 'state' TV channel, a private TV channel and Russian TV channels are available in the RoA.[180]

The situation for civil society appears to be similar in the NKR, with many organisations engaged in the social and humanitarian field, including the area of women's rights and the rights of persons with disabilities.[181] It is reported that NGOs do not generally have difficulties operating or registering with the NKR Ministry of Justice.[182] It is, however, noted that there are very few NGOs that openly challenge fundamental NKR-government policies, a fact that is attributed inter alia to the general 'unipolarity' of Karabakh society, in particular when it comes to policies directed towards Azerbaijan, the parent state from which the NKR broke away in 1991.[183] The media in the NKR faces few restrictions, with 'no reports of harassments of journalists'.[184] Unlike in the parent state Azerbaijan, international radio stations like Radio Free Europe/Radio Liberty (RFE/RL) broadcast in the NKR;[185] there is a 'state' TV channel, and Armenian and Russian TV channels are also available. There are few independent local media outlets, something that is, however, attributed more to the very small NKR-market when it comes to readership and funding than to governmental repression.[186]

The environment for civil society organisations and the media in Transnistria appears more restrictive than in both the RoA and the NKR: whilst numerous civil society organisations operate in the region, including in the field of human rights monitoring,[187] they 'do not enjoy a safe and enabling environment'.[188] The UN Special Rapporteur on Human Rights Defenders visiting Transnistria in 2018 concluded that this was due to among other things various forms of intimidation faced by human

---

180   *Ibid.* 28.

181   Shvedov (n 176).

182   Kolstø and Blakkisrud (n 90) 147.

183   *Ibid.* 147; also Berg and Mölder, 'Who is Entitled to "Earn Sovereignty"? Legitimacy and Regime Support in Abkhazia and Nagorno Karabakh' (2012) 18 *Nations and Nationalism* 527, 541.

184   Kolstø and Blakkisrud (n 90) 148; see also Nahapetyan, 'Nagorno-Karabkh between a Rock and a Hard Place' (*OpenDemocracy*, 13 July 2015) <www.opendemocracy.net/en/can-europe-make-it/azerbaijans-war-against-western-institutions-why-bakus-cr/> accessed 21 March 2021

185   Nahapetyan (n 184).

186   Kolstø and Blakkisrud (n 90) 148.

187   Hammarberg Report on Human Rights in Transnistria 2013 (n 125) 41.

188   Report of the UN Special Rapporteur on the Situations of Human Rights Defenders – Mission to Moldova (15 January 2019) UN Doc A/HRC/40/60/Add.3 [70].

rights defenders and NGOs from the side of the Transnistrian 'security services'; to bureaucratic hurdles,[189] such as the need to coordinate all civil society activities with the authorities in advance and the introduction of a new section into the Transnistrian law on NGOs in 2017, putting restrictions on organisations to receive foreign funding.[190] The UN Special Rapporteur also reports that 'media outlets are placed under tight control and censorship is exercised',[191] and that journalists have faced intimidation through arbitrary arrests and prosecution.[192] Overall, the media landscape in Transnistria is heavily dominated by 'state'-controlled outlets.[193] However, in line with the observation above that the Transnistrian 'regime' is a hybrid one,[194] it would be wrong to conclude that the media is 'simply [a] transmission belt [...] for the executive wishes'.[195] A certain degree of press freedom does exist, evidenced by the presence of some small but vocal independent media outlets.[196]

The picture is equally mixed for civil society organisations and the media in Somaliland. NGOs have been active in Somaliland since the early 1990s,[197] and have contributed to the development of a more pluralistic and inclusive 'democratic society' by advocating for women's and minorities' rights, including their increased political participation.[198] They have

---

189   Hammarberg Report on Human Rights in Transnistria 2013 (n 125) 41.
190   UN Special Rapporteur on Human Rights Defenders - Mission to Moldova (n 188) [71]-[73].
191   *Ibid.* [71]; see also, Promo-LEX, 'Freedom of Expression in the Transnistrian Region of the Republic of Moldova: 2016 Retrospective' (2016) 11-13.
192   UN Special Rapporteur on Human Rights Defenders - Mission to Moldova (n 188) [74]; see also Chiveri, 'The Media Situation, Perspectives, Contacts and Mutual Perception between Journalists from Both Banks of Nistru River' (IPRE/Hans Seidel Stiftung, June 2016), 6-8, <http://ipre.md/2016/06/23/studiu-situatia-in-domeniul -media-perspectivele-contactele-si-perceptia-jurnalistilor-de-pe-ambele-maluri -ale-nistrului/?lang=en> accessed 28 March 2021.
193   Chiveri (n 192) 5.
194   Protsyk (n 93).
195   *Ibid.* 178.
196   Chiveri (n 192) 5-6; Brusa, 'Transnistria: Journalism beyond the Nistru', (*OBC Transeuropa*, 24 July 2018) <www.balcanicaucaso.org/eng/Areas/Transnistria/ Transnistria-journalism-beyond-the-Nistru-189247> accessed 29 March 2021.
197   See eg Report by the UN Special Rapporteur on the Situations of Human Rights in Somalia' (16 January 1998) UN Doc E/CN.4/1998/96 [77]; Report by the UN Special Rapporteur on the Situations of Human Rights in Somalia' (18 February 1999) UN Doc E/CN.4/1999/103 [107]-[109].
198   Report of the Independent Expert on Assistance to Somalia in the Field of Human Rights (14 January 2002) UN Doc E/CN.4/2002/119 [106], 111-112; Report of the Inde-

DE FACTO INDEPENDENT REGIMES AND OVERARCHING HR DUTIES   61

operated relatively unrestricted.[199] However, organisations have faced severe resource constraints, and some have been harassed by the Somaliland 'security services', for example through arbitrary arrests of prominent members.[200] The latter also affects journalists,[201] with UN reports confirming that Somaliland authorities maintain 'tight control over the media',[202] including by prohibiting the setting up of private FM stations, the closing down of critical tv stations,[203] and by intimidating editors of independent newspapers.[204] This, however, does not mean that the Somaliland media did not make a considerable contribution to the democratisation and political stabilisation of Somaliland: it 'clearly provided a forum for controversial discussions between the government and political parties'.[205]

4 In Place of a Conclusion: Potential Implications for the Development of International Law Binding de Facto Independent Regimes and other Non-state Actors with Control over Populations

The above analysis establishes that the RoA, the NKR, Transnistria and Somaliland have not only announced in their respective constitutions

---

pendent Expert on the Situation of Human Rights in Somalia (28 October 2015) UN Doc A/HRC/30/57 [33], [39].

199 Report UNSR Somalia 1998, (n 197) [77].

200 Report UNSR Somalia 2000, (n 128) [106]-[107]; Report of the UN Independent Expert on the Situation of Human Rights in Somalia (24 August 2020) UN Doc A/HRC/45/52 [51].

201 Report UNSR Somalia 1999, (n 197) [106]; Report UNSR Somalia 2010 (n 155) [70]; Report UNSR Somalia 2011 (n 131) [47]; Report of the UN Independent Expert on the Situation of Human Rights in Somalia (6 September 2017) UN Doc A/HRC/36/62 [32]; Report UNSR Somalia 2019 (n 105) [84]. Demeke, 'Freedom of Press and Democratisation in Somaliland: Promises and Challenges' 2013 (SORADI, *Somaliland Press Freedom and Challenges,* Report) <https://ke.boell.org/sites/default/files/press_freedom-opportunities_and_challenges.pdf> accessed 28 March 2021 67, 79.

202 Report UNSR Somalia 2012 (n 132) [76]; see also Demeke (n 201) 76, 78-79.

203 Report of the Independent Expert of the UN Commission on Human Rights on Assistance to Somalia in the Field of Human Rights (31 December 2002) UN Doc E/CN.4/2003/115 [33]; Report UNSR Somalia 2012 (n 132) [76].

204 Report UNSR Somalia 2002 (n 203) [34]; Höhne, 'Newspapers in Hargeisa: Freedom of Speech in Post-Conflict Somaliland' (2008) 43 *Afrika Spectrum* 91; Demeke (n 201) 76, 78-79.

205 Demeke (n 201) 77; see also Höhne (n 204).

that they wish to adhere to human rights law but that they, as a matter of fact, have taken considerable steps to comply with overarching human rights duties. They built and continue to build institutions through which they can secure human rights found in global and regional human rights treaties. They have, though to varying degrees, taken steps to democratise their institutions, by holding multi-party parliamentary and presidential elections, by setting up independent judiciaries, and by taking steps to create an enabling environment for equal political participation and the protection of human rights in their 'territories'. This, in turn, allows them to adopt domestic legislative and policy measures specifying and contextualising human rights and the modes of their implementation in light of local circumstances that comply with, or come close to complying with, the human rights legality standard and democratic principles. They are thus likely to respect and protect the political equality of individuals who come under their influence and control, and progressively implement human rights in light of the collective preferences of the affected rights-holders. Moreover, as indicated in the introduction, de facto adherence to overarching human rights duties will allow these entities to implement many other 'negative' and 'positive' human rights duties arising from specific human rights, all of which require duty-bearers to adopt (democratically legitimised) legislation to for example *non-arbitrarily* detain, to *fairly* try individuals charged with criminal offences, to set up *competent* courts, and to limit (balance) human rights only to an extent *necessary in a democratic society*.

Given this de facto compliance of the four entities examined here, a strong argument can be made that they – and potentially other entities that are able to comply with overarching human rights duties – should be recognised as full human rights duty-bearers in the same way as states that sign and ratify human rights treaties. There are two arguments that support this suggestion further. First, as maintained by the present author elsewhere,[206] entities that de facto adhere to overarching human rights obligations are also highly likely to respect and protect the right to self-determination of the people (and their political community) over which they exercise control and authority. As a collective right, the right to self-determination gives 'all peoples' (i.e. the entire population of a

---

206   Müller (n 70).

DE FACTO INDEPENDENT REGIMES AND OVERARCHING HR DUTIES   63

state[207] and/or (political) sub-groups[208]) the right to 'freely determine their political status and freely pursue their economic, social and cultural development'.[209] Importantly, common art 1 ICCPR/ICESCR obliges states as duty-bearers to set up a government 'representing the whole people belonging to the[ir] territory without distinction of any kind',[210] that enables such political, social, economic and cultural self-determination in an inclusive fashion, i.e. by respecting the political equality of all individuals in this territory and, in addition, without discriminating against any sub-group.[211] A non-state collective entity genuinely complying with these obligations under the right to self-determination should potentially be recognised as a full human rights duty-bearer – something that has been, even if very indirectly and rather quietly, acknowledged by the ECtHR in its inadmissibility decision in *Azemi v. Serbia*.[212]

Second, recognising these de facto independent regimes as full human rights duty-bearers helps to close important gaps in human rights protection. In the four cases discussed above, it is questionable whether either the parent or patron states of the RoA, the NKR, Transnistria or Somaliland (with the latter not having a patron state), are in fact able and willing to take on full human rights duties towards the individuals living in these de facto independent regimes. Nor is it clear whether – in cases where de facto independent regimes comply with the overarching human rights duties discussed above as a matter of fact and make clear efforts to implement many other duties arising from concrete human rights – either the

---

207   Eg Cassese, *Self-Determination of Peoples: A Legal Reappraisal* (CUP, 1995) 59-60, 102, 327, 364; Raič, *Statehood and the Law of Self-Determination* (Hart, 2002) 244-47; McCorquodale, 'Self-Determination: A Human Rights Approach' (1996) 43 *International and Comparative Law Quarterly* 587, 866-68; Mégret, 'The Right to Self-Determination: Earned, Not Inherent' in Tesón (ed) *The Theory of Self-Determination* (CUP, 2018) 45-69, 58.

208   As envisaged in the Declaration on Principles of International Law concerning Friendly Relations and Cooperation with the Charter of the United Nations (24 October 1970) UNGA Res 2626 (XXV) UN Doc A/RES/2626(XXV); Raič (n 207) 247-72; Mégret (n 207) 45-69; McCorquodale (n 207) 867-68.

209   ICCPR art 1; ICESCR art 1

210   Vienna Declaration and Programme of Action, (25 June 1993) UN Doc A/CONF.157/23 [2]; also 1970 Declaration on Friendly Relations (n 208); HRC, General Comment 12: The Right to Self Determination (12 April 1984) UN Doc HRI/GEN/1/Rev.9 [6].

211   Reinforced by independent non-discrimination rights in human rights treaties, eg ICCPR arts 3, 26; and ICESCR art 2(2).

212   *Azemi v Serbia* App no 11209/09 (ECtHR, 5 November 2013). For the full argument, see Müller (n 70).

parent or patron state would enjoy the same (democratic) legitimacy as the institutions set up by the de facto independent regimes that arguably allow them to secure the equal human rights of the affected populations in line with the genuine collective preferences of these populations. This does not inevitably imply that recognising these specific de facto independent regimes as full human rights duty-bearers also means that they should be recognised as independent states. The fact that their authority is exercised over groups of individuals (forming a political community) with these individuals' consent, entrenched in democratic law-making procedures, will arguably strengthen their demand for statehood. However, other solutions arrived at through fair and inclusive negotiations and compromises that respect individual human rights and the right to self-determination are also thinkable and should not be excluded. Among them are federal or consociational arrangements, or arrangements granting regional autonomy to allow for accurate representation of minorities and other sub-groups within larger 'democratic societies' of patron or parent states and their institutional structures.[213]

Questions can be raised about the potential human rights duties of armed non-state entities that are unable and/or clearly unwilling to comply with the overarching human rights duties discussed above. It is submitted here that such entities should *not* be recognised as human rights duty-bearers under international law, be it as a matter of custom or by permitting ratifications of international human rights treaties. Whilst a full justification for this submission cannot be provided here,[214] two primary reasons shall be mentioned, and two primary objections be refuted.

First, armed non-state actors that cannot genuinely claim and show that they exercise authority over individuals in order to secure these individuals' human rights on an equal basis, but exercise it because they wish to implement their economic-exploitative, ethno-nationalistic, religious-exclusionary or even genocidal aims, or aims that are in any other way in the interest of, if at all, a limited group of individuals who come under their influence and control, will be unable to comply with human rights obligations in any meaningful way. Their exercise of, by definition exclu-

---

213   For different ways in which (internal) self-determination of various groups and minorities can be exercised within a state implementing the requirement of individual political equality and representativeness in plural societies, see Weller and Wolff, 'Self-determination and Autonomy' in Weller and Wolff (eds), *Autonomy, Self-Determination and Conflict Resolution: Innovative Approaches to Institutional Design in Divided Societies* (Routledge, 2005) 1-25.

214   But see Müller (n 70).

sively coercive authority, is also unlikely to gain the trust and approval of individuals affected, and it will therefore be unlikely that it will be sustainable over a long period of time. Whilst comprehensive studies on long-term public approval of de facto independent regimes' or other non-state armed actors' administrations are, to the present author's knowledge, so far unavailable, there are indications that institutions set up by so-called 'predatory rebel groups' such as the National Patriotic Front of Liberia (NPFL), operating in Liberia between 1989 and 1996 rarely gain the sustained support of affected populations. 'Civil administrations' run by such groups have been described as all but façades for their criminal and exploitative activities.[215] The same can be said for groups with religious-exclusionary ideologies. For example, there are reports that affected populations were initially relieved when the so-called Islamic State (ISIS) set up a justice system in territories it controlled. They saw it as preferable to a complete absence of law and order and/or alternative justice and governance offered by repressive governments or other armed groups,[216] even though they might not have shared ISIS's ideology. In the longer-term, however, people 'inured to the harshness of IS rule begin to object to the cost of the services being supplied',[217] leading to large-scale popular dissent. By contrast, there are indications that the institutions set up in the four de facto independent regimes discussed in section 3 enjoy considerable popular support.[218]

Second and relatedly, international law should arguably not empower these entities and legitimise the exercise of their authority through recognising them as human rights duty-bearers prematurely. As mentioned, doing so will not only pose human rights duties on these entities, but will also endow them with considerable rights and

---

215   Reno, 'Predatory Rebellions and Governance: The National Patriotic Front of Liberia' in Arjona *et al.* (eds), *Rebel Governance in Civil War* (CUP, 2017) 279-82.

216   Revkin, 'ISIS' Social Contract: What the Islamic State Offers Civilians' (*Foreign Affairs*, 10 January 2016) <www.foreignaffairs.com/articles/syria/2016-01-10/isis-social-contract> accessed 29 March 2021; and Ledwidge, *Rebel Law: Insurgents, Courts and Justice in Modern Conflict* (C Hurst & Co, 2017) 78-79.

217   Ledwidge (n 216) 82; Revkin, 'The Experts Weigh in: Is ISIS Good at Governing?' (*Brookings Online*, 20 November 2015) <www.brookings.edu/blog/markaz/2015/11/20/experts-weigh-in-is-isis-good-at-governing/> accessed 28 March 2021.

218   Concerning RoA, the NKR and Transnistria see Berg and Mölder (n 183) 538-42 and Caspersen, 'Degrees of Legitimacy: Ensuring Internal and External Support in the Absence of Recognition' (2015) 66 *Geoforum* 184; concerning Somaliland, see Pegg and Kolstø, 'Somaliland: Dynamics of Internal Legitimacy and (Lack of) External Sovereignty' (2015) 66 *Geoforum* 193, 294-97; Kaplan (n 155) 144.

privileges to exercise public authority, ranging from rights to detain and try individuals to rights to exercise far-reaching legislative functions in the name of the 'political communities' over which they preside. Such privileges should arguably not be granted lightly to various types of collective non-state entities with discriminatory or exploitative aims.

Against these two arguments it can first be objected that rejecting the proposition that all de facto independent regimes and other armed non-state actors should become human rights duty-bearers, including those with clearly discriminatory ideologies or exploitative aims, will undermine the protection of individuals affected by these entities. After all, expanding human rights obligations to as many actors as possible is often supported by the argument that this is needed for ensuring more effective protection of individuals.[219] Second, it can be objected that the threshold proposed here at which de facto independent regimes should be recognised as full human rights duty-bearers does not equally apply to states, many of which do, as a matter of fact, not protect human rights through democratic institutions within their jurisdictions but are nonetheless recognised as human rights duty-bearers in relation to the individuals who come under their jurisdiction.

Concerning the first objection, it can be observed that limiting the number of de facto independent regimes that shall potentially be recognised as full human rights duty-bearers in the way suggested here does not mean that improvements in the protection of individuals affected by other types of armed non-state actors in international law shall not be pursued. Rather, it means that it might be normatively more convincing to rely on IHL, including the law of occupation, to achieve this. This will legitimise the authority exercised by these entities to a much lesser degree but at the same time increase the protection of affected individuals. This is because IHL, including the law of occupation, is built on a more technocratic, top-down normative logic containing relatively clear permissions and prohibitions addressing all types of armed actors. This normative logic is rather different from the equality- and democracy-based

---

219 See eg Bellal et al 'International Law and Armed Non-state Actors in Afghanistan' (2011) 93 *International Review of the Red Cross* 47, 71; Tan, 'Filling the Lacuna: *De Facto* Regimes and Effective Power in International Human Rights Law' (2019) 51 *International Law and Politics* 435, 444-50; Clapham, 'Detention by Armed Groups under International Law' (2017) 93 *International Law Studies* 1 at 21; Murray, *Human Rights Obligations of Non-State Armed Groups* (Hart, 2017) 10; and Fortin, *The Accountability of Armed Groups under Human Rights Law* (OUP, 2017) 35-68.

bottom-up normative grounding of human rights law.[220] In addition, so-called 'responsibilities for human rights'[221] can be developed binding armed non-state actors, in particular weaker groups that are not in control of territories.[222]

Concerning the second objection: the higher demands that should potentially be put on de facto independent regimes than on states seem justified based on the general 'presumptive legitimacy'[223] to exercise public authority that states enjoy in today's international legal system that non-state actors do not (and arguably should not) benefit from to the same extent. When states sign and ratify human rights treaties, it is presumed that they are willing and able to secure the equal human rights of rights-holders under their jurisdiction through democratic institution,[224] something that cannot presumed for de facto independent regimes, armed non-state actors or other non-state actors such as multinational corporations or wealthy private foundations or trusts, as long as these entities remain unable to sign these treaties. Setting the standard high for de facto independent regimes and other private entities is not only justified by the aforementioned authority-legitimising effects that recognising non-state actors as human rights duty-bearers will have, but also by the need to avoid various other problems that can arise when an increasing number of non-state entities – including potentially corporations – are recognised as human rights duty-bearers on a par with states. Among these difficulties are problems of overlapping and competing (domestic) law-making by 'legitimate' institutions, as well as so-called 'problems of many hands'.[225] The latter can lead to 'buck passing',[226] i.e. allowing all potential state and non-state duty-bearers to deny responsibility for hu-

---

220 See n 11; also elaborated on in Müller (n 70).

221 For the notion of 'responsibilities for human rights' see Besson, 'The Bearers of Human Rights Duties and Responsibilities for Human Rights: A Quiet (R)evolution' (2015) 32 *Social Philosophy and Policy* 244.

222 Müller (n 70)

223 On the idea of 'presumptive legitimacy' of statehood, see Mégret, 'Detention by Non-State Armed Groups in Non-International Armed Conflict: International Humanitarian Law, International Human Rights Law and the Question of Right Authority' in Heffes, Kotlik and Ventura (eds), *International Humanitarian Law and Non-State Actors: Debates, Law and Practice* (2020) at 183; also Müller (n 70).

224 This comes through in particular in ECtHR- and treaty body jurisprudence, that regularly *presumes* states' (human rights) jurisdiction over their own territories.

225 Nollkaemper, '"Failures to Protect" in International Law', in Weller (ed), *The Oxford Handbook of the Use of Force in International Law* (OUP, 2015) 438-463, 454.

226 *Ibid.* 456-57.

man rights violations through acts and omissions by pointing to the potentially unfulfilled overlapping duties binding other actors.

3 The 'Unwilling or Unable' Doctrine Unmasked

A Case Study of ISIL in Syria

Sarah McGibbon *

Abstract

The unwilling or unable doctrine has been extensively discussed in international law scholarship, particularly since the November 2015 Paris bombing by the Islamic State of Iraq and the Levant (ISIL). Its use by states to carry out air strikes within Syrian territory against militant ISIL forces has elicited much debate on the scope of the doctrine. However, existing scholarship has failed to interrogate adequately the underlying theoretical framework (or lack thereof) of the doctrine. Consequently, its inherently political nature and application has not been challenged. Nor has its implications for attribution in relation to nonstate armed groups (NSAGs).

This paper begins with a holistic exploration of the conceptual framework of the prohibition of the use of force in international law and the exceptions thereto. It is followed by a brief review of state practice as well as an examination the use of the unwilling or unable doctrine in relation to the ongoing military activity in Syria. It proceeds to attempt to classify the doctrine/identify its place in the legal framework of international law.

Ultimately, the paper argues that the manipulation of the boundaries of the unwilling or unable doctrine is fundamentally premised on political will rather than legal theory which has, in turn, resulted in theoretical incoherence. It further argues that the unwilling or unable doctrine is, in fact, a policy rather than a legal doctrine and that the application of this policy results in the incorporation of the domestic law concept of strict liability in the public international law framework.

---

* PhD Researcher, Maastricht University, Faculty of Law.

Keywords

Unwilling or unable – use of force – self-defence – attribution – state responsibility

1   Introduction

The 'unwilling or unable' doctrine has been extensively discussed – in a variety of contexts – in international law scholarship, particularly since the November 2015 Paris attacks.[1] Its use (and arguably abuse) by states to carry out air strikes in Syrian territory against the militant forces of the Islamic State of Iraq and the Levant (ISIL) have elicited much debate on the scope of the doctrine.[2] However, existing scholarship has failed to explore adequately the underlying theoretical framework (or lack thereof) of the doctrine and, consequently, to reveal and challenge its true nature.[3]

It is because the terms 'unwilling' and/or 'unable', and most particularly their usage together as 'unwilling or unable', have become ubiquitous in political and legal discussions about global terrorism that it is crucial to subject the doctrine to more rigorous scrutiny. The use of force is an action with grave, extensive and often irreversible implications; it is not something that should be resorted to lightly or on questionable grounds.[4]

---

1   See, for example, Ashley Deeks, 'Unwilling or Unable: Toward a Normative Framework for ExtraTerritorial Self-Defense' (2012) 52 Virginia Journal of International Law 483; Nicholas Tsagourias, 'SelfDefence Against Non-State Actors: The Interaction Between Self-Defence as a Primary Rule and Self-Defence as a Secondary Rule' (2016) 29 Leiden Journal of International Law 801; Olivia Flasch, 'The Legality of the Air Strikes Against ISIL in Syria: New Insights on the Extraterritorial Use of Force Against Non-State Actors' (2016) 3 Journal on the Use of Force and International Law 37; Olivier Corten, 'The "Unwilling or Unable" Test: Has It Been, and Could It Be, Accepted?' (2016) 29 Leiden Journal of International Law 777; Jutta Brunnée and Stephen J Toope, 'Self-Defence Against Non-State Actors: Are Powerful States Willing But Unable to Change International Law?' (2018) 67 International and Comparative Law Quarterly 263.

2   This is discussed extensively later in the paper, in particular in section 5.

3   For a brief but helpful consideration of the various theoretical underpinnings of the doctrine, see Donette Murray, 'Flawed and Unnecessary: The "Unwilling or Unable" Doctrine Pertaining to States' Use of Force in Self-Defence Against Non-State Actors' (2017) 30 Hague Yearbook of International Law 59.

4   The architects of the UN Charter built this idea into article 2(4) of the Charter, which is discussed in further detail in the following section.

The use of force by states against ISIL in Syria is a fitting case study for this topic for two reasons. First, although ISIL's territorial presence in Syria has declined in recent years,[5] at the time of the air strikes following the Paris attack in November 2015, ISIL factually controlled a considerable portion of *de jure* Syrian territory.[6] It was (and may continue to be)[7] a non-state armed group (NSAG) that bore a close resemblance to a state, traditionally understood. This affords us a particularly interesting perspective from which to juxtapose the use of force directed at states against the use of force directed at NSAGs. Second, it is a (relatively) recent example of the invocation of the unwilling or unable doctrine, which allows us to assess the development of the doctrine over a longer period and in light of more recent developments in academic scholarship.

This paper begins the case study by examining the conceptual foundations of the prohibition of the use of force in international law (section 2). Following this, there is a brief review of state practice, including the use of the unwilling or unable doctrine in relation to the 2014/2015 military activity in Syria (section 3). The paper then attempts a classification of the unwilling or unable doctrine, considering the themes

---

5   See 'Timeline: The Rise, Spread, and Fall of the Islamic State | Wilson Center' <https://www.wilsoncenter.org/article/timeline-the-rise-spread-and-fall-the-islamic-state> accessed 8 June 2021 for a concise but comprehensive overview of the decline of ISIL.

6   In October 2016, for example, ISIL held 21 428m2 in Syrian territory. This figure was calculated using the Institute for the Study of War's (ISW) map showing ISIL's territorial control (as at 13 October 2016), <http://understandingwar.org/sites/default/files/Oct13%20EDITS%20COT_0.pdf> accessed 6 June 2021) and Population Explorer <https://populationexplorer.com/> accessed 6 June 2021. This amounts to approximately 1 829 210 people under the rule of ISIL in Syria alone. This figure has been calculated using the ISW territorial control map above recreated in the Population Explorer tool referenced directly above. The population figures are obtained by Population Explorer from Landscan (more information: <http://web.ornl.gov/sci/landscan/>), which algorithm uses spatial data and imagery analysis technologies to disaggregate census counts within an administrative boundary. The Population Explorer tool is configured to use the 2014 Landscan dataset, therefore, these numbers are approximate only and some allowance should be made for internal displacement and exiting refugees.

7   This complex issue is beyond the scope of this paper. For further information on ISIL's state-like attributes, and the continuing reaction to it, see for example Seth Jones and others, 'Rolling Back the Islamic State' (RAND Corporation 2017); Benjamin Nussberger, '"Sustainable Self-Defense"? How the German Government Justifies Continuing Its Fight against ISIL in Syria' <https://www.ejiltalk.org/sustainable-self-defense-how-the-german-government-justifies-continuing-its-fight-against-isil-in-syria/> accessed 8 June 2021.

of consent, authorisation and self-defence (section 4). Thereafter, it enunciates the conceptual challenges posed by the use of the doctrine (section 5). In this section of the paper, it is argued that the unwilling or unable doctrine is, in fact, a policy masquerading as a legal doctrine and that the application of this policy results in the incorporation of the domestic law concept of strict liability in the public international law framework (i.e. there is a shift in the standard of attribution in state responsibility). It is further argued that this has, in turn, resulted in theoretical incoherence. Finally, the paper closes with some concluding remarks (section 6).

2 Conceptual Foundations of the Prohibition of the Use of Force

As a starting point, it is necessary to situate the use of the unwilling or unable doctrine within the greater scheme of the prohibition on the use of force in international law. This allows us to have a greater comprehension of the problems identified later in this paper.

Article 2(4) of the UN Charter contains the general prohibition on the use of force:

> All Members shall refrain in their international relations from the threat or use of force against the territorial integrity or political independence of any state, or in any other manner inconsistent with the Purposes of the United Nations.

This article has been called 'a cornerstone of the United Nations Charter',[8] with the International Court of Justice (ICJ),[9] the International Law Commission (ILC)[10] and the majority of scholars even accepting that it is an

---

8   *Armed Activities on the Territory of the Congo* (*Democratic Republic of the Congo v Uganda*) ICJ Reports 2005 p 167 at 223.

9   See *Military and Paramilitary Activities In and Against Nicaragua* (*Nicaragua v United States*) [1986] ICJ Rep 14 (*Nicaragua*) at para. 190, as well as the separate opinion of President Singh at para. 153 and the separate opinion of Judge Sette-Camara at para. 199.

10 In its commentary on the draft Vienna Convention, the ILC identified article 2(4) of the UN Charter as 'a conspicuous example' of *ius cogens*. Again, in 2001, it stated that 'it is generally agreed that the prohibition of aggression is to be regarded as peremptory' (see the final text with commentary in James Crawford, *The Inter-*

THE 'UNWILLING OR UNABLE' DOCTRINE UNMASKED

ius cogens norm.[11] It is not necessary to take a firm stand on this question for the purpose of this paper.

The UN Charter itself, however, contains two justifications for the use of force that would otherwise be prohibited by this article, namely self-defence (article 51) and authorisation by the United Nations Security Council (UNSC) (Chapter 7).[12] Some scholars call these justifications 'exceptions' to the rule contained in article 2(4).[13] Regardless of the nomenclature, these are the recognised 'grounds on which the use of armed force by a [s]tate can be justified today on the basis of a norm in international law'.[14]

It goes without saying that both of the justifications represent situations where consent has not been obtained from the state against which force is being used. The more pertinent question in contemporary public international law debates is the effect of consent on the prohibition.[15] It is necessary to highlight at this point that there is some debate whether consent to use force/intervene (for example, to offer humanitarian as-

---

national Law Commission's Articles on State Responsibility: Introduction, Text, and Commentaries (Cambridge University Press 2002).

11 See, for example, Olivier Corten and Bruno Simma, *The Law Against War: The Prohibition on the Use of Force in Contemporary International Law* (Hart Publishing 2012) at 199 *et seq* and Yoram Dinstein, *War, Aggression and Self-Defence* (6th edn, Cambridge University Press 2017) at 110 as two prominent examples from this majority. However, there are scholars questioning this status. See, for example, James A Green, 'Questioning the Peremptory Status of the Prohibition of the Use of Force' (2010) 32 Michigan Journal of International Law 215; U Linderfalk, 'The Effect of Jus Cogens Norms: Whoever Opened Pandora's Box, Did You Ever Think About the Consequences?' (2007) 18 European Journal of International Law 853.

12 There is, strictly theoretically-speaking, a third justification contained in the UN Charter, namely measures against former enemy states (article 107 read with article 53). However, it is largely accepted that this justification is obsolete given that the former enemy states are now UN member states and, as such, have become peace-loving states in accordance with article 4(1) of the Charter. The opposite conclusion would also result in a violation of those states' sovereignty under article 2(1). (In this regard, see Oliver Dörr and Albrecht Randelzhofer, 'Ch.1 Purposes and Principles, Article 2(4)' in Bruno Simma, Hermann Mosler and Andreas Paulus (eds), *The Charter of the United Nations: A Commentary* (3rd edn, Oxford University Press 2012) at 219.) This conclusion is confirmed by the ICJ's failure to include this as a lawful use of force in its advisory opinion on the *Legality of the Threat or Use of Nuclear Weapons* ICJ Reports 1996, p 226 at para. 38.

13 See, for example, Crawford *Brownlie's Principles of International Law* (8th edn, Oxford University Press 2012) at 747.

14 Dörr and Randelzhofer (n 12) at 218.

15 The importance of understanding this effect will become apparent when considering the legal framework of the unwilling or unable doctrine itself.

sistance) renders the UN Charter prohibition inapplicable, or whether it falls under one of the justifications named above.

In the former case, scholars argue that valid consent implies that the use of force is not against the political independence or territorial integrity of the requesting state and, therefore, the force falls outside the scope of the prohibition contained in article 2(4).[16] Alternatively, there is no use of force in the attacking state's international relations because the consent means that the situation is instead one where two states are co-operating together within an internal strife.[17] Under either approach, the military action would thus not amount to a 'justification' or 'exception' per se to article 2(4), as these terms connote that the type of force contemplated would, in principle, be covered by the prohibition on the use of force.[18]

Conversely, following the latter line of debate, both Erika De Wet and John Perkins submit that consent does not automatically mean that military action is not 'against the territorial integrity or political independence' of the state.[19] If this approach is taken, consensual use of force in fact constitutes an exception to article 2(4).[20] However, the legal basis for the existence of such an exception outside the scope of the two set out in the UN Charter itself is unclear. It is beyond the scope of this paper to conduct a state practice review to determine whether this exception exists in customary international law, but it is doubtful.[21]

Regardless of the school of argument, it is worth noting that in *Nicaragua* the ICJ stated that 'it is difficult to see what would remain of the principle of non-intervention in international law if intervention, which

---

16   Erika de Wet, 'The Modern Practice of Intervention by Invitation in Africa and Its Implications for the Prohibition of the Use of Force' (2015) 26 European Journal of International Law 979 at 980.

17   Karine Bannelier and Theodore Christakis, 'Under the UN Security Council's Watchful Eyes: Military Intervention by Invitation in the Malian Conflict' (2013) 26 Leiden Journal of International Law 855France launched Operation Serval against several terrorist armed groups in January 2013. The French troops were assisted by a Chadian contingent and by forces progressively deployed by other African countries within a UNSC authorized African force (Resolution 2085 at 860.

18   De Wet (n 16).

19   *Ibid.* and John Perkins, 'The Right of Counterintervention' (1987) 17 Georgia Journal of International and Comparative Law 171.

20   De Wet (n 16).

21   It is worth noting that the ICJ has held that even where an attack does not breach article 2(4), it may nonetheless violate the non-intervention norm or the norm in respect of sovereignty. See *Nicaragua* (n 9) at para. 205 and *Corfu Channel Case (UK v Albania)* (Merits) [1949] ICJ Rep 4 (*Corfu Channel*) at 35.

THE 'UNWILLING OR UNABLE' DOCTRINE UNMASKED 75

is already allowable at the request of the government of a State, were also to be allowed at the request of the opposition'.[22] Unfortunately, the ICJ failed to elaborate on its reasoning in this regard, but it is support for the argument that consent, in one way or another, negates the prohibition on the use of force. I am therefore of the view that validlygranted consent renders article 2(4) of the UN Charter inapplicable for the reasons set out above.[23]

Once it is established that consent in *any form* is absent, it is then necessary to interrogate whether the unwilling or unable doctrine falls into one of the justifications outlined in the UN Charter, namely self-defence (article 51) or UNSC authorisation (Chapter 7). However, before delving into the theoretical difficulties surrounding the doctrine, it is prudent to conduct a brief historical survey of its use.

3   Historical Use of the Unwilling or Unable Doctrine against Non-State Actors

The first appearance of the unwilling or unable doctrine appears to be in relation to Israel's incursions into Lebanon from the 1970s onwards.[24] Previously, Israel had justified its attacks directed at terrorist bases on the ground that Lebanon deliberately harboured these groups on its territory. However, the argument was broadened in the 1970s to provide that even if Lebanon did not actively support or deliberately harbour these groups, Israel could act in selfdefence if Lebanon was either unwilling or unable to prevent cross-border attacks.[25]

---

22   *Nicaragua* (n 9) at para. 246. Emphasis added.
23   It is also interesting to note that, in the context of international humanitarian law, the International Committee of the Red Cross (ICRC) has recognised that consent to the use of armed force by one state on the territory of another state rules out the classification of that use of force as an International armed conflict (ICRC 2016 Commentary on Geneva Convention I for the Amelioration of the Condition of the Wounded and Sick in Armed Forces in the Field, Geneva, 12 August 1949 available at <https://ihl-databases.icrc.org/applic/ihl/ihl.nsf/Comment.xsp?action=openDo cument&documentId=BE2D518CF5DE54EAC1257F7D0036B518#96_B> (accessed 31 March 2021) at para. 259).
24   Kinga Tibori-Szabó, 'The "Unwilling or Unable" Test and the Law of Self-Defence' in Christophe Paulussen and others (eds), *Fundamental Rights in International and European Law: Public and Private Law Perspectives* (Asser Press 2016) at 76.
25   *Ibid.* at 77. See, for example, Israel's statement in 1972 from UN Yearbook 1972, p 158. See also SCOR, 33rd Session, 2071st meeting (17 March 1978) UN Doc. S/PV.2071 at

This approach continued to be followed by Israel into the 1980s. In July 1981 Israel argued before the UNSC that '[m]embers of the Council need scarcely be reminded that under international law, if a state is unwilling or unable to prevent the use of its territory to attack another state, the latter state is entitled to take all necessary measures in its own defence'.[26] These arguments were largely met with strong opposition, and the vast majority of UNSC resolutions at the time condemned Israeli conduct.[27]

The US also developed a similar line of reasoning in the 1980s.[28] In 1985 (where it abstained from voting for a resolution condemning Israel's raid against Palestinian Liberation Organisation headquarters) it stated that 'it is the responsibility of each state to take appropriate steps to prevent persons or groups within its sovereign territory from perpetrating such acts'.[29]

The unwilling or unable argument was further invoked by a small number of states in the 1990s. However, there was a noticeable shift in the reaction to the use of this reasoning in 1998 when the US bombed Al-Qaeda targets in Sudan and Afghanistan in response to the bombing of the US embassies in Kenya and Tanzania.[30] The reaction to the bombing was mixed, with traditional US allies mostly supporting it, and Russia, China, Pakistan, Libya and Iraq condemning the action.[31] This shift could have been due to the fact that an increasing number of governments was

---

para. 53; UN Yearbook 1979, p 332: 'Israel said it was exercising its inherent right of self-defence. If states were unwilling or unable to prevent terrorists from operating out of their countries, they should be prepared for reprisals.'

26 SCOR, 36th Sess., 2292nd meeting (17 July 1981) U.N. Doc. S/PV.2292 at 54.

27 See SC Res 280 (1970); SC Res 316 (1972); SC Res 332 (1973); SC Res 450 (1979); SC Res 467 (1980). However, also see SCOR, 30th Session, 1860th meeting (5 December 1975) UN Doc S/PV.1860 at paras. 3-5 (where the United States (US) vetoed a resolution condemning Israel on the basis that progress could not be achieved with one-sided resolutions that left Israel believing that it was the victim of discrimination and bias on the part of the UN); and SCOR, 40th Session, 2515th meeting (4 October 1985) UN Doc S/PV.2615 at para. 252 (where the US argued that a state subjected to terrorist attacks had the right to defend itself and states had a responsibility to prevent their territory from being used by terrorists).

28 Tibori-Szabó (n 24) at 78.

29 SCOR, 40th Session, 2615th meeting (4 October 1985) UN Doc S/PV. 2615 at para. 252.

30 Tibori-Szabó (n 24) at 78-79.

31 'US allies back missile strikes, Yeltsin sides with Muslims' (*The Irish Times*, 22 August 1998) <https://www.irishtimes.com/news/us-allies-back-missile-strikes-yeltsin-sides-with-muslims-1.185482> accessed 29 March 2021 and 1998 UN Yearbook, p 185.

THE 'UNWILLING OR UNABLE' DOCTRINE UNMASKED 77

realising the growing threat caused by the greater independence and danger of terrorist organisations. However, this particular instance is not necessarily helpful in determining this given that the reasoning adopted by the US for the bombings more closely follows the previous argument of harbouring than that of the unwilling or unable argument.[32]

In tandem with these developments before the UNSC, the ICJ was presented with the opportunity to consider the responsibility of states for the acts of apparent non-state actors in the landmark *Nicaragua* case.[33] After the Court found that US participation in the activities of the *contras* (even if decisive) was not sufficient for the purpose of attributing their conduct to the US,[34] it laid down what would become known as the effective control test:

> For this conduct to give rise to legal responsibility of the United States, it would in principle have to be proved that that State had effective control of the military or paramilitary operations in the course of which the alleged violations were committed.[35]

This test would go on to be incorporated in the articles on the Responsibility of States for Internationally Wrongful Acts (ARSIWA)[36] as article 8, which provided that '[t]he conduct of a person or group of persons shall be considered an act of a state under international law if the person or group of persons is in fact acting on the instructions of, or under the direction or control of, that state in carrying out the conduct'.

However, the International Criminal Tribunal for the former Yugoslavia (ICTY) deemed the effective control test too restrictive. The ICTY instead differentiated between private persons performing specific acts on behalf of a state on the territory of another, and individuals forming a structured and organised group to carry out acts for the purpose of establishing individual criminal responsibility. It found (in relation to the

---

32   Tibori-Szabó (n 24) at 80.

33   *Nicaragua* (n 9).

34   *Ibid.* at para. 115. At para. 109, the Court found that there was no basis on which it could be said that the US 'actually exercised' a degree of control over the *contras* such that they would be considered an organ of the US government or acting on its behalf. The Court continued in para. 110 to find that, for legal purposes, the *contras* could not be equated with the US government.

35   *Ibid.* at para. 115.

36   Responsibility of States for Internationally Wrongful Acts, G.A. Res. 56/83, U.N. GAOR, 56th Sess. (12 December 2001) U.N. Doc. A/RES/56/83.

latter) that a test of 'overall control' was more suitable than the 'effective control' test.[37] This entails that a state had a role in organising, coordinating or planning the military action, in addition to financing, training, equipping or providing operational support for the group. By comparison, the ICJ subsequently found this test unpersuasive.[38]

Therefore, in short, prior to the events of 11 September 2001 (9/11) the underlying assumption was that acts of NSAGs had to be imputed to a state in order for self-defence to be available. Selfdefence against non-state actors was always exercised as part of selfdefence against the state that controlled or sent them. The unwilling or unable doctrine was largely rejected, except by the states that invoked it.[39]

Post 9/11, UNSC Resolutions 1368 and 1373 have been interpreted by many as unequivocally acknowledging the right of self-defence against terrorist attacks as such.[40] However, questions regarding imputing the attacks to a state deliberately harbouring the NSAG remained widely debated.[41] The US focus on the Taliban as being linked to Al-Qaeda and

37   *Prosecutor v Duško Tadic*, Appeals Chamber, Appeals Judgment, ICTY, Case No. IT-94-1-A, 15 July 1999 at paras. 118-120, 137 and 145.

38   *Application of the Convention on the Prevention and Punishment of the Crime of Genocide (Bosnia and Herzegovina v. Serbia and Montenegro)* ICJ Reports 2007 p. 43 at paras. 403-404.

39   Tibori-Szabó (n 24) at 82. Later in this paper it will become apparent that the contemporary position – whereby states rely on the unwilling or unable doctrine to invoke the right to self-defence in cases where there is neither effective nor overall state control of NSAGs – is not a great departure from the pre-9/11 position. This is due to the fact that by invoking this dubious doctrine, victim states and third-party states still impute liability for the actions of NSAGs to the state in whose *de jure* territory they operate.

40   *Ibid.* See also Jack Beard, 'America's New War on Terror: The Case for Self-Defense under International Law and the War on Terrorism: Military Action Against Terrorists Under International Law' (2001) 25 Harvard Journal of Law & Public Policy 559. For a contrasting view, see Antonio Cassese, 'Terrorism Is Also Disrupting Some Crucial Legal Categories of International Law' (2001) 12 European Journal of International Law 993"container-title":"European Journal of International Law","DOI":"10.1093/ejil/12.5.993","ISSN":"0938-5428","issue":"5","journalAbbreviation":"European Journal of International Law","page":"993-1001","source":"Silverc hair","title":"Terrorism is Also Disrupting Some Crucial Legal Categories of International Law","volume":"12","author":[{"family":"Cassese","given":"Antonio"}],"iss ued":{"date-parts":[["2001",12,1]]}}}],"schema":"https://github.com/citation-style -language/schema/raw/master/csl-citation.json"} at 996-97.

41   See, for example, Thomas Franck, 'Terrorism and the Right of Self-Defense' (2001) 95 American Journal of International Law 839; Christopher Greenwood, 'International Law and the Pre-Emptive Use of Force: Afghanistan, Al-Qaida, and Iraq' (2003) 4 San Diego International Law Journal 7 at 25.

THE 'UNWILLING OR UNABLE' DOCTRINE UNMASKED

allowing them to operate in Afghanistan still shows the importance of linking the host state and the NSAG. Operation 'Enduring Freedom' received almost unanimous support. Kinga Tibori-Szabó argues that this could be seen as evidence of a shift towards accepting the argument that NSAG attacks could be imputed to host states,[42] but that still allocates importance to a nexus between the NSAG and the host state.

Russia has also used this doctrine to justify its incursions into Georgia to prevent further crossborder attacks by Chechen rebels. However, instead of alleging a link between the Georgian government and Chechen rebels, it suggested an unwillingness on the part of the territorial government to stop attacks on Russian territory.[43] It stated:

> If the Georgian leadership is unable to establish a security zone in the area of the Georgian-Russian border, continues to ignore UNSC resolution 1373 (2001) of 28 September 2001, and does not put an end to the bandit sorties and attacks on adjoining areas in the Russian Federation, we reserve the right to act in accordance with Article 51 of the Charter of the United Nations, which lays down every member State's inalienable right of individual or collective self-defence.[44]

This argument is similar to the approach taken by Israel in respect of Lebanon's inability to prevent Hezbollah from launching cross-border attacks against Israel.[45] Israel continued to rely on its previous arguments and, in 2006, justified its incursion into Lebanese territory on the basis of '[t]he ineptitude and inaction of the Government of Lebanon [that] has led to a situation in which it has not exercised jurisdiction over its own territory for many years'. It further claimed that '[r]esponsibility for this belligerent act of war lies with the Government of Lebanon, from whose territory these acts have been launched into Israel'. It further claimed that responsibility lay with Iran and Syria, 'which support and embrace those who carried out this attack'.[46]

---

42   Tibori-Szabó (n 24) at 83.

43   Letter dated 11 September 2002 from the Permanent Representative of the Russian Federation to the United Nations addressed to the Secretary-General (11 September 2002) UN Doc S/2002/1012.

44   *Ibid.*, Annex at p 3.

45   Tibori-Szabó (n 24) at 83.

46   Identical Letters dated 12 July 2006 from the Permanent Representative of Israel to the United Nations addressed to the Secretary-General and the President of the Security Council (12 July 2006) UN Doc S/2006/515.

It is striking that although Israel relies on Lebanon's inability to control the Hezbollah-occupied territory, it also imputes the attacks to the Lebanese government due to its inaction.[47] In this instance, several UNSC members, including Argentina, Australia, Brazil, Canada, Denmark, Greece, Guatemala, Peru, Slovakia, Turkey, the United Kingdom (UK) and the US, acknowledged Israel's right of self-defence against Hezbollah.[48] Although there were some condemnations, there was general support for Israel's actions in the UNSC debates. This is potentially indicative of a growing acceptance of the view that the right of self-defence could be invoked against NSAGs.[49]

In 2007 and 2008 Turkey offered no justification for its use of force in Iraq against PKK elements. However, the general reaction of states focused on the proportionality of the use of force rather than the right to use it.[50]

It is possible to argue that these actions are indicative of a more permissive approach being adopted towards the argument that states may defend themselves against armed attacks by NSAGs in the territory of another state even where there is no link between the 'host' state and the NSAG concerned. The key factor is that the state is unwilling or unable to prevent the attacks itself.[51] However, this may be called into question by Ecuador's condemnation of Colombia's use of force against FARC rebels on Ecuador's territory in March 2008. It was only the US that expressed its support for Colombian action, while the Organization of American States also condemned it.[52]

The value of an historical survey in determining where the unwilling or unable doctrine fits into the greater scheme of public international law is not to be underestimated. It usefully illustrates that although it has existed in some form or another for decades, it is only really since 2012, when Ashley Deeks published her seminal article on the subject,[53] that

---

47   Tibori-Szabó (n 24) at 84.
48   SCOR, 61st session, 5489th meeting (14 July 2006) UN Doc S/PV.5489 at pp 12, 14, 15 and 17; SCOR, 61st session, 5493rd meeting (21 July 2006) UN Doc S/PV.5493 at pp 17 and 19; and SCOR, 61st session, 5493rd meeting (21 July 2006) UN Doc S/PV.5493 (Resumption1) at pp 9, 19, 27, 28, 39 and 41.
49   Tibori-Szabó (n 24) at 84.
50   *Ibid.*
51   *Ibid.* at 85.
52   Tom Ruys, *'Armed Attack' and Article 51 of the UN Charter: Evolutions in Customary Law and Practice* (Cambridge University Press 2010).
53   Ashley Deeks, 'Unwilling or Unable: Toward a Normative Framework for Extraterritorial Self-Defense' (2012) 52 Virginia Journal of International Law 483.

THE 'UNWILLING OR UNABLE' DOCTRINE UNMASKED

we have seen it play a more prominent role in international affairs. This is especially so in the collective reaction to the attacks in Paris in November 2015.

The position of the US was made clear in a speech by the contemporary US State Department Legal Advisor Brian Egan's keynote address for the American Society of International Law on 4 April 2016, where he stated:

> [I]n the case of ISIL in Syria, as indicated in our Article 51 letter, we could act in selfdefense without Syrian consent because we had determined that the Syrian regime was unable or unwilling to prevent the use of its territory for armed attacks by ISIL.[54]

The article 51 letter to which he refers is the one submitted to the Secretary-General in 2014, which also makes express reference to the right of self-defence being available to states when a host state is unwilling or unable to stop terrorist attacks.[55] It states that '[t]he Syrian regime has shown that it cannot and will not confront these safe havens effectively itself'. It is worth noting, however, that US involvement initially began in 2014 in response to the allegation that chemical weapons had been used by (now former) President Assad, and the action was directed against Syria and its ruling party. Although this was the starting point for their air strikes, subsequent action falls firmly within the response to ISIL attacks.

The UK similarly tried to link its participation in airstrikes to Assad's alleged use of chemical weapons (and the Syrian civil war), and to use this as an attempt to target both threats simultaneously. Although the UK article 51 letters make no express mention of the unwilling or unable doctrine,[56] it was included in the statement to Parliament by (now for-

---

54   Brian Egan, 'International Law, Legal Diplomacy, and the Counter-ISIL Campaign' (Keynote Address for the American Society of International Law, 4 April 2016) <https://www.youtube.com/watch?v=4ol8Fz-ShaY> accessed 29 March 2021.

55   Letter dated 23 September 2014 from the Permanent Representative of the United States of America to the United Nations addressed to the Secretary-General (23 September 2014) UN Doc S/2014/695.

56   Identical Letters dated 25 November 2014 from the Permanent Representative of the United Kingdom of Great Britain and Northern Ireland to the United Nations addressed to the Secretary-General and the President of the Security-Council (25 November 2014) UN Doc S/2014/851; Letter dated 8 September 2015 from the Permanent Representative of the United Kingdom of Great Britain and Northern Ireland to the United Nations addressed to the President of the Security-Council (8 September 2015) UN Doc S/2015/688; Letter dated 3 December 2015 from the Permanent Representative of the United Kingdom of Great Britain and Northern

mer) Prime Minster David Cameron with the Prime Minister on 26 November 2015.[57] In its article 51 letter, Germany makes express mention of the loss of effective control by Syria and notes that states attacked by ISIL from this territory are justified in acting under article 51's self-defence exception. It purported to act under the right to collective self-defence in supporting states attacked by ISIL.[58] Of course, Russia also participated in the airstrikes, but the key difference is that it was done with the consent of the Syrian government.[59]

The 2015 language, although indicating that the use of force was directed at ISIL and not Syria per se, places the use of force (in the mind of the states invoking the unwilling or unable doctrine) squarely within the article 51 right of self-defence, and attempts were made at a proportionality and necessity assessment. However, in these cases, the fact that Russia was acting in Syria with the consent of the Syrian government, casts serious doubt on the veracity of any such purported reliance on the doctrine, and illustrates that Western action is probably politically motivated rather than strictly necessary from a legal perspective.

Despite its more frequent appearance in the dialogue around collective security, it is readily apparent that the theoretical origins of the doctrine and the scope of its application remain unsettled. Although there is growing support for harsher responses to terrorist activities, state practice does not support the use of the unwilling or unable doctrine.[60] It is unclear from a theoretical perspective, however, what exactly state practice should be supporting. It is at this point that the analysis of the article 2(4) framework set out earlier becomes relevant. Those issues will be pertinent in determining a possible classification of the doctrine.

Ireland to the United Nations addressed to the President of the Security-Council (3 December 2015) UN Doc S/2015/928.

57　David Cameron, 'PM Statement Responding to FAC Report on Military Operations in Syria' (Oral Statement to Parliament, 26 November 2015) <https://www.gov .uk/government/speeches/pm-statement-responding-to-fac-report-on-military-operations-in-syria> accessed 29 March 2021.

58　Letter dated 10 December 2015 from the Chargé d'affaires a.i. of the Permanent Mission of Germany to the United Nations addressed to the President of the Security-Council (10 December 2015) UN Doc S/2015/946.

59　Letter dated 15 October 2015 from the Permanent Representative of the Russian Federation to the United Nations addressed to the President of the Security Council (15 October 2015) UN Doc S/2015/792. See the discussion on consent that follows later in this paper for a deeper exploration of this issue.

60　Corten (n 1) at 786.

THE 'UNWILLING OR UNABLE' DOCTRINE UNMASKED

4 Classification of the Unwilling or Unable Doctrine: Consent, Authorisation, Self-defence or Strict Liability?

It should be evident by now that the conceptual waters surrounding the unwilling or unable doctrine are muddy (at best). The historical survey shows the way in which it has been raised and manipulated for decades; and reveals that state practice and *opinio iuris* is lacking. However, state practice is only essential if it is argued that the doctrine forms part of customary international law; but, it is only necessary to go this far if the legal foundation for the use of the unwilling or unable test cannot be located in the UN Charter itself,[61] or if it is determined that it is not a consent issue.

In order to attempt to classify the doctrine, this section proceeds to answer the following question: When could a victim state or third-party state have used force in Syria? The starting point in answering this will be examining consent. The reason for this will be apparent from the discussion that follows.

4.1 *Implied Consent*

There is a school of thought that, by implication, posits that in the case of unwilling or unable states, there is implied consent to use force which means the UN Charter does not find application.[62] It is necessary to highlight at this point that there is some debate in public international law whether consent to use of force/intervention renders the UN Charter inapplicable, or whether it falls under one of the justifications. A brief overview of this debate has already been set out in section 2 above.[63]

---

61 *Charter of the United Nations*, 24 October 1945, 1 UNTS XVI.
62 See, for example, Kenneth Watkin, 'Letter to the Editor: "Lines in the Sand" – A Reply to Professor Haque' (*Just Security*, 24 October 2016) <https://www.justsecurity.org/33792/letter-editor-lines-sand-a-reply-professor-haque/> accessed 6 June 2021; Chris Ford, 'Implicit Consent and the Use of Force in Syria' (*Just Security*, 2 November 2016) <https://www.justsecurity.org/34072/implicit-consent-force-syria/> accessed 6 June 2021.
63 It is beyond the scope of this chapter to give a more comprehensive overview. For greater detail, see Laura Visser, 'May the Force Be with You: The Legal Classification of Intervention by Invitation' (2019) 66 Netherlands International Law Review 21.e.g. its name and its place within the rules of jus ad bellum. This article seeks to clarify and resolve these issues. First, an analysis is conducted into what the two terms intervention and invitation actually entail. The term intervention is contrasted with the use of force and the entire concept of intervention by invitation is differentiated from collective self-defence. It is concluded that the threshold of

However, it is necessary for the purpose of the arguments I make going forward to reiterate that my view is that consent means that article 2(4) of the UN Charter does not apply, so there is no need to delve into the justifications in the case where consent is obtained.[64]

However, this raises the further question of whether it is necessary for the consent to be explicit in order to be valid, or whether implicit consent suffices. In its commentary on draft article 29 of the 1996 version of AR-SIWA[65] (now article 20) dealing with consent as a circumstance precluding wrongfulness in state responsibility law, the ILC noted that in order to have the legal effect of precluding wrongfulness, the consent must be 'valid in international law, clearly established, really expressed (which precludes merely presumed consent), internationally attributable to the State and anterior to the commission of the act to which it refers'.[66] It is worth noting that while this author acknowledges that there are those who firmly support a distinction between the so-called primary and secondary rules of international law who may suggest that reliance on this commentary conflates the primary and secondary rules by implying that consent is a circumstance precluding wrongfulness,[67] there appears to

---

force has been met and thus the focus should be placed on the rules regulating this field of law, rather than the rules of non-intervention. The concept would be more aptly labelled as the use of force by invitation. Second, this article examines where intervention by invitation finds its place in relation to the prohibition of the use of force. Alternative perspectives are investigated encompassing the scope of Article 2(4

64   Once it is determined that consent is absent, it is then necessary to interrogate whether the unwilling or unable doctrine falls into one of the justifications outlined in the UN Charter, namely self-defence (article 51) or UNSC authorisation (Chapter 7).

65   Draft Articles on State Responsibility with Commentaries Thereto adopted by the International Law Commission on First Reading, January 1997 <https://legal .un.org/ilc/texts/instruments/english/commentaries/9_6_1996.pdf> accessed 29 March 2021.

66   International Law Commission, 'Yearbook of the International Law Commission' (1979) II part 2 at 112.

67   Consent as a circumstance precluding wrongfulness as contemplated in article 20 of ARSIWA is arguably not *directly* applicable when considering whether article 2(4) is rendered inoperative by consent (in one form or another) because this problem is not an issue of state responsibility (a 'secondary' rule question) but one concerning the scope of the 'primary' rule. See, for a more detailed explanation, Théodore Christakis and Karine Christakis Mollard-Bannelier, 'Volenti non fit injuria ? Les effets du consentement à l'intervention militaire' (2004) 50 Annuaire Français de Droit International 102 at 10411. See also James Crawford, *State Responsibility : The General Part* (Cambridge University Press 2013) at 64. However,

THE 'UNWILLING OR UNABLE' DOCTRINE UNMASKED

be no reason why this standard should not apply in understanding what consent means in this context and in respect of considering whether article 2(4) has been infringed at the primary law level.

The ICJ seems to confirm that implicit consent is indeed possible. In its *Armed Activities* judgment, the Court states:

> The Court believes that both the absence of any objection to the presence of Ugandan troops in the DRC in the preceding months, and the practice subsequent to the signing of the Protocol, support the view that the continued presence as before of Ugandan troops would be permitted by the DRC by virtue of the Protocol.[68]

Importantly, it goes on to state:

> While the co-operation envisaged in the Protocol may be reasonably understood as having its effect in a continued authorization of Ugandan troops in the border area, *it was not the legal basis for such authorization or consent. The source of an authorization or consent to the crossing of the border by these troops antedated the Protocol* and this prior authorization or consent could thus be withdrawn at any time by the Government of the DRC, without further formalities being necessary.[69]

Thus, although there was no *written* consent prior to the signature of the Protocol on Security along the Common Border (signed on 27 April 1998), the consent nevertheless existed. Consent may therefore be express or implied.

As already alluded to earlier in this chapter, the issue of consent has also been considered in the area of international humanitarian law, both

---

there are many scholars who do not see the need to maintain such a distinction. In particular, Willem Riphagen warned that the distinction 'should not be carried so far as to dissimulate the essential unity of the structure of international law as a whole'. Willem Riphagen, 'Second Report on the Content, Forms and Degrees of International Responsibility (Part 2 of the Draft Articles)' in International Law Commission, 'Yearbook of the International Law Commission' (1981) 2, part 1 at 82, para. 31. See also Daniel Bodansky and John Crook, 'Symposium on the ILC's State Responsibility Articles: Introduction and Overview' (2002) 96 American Journal of International Law 773. at 780-1 where they note that this distinction is arbitrary.

68   *Armed Activities on the Territory of the Congo* (*Democratic Republic of the Congo v Uganda* ICJ Reports 2005, p 168 at para. 46.

69   *Ibid.* at para. 47. Emphasis added.

by scholars and the ICRC. In particular, in its 2016 Commentary on the Geneva Conventions, the ICRC considers consent in the context of classifying a conflict as an international armed conflict.[70] The argument relies on Dapo Akande's scholarship on the same issue (among others) to indicate that consent by the host state in the case of the use of armed force against a NSAG operating in foreign territory precludes classification as an international armed conflict, as the consenting host state is not engaged in the conflict with the other (foreign) state.[71]

As already discussed, article 20 of ARSIWA lists 'valid consent' as a circumstance precluding wrongfulness in the case of determining state responsibility. In its commentary, the ILC clarifies this concept as requiring that consent be 'really expressed'.[72] It later goes on to indicate that as long as consent is 'clearly established', it may be tacit or implicit (but never presumed).[73] As set out, this seems to align with the ICJ's interpretation of consent in the context of breaches of article 2(4) in *Armed Activities*.

Whether consent has been granted (in any form) is a factual matter to be determined on a casebycase basis. In the case of Syria, Chris Ford argues that there are 'objective facts' which point to Syria having granted tacit consent to the US and coalition forces to conduct airstrikes against ISIL on Syrian territory.[74] These facts include that Syria has not formally objected to these airstrikes whereas, in the case of past incursions onto its territory for various reasons, it has placed its objections on record with the UNSC.[75] He is of the view that these push the situation beyond the bounds of mere presumed consent.

---

70   ICRC Commentary (n 23) at paras. 257-64.

71   *Ibid.* at paras. 260 and 263. This view relies on Dapo Akande, 'Classification of Armed Conflicts: Relevant Legal Concepts' in Elizabeth Wilmshurst (ed), *International Law and the Classification of Conflicts* (Oxford University Press 2012).transnational armed groups and organized criminal gangs, the need for clarity of the law is all-important. The case studies selected for analysis are Northern Ireland, DRC, Colombia, Afghanistan (from 2001, in particular, at 73.

72   International Law Commission (n 66).

73   *Ibid.*

74   Ford (n 62).

75   See Letter dated 18 June 2014 from the Permanent Representative of the Syrian Arab Republic to the United Nations addressed to the Secretary-General (20 June 2014) UN Doc S/2014/426; Identical letters dated 3 October 2014 from the Chargé d'affaires a.i. of the Permanent Mission of the Syrian Arab Republic to the United Nations addressed to the SecretaryGeneral and the President of the Security Council (8 October 2014) UN Doc A/69/2014-S/2014/719; Identical letters dated 11 December 2014 from the Permanent Representative of the Syrian Arab Republic

THE 'UNWILLING OR UNABLE' DOCTRINE UNMASKED

However, Ford correctly raises the question of whether there is an obligation on Syria to express its lack of consent. He (again, correctly) observes that no such obligation appears to exist in international law and astutely notes that the fact that consent cannot be presumed militates against such an obligation.

The effort to identify the facts allegedly in support of Syria having granted tacit consent has failed to consider the facts indicative of the opposite conclusion. Given that there does not appear to be any obligation to take formal steps to object to the use of force in question, it is not enough simply to point to historical situations as evidence of a particular contemporary stance. There is no objective indication as to why its position on western involvement may have changed. This is especially so in a factual setting where Syria was faced with the task of suppressing an extreme terrorist network within its borders. This was also at a time when ISIL's territorial possession was steadily increasing. In addition, Syria invited Russia to step in and assist with the fight against ISIL. It did not, however, see fit to invite the US or the coalition forces. This decision in itself suggests that tacit consent was never granted. As such, the UN Charter still finds application in this case.[76]

Given that consent was not a legal reason for the use of force in Syria, it is necessary to consider the options provided for in the UN Charter, namely authorisation by the UNSC and self-defence.

4.2 *Authorisation to Use Force*

There are others (scholars and states alike) who have attempted to justify third-party state intervention in Syria on the basis of UNSC authorisation.[77] In relation to Syria, this is done by arguing that resolution 2249

---

to the United Nations addressed to the Secretary-General and the President of the Security Council (15 December 2014) UN Doc S/2014/885.

76   Even if this conclusion is wrong, and consent was obtained, then the UN Charter does not apply and thus state practice and *opinio iuris* in support of the unwilling or unable doctrine is necessary in order for it to be considered customary international law. As has been illustrated, state support for the use of this doctrine in reality is lacking. Therefore, even on the tenuous basis that implied consent may have been granted and is sufficient to displace the article 2(4)-prohibition, proponents of this theory fall short when it comes to any steady ground for the application of the doctrine in real life.

77   See Germany's article 51 letter (n 58) and Belgium's article 51 letter: Letter dated 7 June 2016 from the Permanent Representative of Belgium to the United Nations addressed to the President of the Security Council (7 June 2016) UN Doc S/2016/523. See also Nicholas Tsagourias, 'Self-Defence Against Non-State Actors: The

authorised use of force by its reference to 'all necessary measures'.[78] However, as Corten has pointed out, it is not the purpose of that article to determine the legal outcomes of the resolution, and it is striking that military action in selfdefence is not explicitly mentioned as has been the case in previous cases.[79] He further states that '[i]n those circumstances, to deduce a general agreement consecrating the "unwilling or unable" standard from such a resolution would be misleading'.[80] Christopher Greenwood also appears to be of the view that use of force must be expressly authorised by the UNSC.[81]

4.3   Self-defence

If it cannot be said that use of force in Syria was authorised by the UNSC, it is necessary to turn to the next exception in the UN Charter: article 51. Many scholars attempt to situate the unwilling or unable doctrine within the right to selfdefence, as enshrined in article 51 of the Charter.[82] As has been illustrated in section 3 of this paper, there are numerous states who argue the same. But it weighs heavily that there is no hint of this doctrine within the UN Charter itself, despite the other exceptions/justifications being expressly mentioned.[83]

Interaction Between Self-Defence as a Primary Rule and Self-Defence as a Secondary Rule' (2016) 29 Leiden Journal of International Law 801"plainCitation":"Nicholas Tsagourias, 'Self-Defence Against Non-State Actors: The Interaction Between Self-Defence as a Primary Rule and Self-Defence as a Secondary Rule' (2016 at 824.

78   UNSC Resolution 2249 (2015), adopted at its 7565th meeting, UN Doc S/Res/2249(2015) at para. 5.

79   Corten (n 1) at 791.

80   *Ibid.*

81   Clare Dyer, 'Ousting Saddam Illegal, PM Told' *The Guardian* (8 October 2002) <http://www.theguardian.com/politics/2002/oct/08/uk.iraq> accessed 6 June 2021. Alex Bellamy, 'International Law and the War with Iraq Feature - Legality of the Use of Force Against Iraq' (2003) 4 Melbourne Journal of International Law 497 at 500 also understood Greenwood's statement to have this implication.

82   See, for example, Tibori-Szabó (n 24) at 94, Deeks (n 53) at 487; Georg Nolte and Albrecht Randelzhofer, 'Ch.VII Action with Respect to Threats to the Peace, Breaches of the Peace, and Acts of Aggression, Article 51' in Bruno Simma, Hermann Mosler and Andreas Paulus (eds), *The Charter of the United Nations: A Commentary* (3rd edn, Oxford University Press 2012) at 1418.

83   Tsagourias (n 77)it proposes an alternative framework which combines the primary rule of self-defence to justify the use of defensive force against non-state actors, with the secondary rule of self-defence to excuse the incidental breach of the territorial state's sovereignty.","container-title":"Leiden Journal of International Law","DOI":"10.1017/S0922156516000327","ISSN":"0922-1565, 1478-9698","issue":"3","journalAbbreviation":"Leiden Journal of International

THE 'UNWILLING OR UNABLE' DOCTRINE UNMASKED

States no longer appear to dispute that NSAGs can mount armed attacks in the technical sense; instead the debate focuses on the degree of state involvement required in order to *attribute* that conduct of the NSAG to the host state in order to justify actions in self-defence.[84] This is where the framework becomes even more complex. The conceptual difficulties that arise under the self-defence model are dealt with in detail in the next section. In short, the section argues that the unwilling or unable doctrine does not fall under article 51, and that article 51 was not a suitable basis for the use of force in Syria. Instead, it suggests that the unwilling or unable doctrine presents a fourth possibility to justify such force, namely, the introduction of strict liability for host states.

5   Self-defence, Attribution and Politics: Conceptual Challenges Posed by the Current Status of the Unwilling or Unable Doctrine

The true unwilling or unable test presupposes the absence of any link between the host state and the nonstate actor,[85] which makes its consideration under the rubric of attribution somewhat ironic. However, a state practice review demonstrates that reliance on the various grounds for invocation of the right to self-defence against NSAGs does not reveal any clear conceptual distinction between any harbouring arguments and reliance on the true unwilling or unable test. In addition, when unwillingness or inability to deal with the threat has been invoked, it is often coupled with a reminder that all states are responsible for preventing terrorist groups from operating on their territory, derived from *Corfu Channel*.[86]

Where the true unwilling or unable test has been relied upon, the unwillingness invoked is usually some form of inaction of the ruling govern-

---

Law","language":"en","page":"801-825","source":"DOI.org (Crossref at 821 argues that in cases of self-defence against NSAGs conducted in the territory of a host state (such as the case in Syria) a so-called secondary rule of self-defence is implicated.

84   Christine Gray, *International Law and the Use of Force* (3rd edn, Oxford University Press 2008) at 130.

85   Tibori-Szabó (n 24) at 87.

86   In *Corfu Channel* (n 21) at 22, the ICJ noted that every state has an 'obligation not to allow knowingly its territory to be used for acts contrary to the rights of other states'.

ment in the face of NSAGs operating in its territory.[87] This can be a very subjective claim that is open to significant manipulation.[88] Can a refusal of outside help (or at least, refusal of help from some third-party states) be construed as unwillingness? This is certainly what has happened in respect of the situation in Syria, where Russia was acting on Syria's invitation, but other parties persisted in intervening despite Syria's refusal of consent. In particular, this is illustrated by Egan's justification of the continuing US intervention in Syria in the wake of the November 2015 Paris attack.[89]

Inability, on the other hand, may appear to be a more objective measure, however the interpretation of this concept also presents difficulties. In particular, the question of whether unsuccessful measures taken against non-state actors constitutes 'unable' for the purpose of the unwilling or unable test.[90] Closely linked to this is the question of territorial control by the government of the host state. A number of states have also referred to the Syrian government's loss of effective control of the territory held by ISIL as being an indication of unwillingness or inability to address the threat posed by the group. This issue is crucial to understanding the modern unwilling or unable test so this paper shall return to it shortly. For purposes of this discussion, it suffices to suggest that this particular reason falls more into the category of inability, rather than unwillingness. A pertinent example of this is the reasoning offered by Germany in its article 51 letter to the UNSC in December 2015:

> ISIL has occupied a certain part of Syrian territory *over which the Government of the Syrian Arab Republic does not at this time exercise effective control.* States that have been subjected to armed attack by ISIL originating in this part of Syrian territory, are therefore justified under Article 51 of the Charter of the United Nations to take necessary measures of self-defence, even without the consent of the Government of the Syrian Arab Republic. Exercising the right of collec-

---

87   See, from section 3 for example, Israel's justifications for incursions into Lebanon in the 1970s (n 25) and the US justifications for the 2015 air strikes on Syria in the US article 51 letter (n 55).

88   Dawood Ahmed, 'Defending Weak States Against the "Unwilling or Unable" Doctrine of Self-Defense' (2013) 9 Journal of International Law and International Relations 1 at 14.

89   Egan (n 54).

90   Tibori-Szabó (n 24) at 89.

THE 'UNWILLING OR UNABLE' DOCTRINE UNMASKED 91

tive selfdefence, Germany will now support the military measures of those States that have been subjected to attacks by ISIL.[91]

Tibori-Szabó has also questioned where an analysis of these elements fits in the context of selfdefence,[92] which is – after all – when this doctrine is most-often invoked. He suggests that 'assessing the necessity and proportionality of the defensive action [under the analysis of selfdefence] may also need to encompass analysing the unwillingness or inability of the host state to tackle the terrorist threat itself'.[93] This includes the challenging task of evaluations the host state's capacity and behaviour.[94] Therefore, he argues that express and valid consent should always be sought by the victim state *before* any assessment of the host state's willingness or ability to neutralise any NSAG threat. If the host state does not consent, then its attitude may become part of the assessment.[95]

Importantly, lack of consent should not be equated to an unwillingness to tackle the problem.[96] A host state may refuse another (possibly victim) state's request to use force within the host state's borders for myriad reasons, including concerns about the particular means and methods of force to be used and questions about the repercussions thereof.[97] Similarly, the scale of the measures taken by a host state with inferior military capabilities to the victim state should not be equated with inability.[98] The analysis of the state's ability or willingness must be more than a snapshot in an otherwise volatile context.[99]

---

91 Germany's article 51 letter (n 58). Emphasis added. This wording will also be considered again in this paper.

92 Tibori-Szabó (n 24) at 89. Deeks (n 53) at 495 previously suggested that the doctrine falls within the necessity evaluation, which has subsequently been supported by Brunnée and Toope (n 1) at 264.

93 *Ibid.* at 90.

94 Douglas Cantwell, '"Unwilling or Unable" in the Legal Adviser's ASIL Speech' (*Lawfare*, 12 April 2016) <https://www.lawfareblog.com/unwilling-or-unable-legal -advisers-asil-speech> accessed 6 June 2021.

95 This mirrors the necessity characterisation adopted by Deeks (n 53) and Brunnée and Toope (n 1).

96 Tibori-Szabó (n 24) at 92.

97 Ntina Tzouvala, 'TWAIL and the "Unwilling or Unable" Doctrine: Continuities and Ruptures' (2015) 109 American Journal of International Law 266.

98 Ahmed above n 88 at 18. The maxim *ultra posse nemo obligatur* is relevant in this instance, and is discussed in more detail in Paulina Starski, 'Right to Self-Defence, Attribution and Non-State Actor' (2015) 75 ZaöRV 455 at 481.

99 Tibori-Szabó (n 24) at 92.

However, these problems – although important – tend to be more pragmatic than conceptual. What the preceding analysis has shown is that when dealing with attacks by NSAGs, a more onerous level of attribution is used when determining whether the right of self-defence may be exercised against a thirdparty state (i.e. the host state), what this paper calls a shift to the standard of strict liability. In order to better understand this, the concept of control needs to be clarified. But first, it is prudent to consider (albeit briefly) the relevant provisions on state responsibility.

5.1 State Responsibility under ARSIWA

The issue of state responsibility is comprehensively dealt with in ARSIWA.[100] Article 1 provides that '[e]very internationally wrongful act of a state entails the international responsibility of that state'. The natural question that follows upon reading this article is: what is an internationally wrongful act? This question is conveniently answered in article 2 which sets out the elements of an internationally wrongful act of a state: (1) conduct consisting of an act or omission; (2) that is attributable to the state under international law; and (3) which constitutes a breach of an international obligation of the state.

Following this clearly set out structure in ARSIWA, it is necessary to distinguish between the attribution of conduct to a state and the breach of an international obligation through that conduct. While that may seem to state the obvious, when discussing terrorism and counterterrorism, these two elements are easy to conflate, probably because of the emotive nature of these topics.

However, Vidmar argues that we need to attach law to the matter of fact.[101] This terse reminder is useful, but it is advice that can get lost when

---

100 See above n 67 for a consideration of the distinction between primary and secondary rules of international law. Starski (n 98) at 468-69 addresses the use of ARSIWA as an interpretive aid for article 51 of the UN Charter.

101 Jure Vidmar, 'Some Observations on Wrongfulness, Responsibility and Defences in International Law' (2016) 63 Netherlands International Law Review 335I argue that international law has a major structural crack: the limited international legal capacity of non-states, and a high threshold of attribution to states. A great deal of international conduct thus remains unregulated. I further explain that this is not only a gap in responsibility but in fact a gap in international legal regulation. The law of international responsibility overlaps with the law of international legal capacity. For the most part, it is thus only states and international organisations which are even conceptually able to violate international law directly. If a certain conduct is not attributable to them, it will not be internationally wrongful. I also suggest that the division between the primary and secondary rules of

THE 'UNWILLING OR UNABLE' DOCTRINE UNMASKED

one considers the conceptual difficulties that come with this seemingly simple assessment.

5.2   Obligations, Conduct and Breach[102]

Let us start by identifying the conduct in question in the Syrian example. Although it is trite that the conduct in question is an omission, the nature of the obligation to which that omission relates is less clear. As noted earlier, the obligation most often called upon is the *Corfu Channel* obligation to prevent (in this case) terrorist attacks emanating from the host state's territory.[103] What exactly this obligation entails, and whether it is one of result or due diligence, is not settled which creates problems when considering possible breaches of this obligation.

An alternative formulation has been suggested by Vincent-Joël Proulx and Bruno Simma: the host state has an obligation to control its territory and 'harmful terrorist activities emanating from its soil'.[104] The implica-

---

international law is confusing and arbitrary, and certainly should not be understood as a sequential order. In the conclusion I argue that scholarship has been perhaps too preoccupied with addressing certain symptoms of the 'great structural crack' in international law, while the real problem lies in the unclear concept of international legal capacity","container-title":"Netherlands International Law Review","DOI":"10.1007/s40802-016-0071-0","ISSN":"1741-6191","issue":"3","journalAbbreviation":"Neth Int Law Rev","language":"en","page":"335-353","source":"Springer Link","title":"Some Observations on Wrongfulness, Responsibility and Defences in International Law","volume":"63","author":[{"family":"Vidmar","given":"Jure"}],"issued":{"date-parts":[["2016",10,1]]}}}],"schema":"https://github.com/citation-style-language/schema/raw/master/csl-citation.json"} at 347.

102   As the primary focus of this paper is attribution, these elements are only dealt with briefly. However, these elements bring their own complexities that deserve attention. See Starski above n 98 at 474-83 for more information.

103   See above n 86. Although this paper mentions 'terrorist attacks' (and other iterations thereof) throughout, it should be noted that there may disagreement between scholars about what exactly this entails. This definitional issue is not the concern of this paper. For further reading on this, see Ben Saul, 'Attempts to Define "Terrorism" in International Law' (2005) 52 Netherlands International Law Review 57. It is also not the aim of this paper to determine whether such attacks meet the gravity threshold for an 'armed attack' per the ICJ's interpretation of article 51 in *Nicaragua* (n 9).

104   Vincent-Joël Proulx and Bruno Simma, *Transnational Terrorism and State Accountability: A New Theory of Prevention* (Hart Publishing 2012) at 172. This might stem from a representation by Israel at a UNSC meeting stating: 'When sovereign States fail to govern responsibly according to their duties under international law, terrorists and other non-State actors seek to take advantage of the void. Similarly, when States support terrorist groups by providing safe haven, weapons, training and financing, they should bear responsibility for the actions of those groups and

tions of this reformulation are discussed in the section dealing with control below. It is worth noting at this point that this formulation appears to be one of result. Regardless of how the obligation is framed, it is crucial that the conduct (the omission in this case) is attributable to the host state. It is sensible to start by examining the concept of control.

5.3   Control and its Importance to Attribution

It is evident from the previous sections that control in some form or another is integral to attribution. Indeed, Proulx and Simma also note that control is a 'central component' in triggering responsibility.[105] However, it appears that there has been some conflation between the notions of control and attribution, which further contributes to the structural problems in the international legal framework for responsibility and non-state actors.

The cornerstone of the concept of control is the *Namibia Advisory Opinion*, from which it is apparent that *physical control of the territory* concerned is sufficient for establishing liability; that is, lack of legal title over a territory does not result in a lack of responsibility in respect thereof.[106] In particular, paragraph 118 states:

> [T]he fact that South Africa no longer has any title to administer the territory [of Namibia] does not release it from its obligations and responsibilities under international law towards other states in respect of the exercise of its powers in relation to this territory. Physical control of a territory, and not sovereignty or legitimacy of title, is the basis of state liability for acts affecting other states.[107]

Therefore, if physical control is the lowest common denominator for liability, it is key to unlocking a significant part of public international law: responsibility. But this theory of control must be weighed against the iconic effective control test established in *Nicaragua*. It is evident (and

---

be held accountable for violations of international law.' See UNSC 5898th Meeting, 27 May 2008 UN Doc S/PV.5898 (Resumption 1) at 7.

105   Proulx and Simma *ibid.* at 165.

106   A correlative conclusion is that responsibility/liability does not result in legitimacy or *de jure* control, but that issue is beyond the scope of this paper.

107   *Legal Consequences for States of the Continued Presence of South Africa in Namibia (South West Africa) Notwithstanding Security Council Resolution 276 (1970)*, Advisory opinion of 21 June, ICJ Reports (1971) 16 at para. 118. Emphasis added.

THE 'UNWILLING OR UNABLE' DOCTRINE UNMASKED

seemingly unquestioned) that the Court considered control (as a concept distinct from dependence) to be decisive.

> The Court has taken the view (paragraph 110 above) that United States participation, even if preponderant or decisive, in the financing, organizing, training, supplying and equipping of the contras, the selection of its military or paramilitary targets, and the planning of the whole of its operation, is still insufficient in itself, on the basis of the evidence in the possession of the Court, for the purpose of attributing to the United States .... For this conduct to give rise to *legal responsibility of the United States*, it would in principle have to be proved that that State had *effective control of the military or paramilitary operations* in the course of which the alleged violations were committed.[108]

Thus, in terms of this judgment, it is effective control that leads to responsibility rather than physical control as per the *Namibia Advisory Opinion*. Effective control and physical control (as factual situations) may overlap in some cases, but this is not always so. For the time-being, it is therefore important to consider them as two distinct legal concepts/standards.

There does appear to be a subtle but important difference between the consequences of effective control and physical control that runs deeper than the nomenclature chosen by the court in each case. As a reminder, *Namibia Advisory Opinion* refers to 'state liability' (for acts affecting other states) while *Nicaragua* refers to 'legal responsibility' (of the state).

There has been some discussion on the interchangeable use of liability and responsibility in English international law texts (for example, their use in United Nations Convention on the Law of the Sea)[109]. Although ARSIWA makes no reference itself to 'liability', the use of this term in the case law around state responsibility and in the commentaries necessitates this brief consideration. Civil lawyers view these as two distinct legal concepts. However, James Crawford rightly points out that this is not the case, and that these words – without the addition of an adjective – are used to mean the same thing in the common law and, as a result, the English texts.[110]

---

108 *Nicaragua* (n 9) at para. 115. Emphasis added.
109 10 December 1982, 1833 U.N.T.S. 397.
110 Crawford (n 67) at 61-3.

Therefore, if the terms liability and responsibility can be equated for the purpose of reading *Namibia Advisory Opinion* and *Nicaragua*, what is the relationship (and distinction) between the physical control and effective control tests? Crucially, the words following 'control' in each instance reveal everything: the *Namibia Advisory Opinion* refers to physical control of territory, while *Nicaragua* refers to effective control of activities/conduct.

This distinction is particularly interesting when reflecting again on the language used by states in their justifications for using force against non-state actors in host states. It is often raised that the host state has lost 'effective control of the territory'.[111] This is a patent misuse of the effective control test; what we should be using is the physical control test. It conflates these two standards.

Loss of physical (territorial) control is a vital pre-condition for the application of the unwilling or unable doctrine. Because of this, there is no chance of grounding the unwilling or unable doctrine being in the physical control test, an easy road to attribution.[112] Therefore, if states wished to use force within the framework of selfdefence, it would be necessary to attach the doctrine in some way to effective control. This has led to the conflation of the two tests, evinced in the language used by states.

If the host state physically controls its territory, it may be responsible under article 1 of ARSIWA as physical control is the foundation for state liability at an international level.[113] *Nicaragua* created the additional effective control test in order to broaden the scope for states to be held responsible,[114] but it does not help facilitate responsibility for host states who have lost territorial control to NSAGs.

Therefore, if no ground for attribution can be found under either the physical or effective control rubrics, there is no attribution of ISIL's conduct to Syria and thus no legal ground for the use of force in Syrian territory under article 51, and victim states have exhausted the extant legal justifications for use of force.

However, some commentators have over the years attempted to shift the narrative on control to the concept of indirect responsibility en-

---

111   See, for example, Germany's article 51 letter (n 58) in relation to ISIL in Syria.
112   The physical control test could only have been helpful in the historical resorts to the doctrine, which in any event amounted to harbouring. See section 3 above.
113   *Namibia Advisory Opinion* (n 107).
114   Particularly for extraterritorial activities.

THE 'UNWILLING OR UNABLE' DOCTRINE UNMASKED

shrined in article 12 of ARSIWA.[115] By doing so, they purportedly sidestep the issues created by the application of the effective control test set out in *Nicaragua*. They do this by noting that paragraph 116 of *Nicaragua* states that 'the United States may be responsible directly in connection with the activities of the contras'.[116]

At first glance, this may appear to be a neat solution grounded in the alleged need for a radical solution to the threat posed to the international order by terrorism (a convenient term that belies the more complex notion of the spectrum of non-state actors). However, in order for this approach to be theoretically sound, it relies on a breach of the obligation to prevent terrorist activities from a state's own territory (primarily by omission),[117] which is only possible in cases where the state concerned retains physical control of its territory. Firstly, and as already discussed earlier, it is not clear what that obligation actually entails – that is, whether it is an obligation of result or an obligation of due diligence. This uncertainty alone warrants a cautious approach to this proposed solution of indirect responsibility. Secondly, and more importantly for the purpose of this paper, this approach does not address the more realistic scenario where a state has lost physical control of the territory from which the terrorist threat emanates. It is not clear that the *Corfu Channel* obligation exists in such a case.

It has also been astutely noted that the concept of control seems ill-suited to address scenarios where states have no control over NSAGs operating within or from within their borders.[118] However, they argue that instead of eschewing the notion of control entirely, the liability should stem from the state's '*failure to control* its territory and harmful terrorist activities emanating from its soil', rather than the traditional *Corfu Channel* obligation.[119] This approach relies on the requirement of knowledge set out in *Corfu Channel*. Ian Brownlie notes that –

---

115   This article reads: 'There is a breach of an international obligation by a state when an act of that state is not in conformity with what is required of it by that obligation, regardless of its origin or character.'

116   Emphasis added. Proulx and Simma (n 104) at 166. Proulx considers indirect responsibility to be the same as what other scholars have called vicarious liability. See Vincent-Joel Proulx, 'Babysitting Terrorists: Should States Be Strictly Liable for Failing to Prevent Transborder Attacks' (2005) 23 Berkeley Journal of International Law 615 at 624.

117   See above n 86.

118   Proulx and Simma (n 104) at 172.

119   *Ibid.* Emphasis added.

where the loss complained of results from acts of individuals not employed by the state, or from activities of licensees or trespassers on the territory of the state, the responsibility of the state will depend on a failure to control. In this type of case questions of knowledge may be relevant in establishing the omission or, more properly, responsibility for failure to act.[120]

Thus, if one were to assess whether Syria has failed to control 'its territory and harmful terrorist activities emanating from its soil', one would have to assess Syria's knowledge of the activities, which would presumably relate to their nature and extent. Establishing the scope of Syria's knowledge is in itself a challenging task. As Christine Chinkin notes, 'the assertion of State responsibility for violations by non-State actors rests upon assumptions of knowledge and control that in many cases States simply do not possess'.[121] But what makes this approach truly formidable is the incoherent framework for the assessment of that knowledge.[122]

There are other legal commentators who have questioned the broad notion of control in the response to terrorism.[123] The arguments all center around the difficulty of attributing the conduct of these groups to states in order to perform counterterrorism measures within the confines of contemporary international law as they see it.[124] However, as clarified earlier, control remains central to responsibility, and that is why it is essential that a cogent account of its operation in the case of attacks by NSAGs is delineated.

---

120   Ian Brownlie, *System of the Law of Nations: State Responsibility Part 1* (Clarendon Press 1983) at 45.

121   Christine Chinkin, 'Human Rights and the Politics of Representation: Is There a Role for International Law?' in Michael Byers (ed), *The Role of Law in International Politics: Essays in International Relations and International Law* (Oxford University Press 2000) at 146. See also Proulx and Simma (n 104) at 171 who note unequivocally that 'evidence of State control is in many instances impossible to demonstrate following terrorist strikes'.

122   See the first paragraphs of section 5 dealing with these issues.

123   For example, see Karl Zemanek, 'Does the Prospect of Incurring Responsibility Improve the Observance of International Law?' in Maurizio Ragazzi (ed), *International Responsibility Today: Essays in Memory of Oscar Schachter* (Brill 2005) at 131.

124   Proulx and Simma (n 104) at 174.

THE 'UNWILLING OR UNABLE' DOCTRINE UNMASKED

5.4 *Strict Liability*

Due to the difficulties posed by the physical (territorial) and effective control tests, states and some scholars have found a neat way to bypass these tests and attribute conduct to host states (regardless of the manner in which the obligation is framed) – the unwilling or unable test. In this instance, it results in the introduction of an entirely new standard of liability to the equation: strict liability.

By circumventing the regular attribution tests and imposing liability on the host state (in this case, Syria) which only maintain *de jure* control over the territory, the unwilling or unable doctrine has (perhaps unwittingly) secreted this onerous form of liability into the international law discourse. The troubling implication of this is that where a state has lost physical control of its territory and has no links to the NSAG, it is nonsensically held to a higher standard of accountability. This may not have been so problematic if there was support for this shift in the UN Charter, ARSIWA, case law or customary international law; however, this is not the case. In relation to the latter, it is prudent to recall that state support for the unwilling or unable doctrine vacillates over time and is in any event not founded on a clear understanding of what the doctrine actually entails. It has, ultimately, been a political issue and is far from being a legal doctrine.

While this conclusion about the true nature of the unwilling or unable doctrine and the opportunities it could bring will undoubtedly delight many states, it may please some scholars too. Proulx first advocated for the incorporation of a strict liability standard to aid (legal) counterterrorism efforts in 2005.[125] This extreme measure is justified, he argued, because of the importance of what is at stake: the 'core of human dignity and security'.[126] These same arguments and calls for change in the international legal order formed the basis of his 2012 publication with Simma, which is also referenced in this paper.[127]

While the intention and aims behind the strict liability model proposed by these authors are laudable, the question of the suitability of strict liability for this purpose is deeply concerning. It is beyond the scope of this paper to conduct a comprehensive analysis and rebuttal,[128]

---

125   Proulx (n 116) at 643ff.

126   *Ibid.* at 650.

127   See above n 104 in its entirety.

128   The aim of this paper was merely to clarify the nature of the unwilling or unable doctrine through examining the conceptual challenges it poses, not to pronounce on its ultimate suitability. To read more on a modified but not dissimilar approach

however, suffice it to say very briefly that this approach: firstly, seemingly upends article 2(4) of the UN Charter; secondly, raises unsettling and complex normative questions about the right to sovereignty for states with less economic and/or military power (which is often linked to and thus compounds a history of intrusion upon sovereignty through events such as, but not limited to, colonialism); thirdly, is open to significant political abuse; and, finally, goes strongly against the cautious approach to importing domestic law concepts into public international law.[129]

Even if one understands the unwilling or unable doctrine as introducing strict liability for dealing with attacks by NSAGs, it is worth noting that this conclusion would not necessarily justify the violation of the host state's sovereignty in selfdefence.[130] In fact, article 5(1) of the definition of aggression (adopted by the General Assembly) states: 'No consideration of whatever nature, whether political, economic, military or otherwise, may serve as a justification for aggression.' Article 1 defines aggression as 'the use of armed force by a State against the sovereignty, territorial integrity or political independence of another State, or in any other manner inconsistent with the Charter of the United Nations'.

The use of force by victim states on the territory of a host state on the basis of the unwilling or unable doctrine is, without a legitimate legal foundation, undoubtedly an act of aggression, despite statements by the aggressors that the attacks are directed at ISIL rather than Syria as a state: it is the *effect*, and not the intention, that is relevant.[131]

However, in terms of article 39 of the UN Charter, the UNSC retains the power to determine whether conduct amounts to an act of aggression. In practice, the UNSC has been reluctant to exercise this power.[132] It does

---

of 'vicarious liability' in these circumstances, see Starski (n 98). For more on the suitability of strict liability for international law more generally (although written in the context of environmental law), see Constance O'Keefe, 'Transboundary Pollution and the Strict Liability Issue: The Work of the International Law Commission on the Topic of International Liability for Injuries Consequences Arising out of Acts Not Prohibited by International Law' (2020) 18 Denver Journal of International Law & Policy 65.29, reprintedin [1986] I Y.B. INT'L L. COMM'N., U.N. Doc. A/CN.4/SER. A/1986 (Part 1

129   On this last point, see Brownlie (n 120) at 37-8 and 40-7.

130   Christian Tams, 'The Use of Force Against Terrorists' (2009) 20 European Journal of International Law 359.at 385.

131   This is apparent from a reading of the definition of aggression. This author is not aware of anything (scholarly or jurisprudentially) to contradict this.

132   Gérard Cohen-Jonathan, 'Chapitre VII: Action En Cas De Menace Contre La Paix, De Rupture De La Paix et D'Acte D'Aggression' in Jean-Pierre Cot and Alain Pellet

THE 'UNWILLING OR UNABLE' DOCTRINE UNMASKED   101

not appear that it has declared any conduct purportedly justified by the unwilling or unable doctrine as an act of aggression.

The possibility remains that even if the conduct does not amount to an act of aggression, it may still constitute a breach of, or threat to, the peace which would be open to condemnation by the UN.[133] Gray notes that historically the UNSC condemned even minor uses of force under this power, but that this no longer appears to be the case.[134]

6   Concluding Remarks

This paper set out to demonstrate that the unwilling or unable doctrine is nothing but a political policy in disguise and that its use results in the incorporation of strict liability in the public international law framework for dealing with armed attacks by NSAGs. Through examining its historical applications, and revisiting states' more recent reliance on it in the Syrian case, it is evident that it is a doctrine lacking in legal pedigree. It has been manipulated for decades to evade the accepted principles of state responsibility and attribution, and it has the potential to further disrupt international law through its unchecked introduction of strict liability.

Practically speaking, the current use of the unwilling or unable doctrine purports to allow victim states and third-party states to hold host states – who have lost physical control of (a part of) their territory – strictly liable for attacks by NSAGs operating on their territory and, as such, authorises those other states to use force on the territory of the liable host state. This approach grants considerable scope to further undermine the prohibition of the use of force and the principle of non-intervention, an outcome that ought to be considered with caution.

While it is evident that we need to find creative solutions to the challenges posed by NSAGs in the modern era, that is no reason to abandon the first principles of public international law, particularly not in favour of a political convenience. Even in her article which triggered a renewed

---

(eds), *La Charte des Nations Unies: Commentaire Article par Article* (2. éd., rev et augm, Économica 1991) at 661.

133   Rosalyn Higgins, *The Development of International Law through the Political Organs of the United Nations* (Oxford University Press 1963) at 181.

134   Gray (n 84) at 182 fn 76.

commitment to the unwilling or unable doctrine, Deeks saw the need for legal certainty and theoretical coherence:

> In a world in which nonstate actors continue actively to threaten states' national security, and in which those nonstate actors know how to take advantage of failed or failing states and ungoverned spaces, it is critical that states responding to those threats proceed carefully in the face of clear, balanced rules.[135]

The purpose of this paper was not to displace the unwilling or unable doctrine and propose an alternative solution to the challenges of modern 'terrorism', but merely to appraise the conceptual difficulties the use of this doctrine creates, hoping to give reason for pause before relying on the doctrine in future.[136] The importance of the exercise conducted in this paper is in allowing the unwilling or unable doctrine to be confronted for what it truly is: not implicit consent, not an exception to the prohibition on the use of force located in the UN Charter, but an imposter; an unsubstantiated attempt to hold states who have lost control of part of their territory to a higher standard of responsibility, regardless of the costs.

---

135   Deeks (n 53) at 538.

136   There are other legal commentators who have attempted to find solutions, both within and outside the scope of the doctrine. See, for example, *Ibid.;* Daniel Bethlehem, 'Self-Defense Against an Imminent or Actual Armed Attack By Nonstate Actors' (2012) 106 American Journal of International Law 770; Proulx and Simma (n 104); Murray (n 3). Donette Murray's solution is particularly interesting because of its approach of considering unwilling and unable separately (at 96-101). That there is a difference between these two concepts shows through in section 5 of this paper, although the potentially deeper consequences of this difference (and any implications relating to the operation of strict liability specifically) have not been discussed.

4 Topoi of Ambiguity: WTO Membership without Statehood

The Case of Separate Customs Territories

*Marios C. Iacovides**

Abstract

This paper is part of a research project that systematically investigates on the basis of precedent the legal rules and practices by which de facto independent regimes which are not recognised as States, of which 'separate customs territories' form part, conduct cross-border trade and the ways in which States and international organisations react to these. The aim is to try to discern the public international law principles, legal rules, historical realities, or functionalist arguments that underpin the de jure or de facto territorial application of international trade rules to de facto independent regimes. The question addressed in this paper is why notions and requirements of statehood are decoupled from issues of the territorial application of the rules in the field of international trade law. To answer that question, I look comprehensively at original WTO Membership in relation to separate customs territories, discuss the acceptance of the WTO Agreement by separate customs territories and the requirements for such acceptance, and explore subsequent accession to the WTO. This study reveals that GATT contracting parties before and WTO Members now have consciously adopted a pragmatic approach to the application of international trade rules to non-state entities and have refrained from bringing claims on sanctions, embargoes, restrictions on trade of dual-use goods, territorial disputes, or issues of recognition connected to territories whose status is ambiguous. This approach has significance for the wider context of including non-state entities in international legal regimes, such as international humanitarian law.

---

* Research Fellow, Faculty of Law, University of Oxford.

Keywords

WTO law – international economic law – international trade and customs law – statehood – separate customs territories

1   Introduction

One of the external functions usually performed by entities effectively controlling a geographically defined area is cross-border trade. To conduct international trade, entities that are recognised by the international community as sovereign States, or groups of such entities that form customs unions and free trade areas having legal personality under public international law, enter into treaties in the form of trade agreements that regulate the terms for the conduct of trade to and from those areas. However, there are also de facto independent regimes controlling geographically defined areas that, although not recognised as States by the international community, nevertheless conduct trade with States, to the extent they are not subject to trade sanctions or embargoes. In international trade law, these territories are usually termed 'separate customs territories',[1] to distinguish them from sovereign States. These territories – *topoi* of ambiguity – are physical places whose status under public international law is (or has been) ambiguous, disputed, in flux, *sui generis*, or in any way unusual.

This article is part of a wider research project whose aim is to systematically investigate, on the basis of precedent, the legal rules and practices by which de facto independent regimes, of which 'separate customs territories' form a part, conduct cross-border trade and the ways in which States and international organisations react to this. The central idea is to try to discern the public international law principles, legal rules, historical realities, or functionalist arguments – the notional places in international trade law that deal with the physical *topoi* to which *topoi* of ambiguity also alludes – that underpin the de jure or de facto territorial application of international trade rules to de facto independent regimes. Put simply, the question that I try to shed light on is why notions and requirements of statehood are decoupled from issues of the territorial application of the rules in the field of international trade law.

---

[1]   See, eg, Marrakesh Agreement Establishing the World Trade Organisation (1994) 1867 UNTS 14 (WTO Agreement), Art XII.

Coming closer to understanding this serves two goals. The first goal is to be able to directly point to legal or practical avenues for the inclusion of de facto independent regimes in the processes and structures that govern international trade, with all the ensuing positive results such inclusion can have for the de facto independent regimes and the people under their control, not to mention the benefits flowing to the whole international community from the general expansion of trade. The second goal is to be able to extrapolate principles and practices to which we can have recourse when trying to find pragmatic solutions to making other fields of public international law applied by and applicable to de facto independent regimes, without disrespecting the sensitivities of States and without disrupting the status quo regarding the requirements of statehood. If the main reason for the relative success of international trade law in accommodating non-state entities is its ability to decouple membership from statehood and thus allow for trade on e.g. WTO terms, can the same approach be adopted in other areas of public international law too, if not by treaty, at least as customary international law through state practice and *opinio juris*? One such field of public international law would be international humanitarian law.

Of special interest for this broader research is whether de facto independent regimes de facto or de jure abide, or have abided, by rules under the General Agreement on Tariffs and Trade (GATT)[2] or World Trade Organization (WTO) law and how GATT contracting parties or WTO Members accommodate or have accommodated that by allowing such territories to officially gain WTO membership. Thus, in this article, I discuss WTO rules regarding membership, which can be traced back to the GATT years, and which allow for de jure membership by 'separate customs territories'. Building on the findings of this article, de facto application of GATT/WTO rules by regimes that were not GATT contracting parties or are not WTO members is explored further in another forthcoming article.[3]

---

2   General Agreement on Tariffs and Trade (30 October 1947), annexed to the Final Act Adopted at the Conclusion of the Second Session of the Preparatory Committee of the United Nations Conference on Trade and Employment, as subsequently rectified, amended or modified (GATT 1947). All references in this article are to the GATT 1947, which is legally distinct from the GATT 1994 (see Article II:4 of the WTO Agreement).

3   M Iacovides, 'Topoi of Ambiguity II – De Facto Application of GATT/WTO Rules by Non-State Entities' (forthcoming 2021).

Separate customs territories, which form the subject-matter of this article, are typically former colonies that are (or have been in the process of) transitioning to independence, but may also be overseas territories of States that form separate customs territories but are not sovereign States in their own right, self-proclaimed States that are not recognised as such by the international community, States whose governing regime at some point in time changed abruptly as a result of revolution or coups d'état, and territories that split from recognised States and either proclaimed independence or acceded to other recognised States. These territories can be characterised as quasi-states and they display many of the characteristics of States.[4] Importantly, they are governed in a relatively stable manner by a 'government' that at least internally enjoys some degree of legitimacy and externally is at least tolerated by States. As will be discussed in this paper, stable entities, inter alia Somaliland, Abkhazia, Northern Cyprus, Nagorno-Karabakh, Transdniestria, South Ossetia, Kosovo, and Palestine, could well join the WTO as separate customs territories, assuming the existing Members would reach a consensus to that effect.

As a corollary, I am not concerned with territories held by non-state armed groups that are involved in non-international armed conflict. Two reasons motivate their exclusion. First, in many cases, international trade with such groups is explicitly illicit, e.g. forbidden by way of United Nations (UN) Security Council Resolutions.[5] Secondly, the governing of many of these territories is entirely fluid and parts of the territory may rapidly shift between the control of different groups. Consequently, any trade they would engage in would be ephemeral. The exclusion means also that I do not in any way investigate the phenomenon of the 'war economy' whereby armed groups or criminal gangs fund their leaders and their activities by illicitly trading in raw materials, such as oil, or illegal substances, such as drugs.

From the outset, I also find it important to note that for the purposes of my research I am neither concerned with any territory's government's claims to independence and statehood, neither do I wish in any way to take sides in the conflicts that may engulf them. These are often the result of complex processes involving intersecting claims and arguments

---

4 They may even satisfy some of the Montevideo criteria on statehood.

5 See, eg, Document S/RES/2199(2015) *Threats to international peace and security caused by terrorist acts* (12 February 2015), adopted under the binding Chapter VII of the UN Charter, condemning any trade in oil and antiquities with the Islamic State in Iraq and the Levant (ISIL, also known as Daesh), the Al-Nusrah Front and other entities designated to be associated with Al-Qaida.

TOPOI OF AMBIGUITY: WTO MEMBERSHIP WITHOUT STATEHOOD   107

regarding self-determination, oppression, exploitation, exclusion, colonialism, political opportunism, ideology, language, culture and religion, to name a few. Moreover, I have only been concerned with the history of these territories to the extent that is necessary in order to understand their peculiarities regarding international trade. Put simply, as far as possible, I am interested only in investigating if and how separate customs territories came to be included as subjects of WTO and GATT law and consequently could engage in trade with other WTO Members.[6]

Expressed in terms of method, I have conducted doctrinal legal positivist research and I have tried, through recourse to recognised legal sources and through well-established legal methods of interpretation, to understand those sources and to present them in a coherent and structured manner. Although I present certain arguments in this article, those arguments are descriptive and inductive and should not be understood as normative.

The rest of this article is structured as follows. In section 2, I discuss original WTO Membership in relation to separate customs territories, with an emphasis on how such territories came to be GATT contracting parties. In section 3, I briefly touch upon acceptance of the WTO Agreement by separate customs territories. In section 4, I consider the third requirement for original WTO Membership, which has to do with attaching valid goods and services schedules of concessions, and how it affects the status of separate customs territories. In section 5, I address accession to the WTO Agreement by separate customs territories. Finally, in section 6, I draw conclusions and explain their significance for the wider context of including non-state entities in international legal regimes, such as international humanitarian law.

2   Original WTO Membership for Separate Customs Territories: GATT Origins

WTO law's subjects include not only States, but also 'separate customs territories'. This is possible because of the WTO's rules on membership. There are two ways for an entity to be officially a WTO Member and

---

6   That said, I do recognise that usage of certain terms, names etc., for these areas may be controversial for some readers and unacceptable for some others. I understand those sensitivities, but at the same time I ask the readers to indulge in my strive to make the choice as objective and apolitical as possible.

thereby be de jure bound by WTO law. The first way is through original WTO Membership as provided for in Article XI of the WTO Agreement. The second is through accession, which is governed by Article XII of the WTO Agreement.[7]

Original WTO Membership was open to all GATT contracting parties as well as the European Communities (as it was then), until 1 January 1997.[8] Article XI:1 of the WTO Agreement imposes three conditions for original membership: (i) being a contracting party to GATT,[9] (ii) accepting the WTO Agreement and the covered agreements, and (iii) annexing valid goods and services schedules to GATT 1994 and the General Agreement on Trade in Services[10] (GATS) respectively. This section deals with the first requirement.

2.1   *GATT Contracting Parties*

As is apparent from the text of Article XI:1 of the WTO Agreement, which specifically mentions the European Communities, statehood is self-evidently not a prerequisite for original membership. This was not an exception made simply for the benefit of the European Communities at the time the WTO Agreement was being negotiated. Looking at the other GATT contracting parties to which original membership was also available, we find Hong Kong and Macau.[11] The former had been a GATT contracting party since April 1986 and the latter since January 1991.[12] Neither is a State, nor was it a State at the time it was 'deemed' to be a GATT contracting party.

Understanding how separate customs territories came to be GATT contracting parties requires having a look at the GATT's provisions on acceptance of, accessions to, and successions to the GATT, found in Articles XXVI and XXXIII. Let us look at those provisions in turn.

---

7   See infra s 5.

8   Art XIV WTO Agreement stipulates that acceptance is open up to two years following the entry into force of the WTO Agreement and the covered agreements. That date was 1 January 1995, meaning that acceptance was possible until 1 January 1997.

9   Or, exceptionally, being the European Communities.

10   General Agreement on Trade in Services, Annex 1B to the WTO Agreement.

11   GATT, Analytical Index: Guide to GATT Law and Practice, updated 6th edn (Geneva, 1995), 1136.

12   See the two WTO Member's respective dedicated webpages on the WTO website, <www.wto.org/english/thewto_e/countries_e/hong_kong_china_e.htm> and <www.wto.org/english/thewto_e/countries_e/macao_china_e.htm> accessed 25 August 2020.

2.2   *GATT Acceptance in Respect of Separate Customs Territories*

Starting with the issue of GATT acceptance, according to Article XXVI:5(a),

> [e]ach government accepting [the] Agreement does so in respect of its metropolitan territory and of the other territories for which it has international responsibility, except such separate customs territories as it shall notify to the Executive Secretary to the Contracting Parties at the time of its own acceptance.

The drafters of the GATT were, thus, aware of the fact that certain contracting parties consisted of or were in control of more than one customs territory and that they might wish to bind only some of them to GATT terms. In fact, it would have been impossible not to have been aware of the matter: a significant portion of the original contracting parties were not only constituted of a metropolitan area from which trade took place, but also of one or more other territories over which they had control, some of which had their own tariffs and regulations.

Pursuant to Article XXVI:5(a) of the GATT, when accepting the Agreement through the Protocol of Provisional Application,[13] some contracting parties (Belgium, France, the Netherlands, and the United Kingdom) explicitly mentioned that the acceptance was limited to their metropolitan territories, a practice which was common for colonial powers entering into treaties, whereas others (Australia, Canada, Luxembourg, and the United States) did not make acceptance subject to any express limitations.[14]

A straightforward lexical reading of the GATT's provision on acceptance confirms that 'separate customs territories' could be included in a metropolitan GATT contracting party's acceptance of all rights and obligations assumed under the Agreement. That, however, did not mean that any such 'separate customs territory' would be assimilated in the metropolitan contracting party's customs territory.

Quite to the contrary, according to Article XXIV:1 of the GATT, which deals with the Agreement's territorial application, each separate customs

---

13   The GATT – as a result of the failure of the 1948 Havana Charter to enter into force and the ensuing non-creation of the International Trade Organization – was for the entirety of its history only applied 'provisionally' by the contracting parties, pursuant to a Protocol of Provisional Application.

14   Document E/PC/T/214.Add.2.Rev.1, Protocol of Provisional Application of the General Agreement on Tariffs and Trade (1 January 1947), para. 1.

territory on behalf of which the agreement would be accepted under Article XXVI, or applied under Article XXXIII or pursuant to the Protocol of Provisional Application, would be treated as if it were *itself* a contracting party. In other words, territories under the same sovereign would have to treat trade between them as international trade, meaning that the principles of non-discrimination and most favoured nation treatment (MFN) would be applicable. Thus, although a 'separate customs territory' could be included in a metropolitan contracting party's acceptance of the GATT, it would keep its *separateness* from that metropolitan customs territory.

It caused grave concerns for colonial powers during the negotiation of the GATT that trade and sovereignty were not necessarily intertwined, and that the cornerstone principles of the GATT would mean that they might not be able to continue giving preferential treatment to goods from territories that, although under their sovereignty, constituted separate customs territories, without breaching the GATT, or without extending the same treatment to territories under the sovereignty of other States.[15] Addressing those concerns necessitated, for instance, adopting express exceptions from MFN treatment with regard to separate customs territories that gave each other preferential treatment, inter alia because they were under common sovereignty or suzerainty.[16]

2.3 *GATT Extension of Territorial Application to Separate Customs Territories*

Beyond acceptance on behalf of separate customs territories by the metropolitan contracting party, Article XXVI:5(b) of the GATT made provision for the extension of such acceptance in respect of any separate customs territory or territories that may have originally been excluded. This possibility was reflected in the Protocol of Provisional Application,

---

15   UN Document E/PC/T/C.II/PV/4, UN Economic and Social Council, Preparatory Committee of the International Conference on Trade and Employment, Verbatim Report of the Fourth Meeting of Committee II, (29 October 1946), 18-20.

16   See Art I:2(b) GATT, referring to "preferences in force exclusively between two or more territories which ... were connected by common sovereignty or relations of protection or suzerainty" *juncto* Annex B to the GATT. See also Document E/PC/T. II/PV/4 (n 15) 18-20 as well as the discussion in Document E/PC/T/33 *Report of the First Session of the London Preparatory Committee of the United Nations Conference on Trade and Employment* (*the London Report*) (October 1946), 14, para. III.C.3(d)(ii) regarding safeguards and non-discriminatory quantitative restrictions in relation to such territories that resulted in the inclusion of an exception to the principle of non-discrimination in Art XIV:3 GATT.

which provided that governments could make effective provisional application of the GATT in respect of any of their territories other than their metropolitan territories after giving notice thereof to the UN Secretary-General.[17]

Such notices were received from Australia (on behalf of Papua New Guinea), Belgium (on behalf of the Belgian Congo), France (on behalf of all overseas territories of the French Union listed in Annex B of the GATT except Morocco), the Netherlands (on behalf of its overseas territories), and the United Kingdom (on behalf of Newfoundland, the Mandated Territory of Palestine, all territories for the international relations of which it was responsible except Jamaica, and later on behalf of Jamaica).[18]

2.4 Succession of Separate Customs Territories to the GATT

In addition to acceptance and extension, the GATT made specific provision for the succession to rights and obligations accruing under the Agreement. Thus, Article XXVI:5(c), provides that:

> If any of the customs territories, in respect of which a contracting party has accepted this Agreement, possesses or acquires full autonomy in the conduct of its external commercial relations and of the other matters provided for in this Agreement, such territory shall, upon sponsorship through a declaration by the responsible contracting party establishing the above-mentioned fact, be deemed to be a contracting party.

Just like with acceptance and extension, the GATT drafters and original contracting parties did not limit the possibility of succession to sovereign States (which would of course be possible under public international law so long as there was continued personality), choosing instead to make it available to 'customs territories'.

This feature was remarkable, in that it set the GATT apart from the practice of international organisations such as ITU, UNESCO, WCO, WMO and FAO.[19] Understanding how Article XXVI:5(c) came to be drafted the way it did will help us shed light on the reasons behind this remarkable feature. In the rest of this section, I trace its origins to the

---

17   Protocol of Provisional Application (n 14) para. 2.

18   GATT Analytical Index (n 11) 917 and fn 40.

19   T Kunugi, 'State Succession in the Framework of GATT' (1965) 59 The American Journal of International Law 268, 286.

International Conference on Trade and Employment (the Conference), by providing a short account of the negotiating history and preparatory works of the GATT, which happened in tandem with the negotiation of the Havana Charter.[20]

In February 1946, the UN's Economic and Social Council decided to call a Conference whose purpose would be, inter alia, to establish an International Trade Organization (ITO) as a UN specialized agency having responsibility over three envisaged international agreements, including one on international trade.[21] To that effect, a preparatory committee was constituted, consisting of a number of States.[22] Subcommittees were created to deal with separate aspects of the negotiations.

At the time the Conference was being convened, Burma, Ceylon, and Southern Rhodesia (as Myanmar, Sri Lanka and Zimbabwe were then respectively called) were in the process of gaining independence from the United Kingdom and they had already been engaged for some time in international trade with some independent States. All three were important trading partners internationally at the time.[23] Consequently, on 28 July 1947, the Economic and Social Council adopted a resolution to invite Burma, Ceylon and Southern Rhodesia to participate in the work of the Conference, noting that 'it [had become] clear during the negotiations ... that [they], although under the sovereignty of a Member of the United Nations, possess full autonomy in the conduct of their external commercial relations'.[24] However, in recognition of these territories' ambiguous status in public international law and in showing deference to the United Kingdom, instead of sending the invitations directly to the territories'

---

20   Document E/CONF.2/FINALACT, UN Conference on Trade and Employment - Held at Havana, Cuba from November 21, 1947, to March 24, 1948 - Final Act and Related Documents - Interim Commission for the International Trade Organization (1 April 1948).

21   UN Document E/22 (6 February 1946), paras. 1 and 3(e), as reproduced in Resolutions adopted by the Economic and Social Council during its 1st session, 23 January 1946-18 February 1946, 183-184 (ESCOR, 1st session).

22   *Ibid.*, para. 6.

23   Burma, for instance, was at the time the world's biggest exporter of rice and teak: See Document E/PC/T/TAC/PV/13, Second Session of the Preparatory Committee of the UN Conference on Trade and Employment – Verbatim Report of the Thirteenth Meeting of the Tariff Agreement Committee (8 September 1947), 14.

24   Document E/62(V), Resolution of 28 July 1947.

TOPOI OF AMBIGUITY: WTO MEMBERSHIP WITHOUT STATEHOOD   113

governments, the Economic and Social Council resolved to send them through the government of the United Kingdom.[25]

In any case, the territories, perhaps emboldened by their inclusion in the negotiations and certainly dissatisfied with being treated as independent with regard to some matters but dependent on the United Kingdom with regard to others, started pushing to become contracting parties to the GATT in their own right and for their governments to be allowed to accept and sign the agreement directly. Their participation in the work of the Preparatory Committees as well as the independent negotiation of future trading terms with other prospective GATT contracting parties, coupled with their demands to be full contracting parties, made it clear to all involved that changes would have to be made to the draft GATT. These changes were also necessary in order to have an approach which would be in line with the one that would come to be adopted in the Havana Charter in respect of ITO.

Thus, at its thirteenth meeting, the Tariff Agreement Committee discussed the position of Burma, Ceylon and Southern Rhodesia at length. During the negotiations regarding the text of what was to become Article XXVI:5(a) of the GATT 1947,[26] a discussion between delegates arose regarding the position of separate customs territories under the agreement. The wording of Article XXIV:3(b), as it then was, provided that the governments of such separate customs territories would be entitled to appoint a representative to the decision-making body of the GATT.[27] The Burmese representative held a long (and within the context of normally mundane trade negotiations, rather passionate) speech during the meeting, asking for the full incorporation of Burma to the GATT and claiming its and other separate customs territories' right to be signatory parties. If Burma could conduct international trade, determine the terms of such trade independently of any sovereign State, negotiate bilaterally with prospective GATT contracting parties, why could it not be a full contract-

---

25   *Ibid.*, 2. The Committee also resolved to send an invitation directly to the government of Indonesia, as it recognised that 'the Indonesian Republic enjoys *in fact* autonomy in the conduct of its external commercial relations': see 3 (emphasis added). However, Indonesia did not participate at the GATT negotiations and never became an original contracting party to that Agreement. For that reason, I have omitted to discuss it at length in this section.

26   See supra, s 2.2.

27   Document E/PC/T/189, Second Session of the Preparatory Committee of the United Nations Conference on Trade and Employment - Draft General Agreement on Tariffs and Trade (30 August 1947), 56.

ing party itself? How could it be required to accept that it would be the United Kingdom and not itself as a separate customs territory that would accept and sign the GATT on its behalf? How could its name not be included in the preambular text?[28]

The ensuing discussion shows how certain States, in particular Australia, Chile, Cuba, and Czechoslovakia, had a hard time accepting the possibility of separate customs territories that were not States, or at least not close to being States, of being full contracting parties to the GATT in their own right. Although they seemed to accept the reality and importance of these separate customs territories' inclusion in international trade as a matter of fact, they expressed concerns regarding what a more formalized participation in international trade agreements would entail for their nebulous international law status.[29]

Here, we see the ambiguous status of these territories, how they both exist and do not exist in the eyes of public international law. As put by the Chilean delegate, 'a separate customs territory which is autonomous in these matters is not politically autonomous, and therefore does such a Government exist? It seems to me contradictory'.[30] We see also different degrees of tolerance or acceptance of this ambiguous status, possibly in direct proportion to each territory's degree of legitimacy in the eyes of recognised States. Thus, most delegates seemed able to accept the contradiction in terms (of existing and not existing as GATT subjects) with regard to Burma, Ceylon and Southern Rhodesia – often going at lengths to express their appreciation for these territories' engagement in international trade, negotiations etc. – but they certainly had trouble accepting that the possibility of full participation could or should be available to *all* other 'hypothetical' separate customs territories.[31]

The United Kingdom which, as a colonial power, was certainly quite invested in the matter, broke the impasse by suggesting the creation of an ad hoc subcommittee to discuss if any changes needed to be made to the draft GATT for hypothetical separate customs territories that might want to join in the future. At the same time, the United Kingdom considered it unnecessary for the subcommittee to discuss specifically the position of Burma, Ceylon and Southern Rhodesia.[32] Representatives of other States

---

28   E/PC/T/TAC/PV/13 (n 23) 9-14.

29   *Ibid.,* 7 and 15-24.

30   *Ibid.,* 7.

31   *Ibid.,* 20.

32   *Ibid.,* 25.

present at the meeting insisted on including in the ad hoc subcommittee's terms of reference also a specific investigation of the position of Burma, Ceylon and Southern Rhodesia.[33] The latter view prevailed in the end.[34]

On 15 September 1947, the ad hoc subcommittee prepared a report which was duly sent to the Tariff Agreement Committee. The report shows that three issues seemed to have been considered relevant by the members of the ad hoc subcommittee for the determination of whether Burma, Ceylon and Southern Rhodesia could participate as full contracting parties in the GATT. They wanted to know, first, whether each of the three territories had the ability to determine and modify its tariffs without the consent of the United Kingdom; secondly, whether they would be able to apply the GATT without reference to the United Kingdom; and thirdly, whether they could enter into contractual relations on commercial matters with foreign governments and if this was in the affirmative if there were any examples of such relations.[35]

In a way, these three questions can be extrapolated as criteria for whether a territory possesses full autonomy in the conduct of its external trade relations, i.e. whether it is a 'separate customs territory' within the meaning of the GATT and by extension of WTO law.[36] Moreover, although the ad hoc subcommittee was aware that the situation with regard to Ceylon was 'fluid',[37] it nevertheless recommended that it be allowed to become a full GATT contracting party just like Burma, which satisfied all three criteria de jure.[38] This makes clear that it was considered sufficient to satisfy the criteria de facto, irrespective of the de jure position of a territory. The de facto satisfaction of the criteria was also explicitly endorsed by the Tariff Agreement Committee.[39]

---

33   *Ibid.,* 24-28.

34   *Ibid.,* 27-28.

35   Document E/PC/T/198, Second Session of the Preparatory Committee of the UN Conference on Trade and Employment — Report of the Ad Hoc Sub-Committee of the Tariff Agreement Committee on paragraph 3 of Article XXIV (15 September 1947), 1.

36   For the same view, see L Wang, 'Separate Customs Territory in GATT and Taiwan's Request for GATT Membership' (1991) 25:5 *Journal of World Trade* 5, 16.

37   Document E/PC/T/198 (n 34) 2.

38   *Ibid.,* 3.

39   Document E/PC/T/TAC/PV/22, Second Session of the Preparatory Committee of the UN Conference on Trade and Employment – Verbatim Report of the Twenty-Second Meeting of the Tariff Agreement Committee (17 September 1947), 22 and 24.

Regarding the second question that the ad hoc subcommittee had to deal with (i.e. whether the territories would be able to apply the GATT without reference to the United Kingdom), several amendments and additions to the draft GATT text of what was then Article XXVI:3(a) were suggested as well as ensuing modifications to the text of Article XXXII.[40] Thus, it is this ad hoc subcommittee that drafted what eventually became Article XXVI:5(c) of the GATT regarding the position of separate customs territories that become autonomous in the conduct of their external trade relations and all other matters provided for by the GATT and are thereafter 'deemed' to be contracting parties upon sponsorship by a metropolitan contracting party – a form of *succession* – as well as Article XXXIII which, alternatively, makes possible the *accession* of new separate customs territories.[41]

Two days after the ad hoc subcommittee's report was circulated, the Tariff Agreement Committee met and confirmed the addition of Article XXVI:5(c) of the GATT.[42] Thus, the question of Burma's, Ceylon's and Southern Rhodesia's demand to be included as contracting party in their own right opened Pandora's box and made possible the subsequent succession of other separate customs territories to the GATT.

However, succession *did* come with certain preconditions attached, namely that a contracting party would already have accepted the GATT on behalf of the customs territory and that the customs territory 'possess[ed] or acquir[ed] full autonomy in the conduct of its external commercial relations and of the other matters provided for in [the GATT].' Moreover, succession was only possible 'upon sponsorship through a declaration by the responsible contracting party establishing [that] fact.' In other words, succession pursuant to Article XXVI:5(c) was only possible for separate customs territories where the GATT already had territorial application by way of either the first or second subparagraph of Article XXVI:5 and where the State formerly responsible for the territory gave its blessing to the succession.

Regardless, it is a remarkable measure of the extent to which the world had changed between the drafting of the original GATT and the coming into being of the WTO on the 1 January 1995 that as of that date, of the total 128 GATT contracting parties almost half (63) had become contracting parties through succes-

---

40   Document E/PC/T/198 (n 34) 3-4.

41   See infra, s 2.5.

42   E/PC/T/TAC/PV/22 (n 38) 25.

TOPOI OF AMBIGUITY: WTO MEMBERSHIP WITHOUT STATEHOOD   117

sion on the basis of Article XXVI:5(c) of the GATT.[43] The large majority
of these 63 contracting parties were former colonies that succeeded as
contracting parties to the GATT as sovereign States having one way or
another obtained their independence from the colonial power. Their succession to the GATT as contracting parties more or less coincided with
their independence. Liechtenstein was a relative anomaly in this regard
as it had been already an independent State for some time when on 1
April 1966 the GATT started being applied in its territory as part of Switzerland's accession to the agreement under Article XXXIII of the GATT
and when it later on became a contracting party in its own right.[44]

Two of the 63 territories that succeeded as contracting parties to the
GATT were customs territories under the international responsibility of
another State. Hong Kong was under the international responsibility of
the United Kingdom and Macau under the international responsibility
of Portugal. Thus, in accordance with the provisions of Article XXVI:5(c)
of the GATT, these two separate customs territories succeeded upon the
United Kingdom's and Portugal's 'sponsorship' respectively.[45]

2.5   *Accession to the GATT*
According to Article XXXIII of the GATT:

> [a] government not party to [the] Agreement, or a government
> acting on behalf of a separate customs territory possessing full

---

43   GATT Analytical Index (n 11) 919.
44   Under the terms of para. 3 of the Protocol for Switzerland's accession to the GATT
      1947, its customs territory was considered to include the one of Liechtenstein by
      virtue of the customs union treaty between the two: Document 14S/6, as referenced
      in Table VI of the Appendix regarding Accessions under Art XXXIII in GATT Ana-
      lytical Index (n 11) 1140. Hence, by accepting the GATT, Switzerland also accepted
      it for the territory of Liechtenstein and up until the declaration of 29 March 1994
      that Liechtenstein should be deemed to be a contracting party in its own right,
      Switzerland had represented the Principality in all matters relating to the GATT.
      See Document L/7440, *Admission of Liechtenstein as a Contracting Party – Certifica-
      tion by the Director-General* (5 April 1994).
45   With regard to Hong Kong, see Document L/5986, Admission of Hong Kong
      as a Contracting Party – Certification by the Director-General (24 April 1986)
      and Document L/5987, Admission of Hong Kong as a Contracting Party –
      Communication from the People's Republic of China (24 April 1986). With regard
      to Macau, see Document L/6806 Admission of Macau as a Contracting Party
      – Certification by the Director-General (14 January 1991) and Document L/6807,
      Admission of Macao as a Contracting Party – Communication from the People's
      Republic of China (14 January 1991).

> autonomy in the conduct of its external relations and of the other matters provided for in [the] Agreement, may accede to [it] on its own behalf or on behalf of that territory [...].

Just like Article XXVI of the GATT, Article XXXIII, thus, does not place any requirement of Statehood regarding accession to the Agreement. Not only does the Article not mention States but uses instead the more ambiguous term 'government'; it also explicitly makes it possible for separate customs territories to accede.

Accession Protocols of acceding contracting parties could include statements concerning provisional application to specific territories, as was the case with Japan, Portugal and Spain.[46] Thus, an acceding metropolitan contracting party could achieve the same result as original contracting parties could through Articles XXVI:5(a) and XXVI:5(b) of the GATT, i.e. to bind or exclude a separate customs territory over which it had sovereignty.

However, in stark contrast to the abundant usage of Article XXIV:5(c) of the GATT, Article XXXIII was never used for the accession of a separate customs territory. The one separate customs territory that did initiate an accession process under this Article was Taiwan.[47] However, its accession was held up by China's accession process;[48] thus, it never actually took place under the provisions of this Article, but instead under the corresponding provisions for accession to the WTO.

2.6 Separate Customs Territories: Other Relevant Provisions

As we saw in the previous subsections, the relevant term used in Articles XXVI and XXXIII of the GATT is 'separate customs territory possessing full autonomy in the conduct of its external commercial relations and of the other matters provided for in this Agreement'. No definition of that type of separate customs territory is provided for in the GATT. However, an agreement like the GATT naturally includes several other provisions

---

46 See Protocols of Accession in Document 4S/7, para. 1(d) (for Japan), Document 11S/20 24, para. 11 (for Portugal), and Document 12S/27, 28, para. 3 (for Spain), all three as referenced in GATT Analytical Index (n 11) 1083.

47 For a detailed account, see L Wang (n 35).

48 Document C/M/259, Council – Minutes of Meeting Held in the Centre William Rappard on 29 September - 1 October 1992 (27 October 1992), 2-3.

TOPOI OF AMBIGUITY: WTO MEMBERSHIP WITHOUT STATEHOOD   119

that are relevant for understanding the provisions regarding acceptance, succession, and accession in relation to separate customs territories.[49]

Thus, a definition of a part of that term, namely 'customs territory', is provided in Article XXIV:2 of the GATT which provides that '... a customs territory shall be understood to mean any territory with respect to which separate tariffs or other regulations of commerce are maintained for a substantial part of the trade of such territory with other territories.'[50] A 'customs territory' is, thereby, defined simply as a matter of fact. The relevant fact is that the territory maintains tariffs or other regulations of commerce for a substantial part of its trade with *other* territories that are *separate* from the tariffs or other regulations of commerce of those trade partners. Thus, although the definition is not for a 'separate' customs territory, essentially, a customs territory for the purposes of Article XXIV:2 of the GATT is determined or constituted antithetically to other customs territories and thus seems, in the present author's opinion, to include the 'separate' epithet. The antithesis establishes the *separateness* that allows a distinction to be made between two territories that are separate customs territories.

Understanding this is helpful, as it means we can have recourse to an additional definition found in the GATT, regarding a form of organisation that contrasts with a 'separate customs territory' – namely, a 'customs union' made up of at least two previously separate customs territories – in order to shed light on the former. That definition is found in Article XXIV:8(a) of the GATT, which holds that a customs union is created when two territories eliminate tariffs and regulatory barriers with respect to substantially all the trade between them and at the same time adopt substantially the same tariffs and regulatory barriers in respect of the rest of the world.

From Article XXIV:8(a) of the GATT we can deduce that a separate customs territory is defined not only in relation to its substantial separateness from other customs territories but also from the substantial absence of tariffs and regulatory barriers *internally* within that territory, which in itself creates indistinctiveness among the physical, political,

---

49   Vienna Convention on the Law of Treaties (22 May 1969) 1155 UNTS 331, entered into force 27 January 1980, Art 31.

50   Art XXIV:2 GATT. This definition, beyond the substitution of 'Chapter' for 'Agreement', is identical to Art 42(2) of the Havana Charter. The text of Art 42(2) Havana Charter was agreed subsequent to the drafting of Art XXIV:2 GATT: See Document E/CONF.2/C.3/87, *Third Committee: Commercial Policy – Report of Working Party No. 8 (Article 42)* (12 March 1948).

or administrative divisions of the territory. We can also deduce that a separate customs territory has both an internal trade aspect and an external one. Noting how the wording is simply declaratory (note the use of the verbs 'are maintained', 'are eliminated', and 'are applied' in Article XXIV:8(a) of the GATT), we can further deduce that both those aspects seem to be simply a matter of fact. This accords with the negotiating history of Articles XXVI:5(c) and XXXIII of the GATT which was presented in the previous subsection.

Importantly, we see also that nowhere in the definition of a customs territory or customs union is there any reference or requirement as to *who* initiates the 'separateness' or its opposite, *who* decides, *who* controls it. The relevant verbs are in the passive form and completely silent as to the actor behind them. This makes it fully possible to have a separate customs territory that is under the sovereignty of another territory, most likely a State.

In the same spirit, the GATT consistently mentions 'governments', not States, as actors that effectuate the Agreement. For instance, the Preamble begins with the words 'The Governments of' before it goes on to list the signatories to the Agreement and the same is true of the opening articles of the Protocol of Provisional Application. Moreover, Article XXXII of the GATT defines the contracting parties to the Agreement as 'those governments which are applying the provisions of [the] Agreement under Article XXVI or XXXIII or pursuant to the Protocol of Provisional Application'. In turn, those Articles also mention 'governments' as the actors which accept the Agreement (Articles XXVI:4 and XXVI:5(a)), succeed to it (Article XXVI:5(c)), or accede to it (Article XXXIII).

This practice has been carried over to the WTO.[51] The WTO Agreement was signed by 'representatives of the governments and of the European Communities members of the Trade Negotiations Committee'.[52] What is more, the WTO Agreement clarifies that the terms 'country' or 'countries' used anywhere in the Agreement or in any of the Multilateral Trade Agreements that make up the body of WTO law, are to be understood to include any separate customs territory Member of the WTO. Similarly

---

51   See WTO Agreement, Art XVI:1 ('the WTO shall be guided by the decisions, procedures and customary practices followed by the Contracting Parties to the GATT 1947 and the bodies established in the framework of GATT 1947.')

52   Final Act Embodying the Results of the Uruguay Round of Multilateral Trade Negotiations, para. 1, available at <https://www.wto.org/english/docs_e/legal_e/03-fa_e .htm> (accessed 22 June 2021).

the term 'national' must be read as pertaining to such a separate customs territory.[53]

3 Acceptance of the WTO Agreement and the Covered Agreements

The previous section dealt with the first requirement for WTO Membership, namely being a GATT contracting party. With regard to the second requirement, acceptance of the WTO Agreement and the covered agreements, in stark contrast to the GATT, the WTO Agreement does not specifically provide for acceptance on behalf of WTO Member's separate customs territories. Does that mean that this possibility does not exist anymore? The answer is no, because such possibility is provided for both directly and indirectly.

Directly, it is made possible as a matter of public international law. Article 29 of the Vienna Convention on the Law of Treaties stipulates that '[u]nless a different intention appears from the treaty or is otherwise established, a treaty is binding upon each party in respect of its entire territory'.[54] For most original Members the area which constitutes their 'entire territory' will also correspond with one and only one customs territory, but that does not have to be the case. Certain WTO Members (for instance, Denmark, France, the Netherlands, New Zealand, the United Kingdom) still have dependent overseas territories, some of which may be separate customs territories. The practice of certain WTO Members regarding their overseas territories has been to explicitly mention the acceptance of the WTO Agreement on behalf of those of their overseas territories they intend to bind (though they do not really have to) and thereby exclude all other territories. In other words, an overseas territory of a WTO Member may be bound by the WTO Member's acceptance of the WTO Agreement.

Indirectly, separate customs territories are also able to accept the WTO Agreement in their own right, so long as they had been GATT contracting parties as of the date of entry into force of the WTO Agreement. This is how Hong Kong and Macau have been able to accept the WTO Agreement. Since the WTO Agreement has been in force since 1995, this possibility is of course no longer available to any other separate customs territories,

---

53   Explanatory Notes to the WTO Agreement.
54   Vienna Convention (n 48) Art 29.

not even those that could have tried to claim that they could be 'deemed' to be contracting parties under Article XXVI:5(c) of the GATT.

4 Attaching Schedules of Concessions to GATT and GATS

Acceptance of the WTO Agreement and, thereby, original WTO Membership has thus been possible for separate customs territories, so long as the responsible metropolitan State was a GATT contracting party and no exclusion was made during acceptance of the WTO Agreement. However, Article XI of the WTO Agreement places a third condition for original membership, namely attaching schedules of concessions to the GATT and the GATS.

Here, things get really muddy regarding separate customs territories, leading to considerable confusion as to which overseas territories of WTO Members are de jure covered by WTO rules. This confusion arises because some WTO Members are part of the European Union's (EU) customs union while also being original WTO Members in their own right and administering overseas territories. EU Member States are covered by the EU schedules of concessions. As such, they have not had to attach schedules of concessions for those of their territories that are part of the EU customs union. However, to the extent that some of their overseas territories are not included in the EU customs union they ought to have done so in order for such territories to be covered by their WTO original membership. In most instances, original WTO Members had valid goods schedules for their overseas territories under the GATT and one could perhaps argue that these could be carried over to the WTO even if they were not explicitly attached.[55] The same, however, is not true regarding services schedules, as the GATS only came about with the creation of the WTO.

Two examples illustrate the confusion and show the likely implications for separate customs territories. The first concerns Aruba and the Antilles, two different overseas territories of the Netherlands.[56] When the Netherlands acceded to the WTO as an original Member, it did so as 'Netherlands (For the Kingdom in Europe and for the Netherlands

---

55 During the GATT era, there was a regularly updated "List of territories to which the General Agreement applies". See further infra n 69.

56 The Netherlands Antilles was dissolved on 10 October 2010.

Antilles)'.[57] However, as a discussion during the Uruguay Round shows, it seems the Netherlands intended also to bind Aruba, since they had presented schedules of tariff concessions for the territory.[58] In any case, these schedules were not in the right format and, thus, their fate as well as the territories' WTO status must have been uncertain for some time. On a technical level, it is unclear how coverage of these two territories as part of Dutch membership was achieved, if at all. For the Antilles, acceptance was clearly in place. For Aruba, acceptance must have taken place at some time before 1 January 1997, when the deadline for accepting the WTO Agreement as original Member expired.[59] In 2008, in two consecutive Notifications to the Committee on Market Access, the Netherlands invoked its rights under Article XXVIII:5 of the GATT to modify the schedules of Aruba and the Antilles, indicating that at some point in time before that, it had submitted valid goods schedules for the territories.[60] The two territories had valid services schedules.[61]

The second example concerns the Faroe Islands (Faroes), a self-governing overseas administrative division, part of Denmark.[62] The Faroes are not part of the EU.[63] The two parties' trade relations are regulated by a bilateral trade agreement.[64] The Faroes has full autonomy in the exer-

---

57 See WTO, Status of WTO Legal Instruments, 2012 edn., available at: <http://www
.wto.org/english/res_e/booksp_e/wto_status_legal_inst12_e.pdf> accessed 25 August 2020, 25.

58 Document MTN.TNC/43, Uruguay Round - Trade Negotiations Committee - Thirty-Seventh Meeting: 30 March 1994 (7 April 1994), 9.

59 See supra, n 8.

60 Document G/MA/224, Invocation of Paragraph 5 of Article XXVIII, Schedule II, Section D – Aruba (8 December 2008); Document G/MA/223, Invocation of Paragraph 5 of Article XXVIII, Schedule II, Section D – The Netherlands-Antilles (8 December 2008).

61 Document GATS/SC/5, The Kingdom of the Netherlands with Respect to Aruba – Schedule of Specific Commitments (15 April 1994); Document GATS/SC/3, The Kingdom of the Netherlands with Respect to the Netherlands Antilles – Schedule of Specific Commitments (15 April 1994).

62 The 1948 Home Rule Act of the Faroe Islands, Act No. 137 (23 March 1948).

63 Art 52 of the Treaty on the European Union (TEU) establishes the applicability of EU Treaties to Denmark, but Art. 355(5)(a) of the Treaty on the Functioning of the European Union (TFEU) stipulates that the territorial scope of the Treaties does not extend to the Faroes. The Faroes are not associated with the EU as an overseas country or territory: See Arts 198-204 and Annex II TFEU.

64 Agreement between the European Community, of the one part, and the Government of Denmark and the Home Government of the Faroe Islands, of the other part, [1997] OJ L 53/2.

cise of its external commercial policy.[65] Thus, it could well be a separate customs territory for the purposes of WTO law.

In 2013, Denmark, in respect of the Faroes, requested consultations with the EU regarding an import ban on Atlanto-Scandian herring and Northeast Atlantic mackerel from the Faroes and a prohibition on the use of EU ports by Faroese and other vessels that fished or transported those fish or their derivatives.[66] A panel was established following Denmark's second request in February 2014. Simultaneously, negotiations continued under the auspices of a working group examining a reallocation of the fishing quotas. By August, Denmark and the EU informed the WTO Dispute Settlement Body (DSB) that the matter had been settled, as an agreement on Faroese fishing quotas for 2014 had been reached and access to the EU market was restored.[67]

Had the parties not found a negotiated solution and had the panel's jurisdiction been disputed by the EU, the panel might have been called to examine the applicability of WTO law to the Faroes as part of Denmark's WTO Membership. Denmark's instrument of acceptance of the WTO Agreement as 'the Kingdom of Denmark' did not include any statement on territorial limitations.[68] In light of Article 29 of the Vienna Convention, this suggests that the WTO Agreement binds Denmark's entire territory, including the Faroes. However, Denmark has no separate schedules for the Faroes and the EU schedules, naturally, only cover the EU customs territory.[69] Thus, an argument could have been made that under Article XI:1 of the WTO Agreement, Denmark's original WTO Membership does not extend to the Faroes. A further complicating factor would have

---

65   Since 2005, the Faroese government has been empowered to represent itself and conclude treaties with States and international organisations in matters devolved to it, such as external trade relations: Act on the Assumption of Matters and Fields of Responsibility by the Faroese Authorities, Act No. 79 (12 May 2005); Act on the Conclusion of Agreements under International Law by the Government of the Faroes, Act No. 80 (14 May 2005).

66   Art 5 of Commission Implementing Regulation 793/2013 of 20 August 2013 establishing measures in respect of the Faeroe Islands to ensure the conservation of the Atlanto-Scandian herring stock, [2013] OJ L 223/1.

67   The restrictive measures were repealed by Commission Implementing Regulation (EU) 896/2014 of 18 August 2014 repealing Implementing Regulation (EU) No 793/2013 establishing measures in respect of the Faroe islands to ensure the conservation of the Atlanto-Scandian herring stock, [2014] OJ L 244/10.

68   Status of WTO Legal Instruments (n 56) 16.

69   The current and historical situation of WTO Members' valid goods schedules is available at <www.wto.org/english/tratop_e/schedules_e/goods_schedules_table_e.htm> accessed 25 August 2020.

been that Denmark had a valid GATT schedule covering the Faroes until it joined the European Communities in 1973.[70] According to the unappealed Panel Report in *Japan – Film*, GATT schedules may create legitimate expectations under certain conditions.[71]

The upshot from these two examples is that original WTO Membership for separate customs territories is not as straightforward as one might think when reading Article XI of the WTO Agreement. It is important to appreciate that separate customs territories of the likes of Aruba and Faroes are the least controversial category of ambiguous territories. Since the politically controversial element is largely missing, these territories demonstrate well how WTO Members and the WTO Secretariat address territorial ambiguities. For instance, the request for consultations and the Minutes of the DSB meetings during which Denmark, in respect of the Faroes, requested the establishment of a panel, do not reveal any doubts on the part of Denmark, the EU, or any other WTO Member as to the Faroes' status. This suggests at least some form of tacit acquiescence to the Faroes being covered by Denmark's membership. This, in spite of the apparent lack of WTO schedules of concessions for the territory and although, to the extent the Faroes constitute a separate customs territory, they would normally need to apply for accession in the event that they were not covered by Denmark's original membership, since the deadline for accepting the WTO Agreement has long expired.

In sum, the territorial scope of WTO membership may be inconclusive even when a territory's status is not in any way disputed. However, WTO Members approach the matter with pragmatism, something that seems to perfectly reflect the pragmatism with which such matters were also dealt during the GATT era. This could have significant implications for trade with disputed areas, for instance Crimea and Eastern Ukraine. I return to this in the last section of this article.

---

70 See GATT, The Territorial Application of the General Agreement - A List of Territories to Which the Agreement is Applied – Addendum, G/5 Add.1 (21 May 1952) and GATT, Application of the General Agreement, G/10 (21 May 1952).

71 Panel Report, *Japan – Measures Affecting Consumer Photographic Film and Paper*, WT/DS44/R, adopted 22 April 1998, paras. 10.61-10.81. Here, the schedules' remoteness in time and the fact that they only cover goods, ought to, in my opinion, have weighed against the creation of legitimate expectations.

5   WTO Accession for Separate Customs Territories

The previous sections dealt with original membership to the WTO. This section briefly deals with accession. Accession to the WTO is governed by Article XII of the WTO Agreement. On a first reading of this provision, in order to accede a territory has to be a State or a separate customs territory possessing full autonomy in the conduct of its external commercial relations and of the other matters provided for in the WTO Agreement and the covered agreements. The term used is identical to the one found in the GATT, thus we can expect that the meaning is the same.

Accession to the WTO includes some indications as to the territory that is intended to be bound by WTO obligations. Thus, for instance, an applicant State or separate customs territory must indicate its territory in the Memorandum on the Foreign Trade Regime that it submits as part of its accession process. The WTO Secretariat circulates the Memorandum and the members of the working party that examines the application can ask for clarifications in various rounds of questions and answers.[72] Hence, any acceding members that administer overseas territories will probably clarify the matter there. It would seem that if WTO Members do not question the territory indicated in the Memorandum, they tacitly accept it as the acceding Member's valid territory. Moreover, especially in cases of acceding separate customs territories, the General Council takes steps to satisfy WTO Members that the territory in question does in fact possess the characteristics required by Article XII of the WTO Agreement.[73] The applicant territory will also have the chance upon depositing the instruments of accession to make Communications, Declarations and Reservations.[74] Thus, through the accession process and its completion, the membership offers its approval as to the applicant's claim of being (at least) a separate customs territory with full autonomy in the conduct of its external commercial relations, and implicitly, also as to the territory on behalf of which it purports to conduct it.

---

72   Document WT/ACC/1, Note by the Secretariat, Accession to the WTO – Procedures for Negotiations under Article XII (24 March 1995), paras. 9-11.

73   E.g., Document WT/GC/M/92, *General Council Minutes of Meeting of 15 February 2005* (7 April 2005), paras. 27-29 (on Montenegro) and paras. 34-36 (on Serbia).

74   For examples, see *Status of WTO Legal Instruments* (n 56). The WTO Agreement does not allow any reservations beyond those specifically provided for in the covered agreements: Art XVI:5 of the WTO Agreement.

WTO Members that may have particular issues with the acceding Member but do not wish to disturb the consensus rule[75] have the possibility (just like the acceding territory does) to invoke Article XIII of the WTO Agreement that provides for the non-application of the Agreement and the covered agreements between particular Members. This has happened numerous times in the past, but only two such invocations have yet to be revoked.[76]

So far there is only one example of a separate customs territory acceding to the WTO, Taiwan, as the 'Separate Customs Territory of Taiwan, Penghu, Kinmen and Matsu (Chinese Taipei)'.[77] Its accession and how it was handled by the WTO Secretariat further confirm the pragmatism with which separate customs territories are dealt with in international trade law. The accession took place almost[78] simultaneously with the accession of China and the WTO Secretariat borrowed from the practices of the International Olympic Committee to avoid thorny issues regarding nomenclature, titles, symbols and the like.[79] China, as is well known, does not recognise Taiwan as a separate state. Yet, once issues of nomenclature, symbols etc. had been agreed, it had no problem accepting that Taiwan is de facto a separate customs territory possessing full autonomy in the conduct of its external commercial relations and of the other matters provided for in the WTO Agreement and the covered agreements.

6   Conclusions Regarding Separate Customs Territories

In this article, we looked at the text and drafting of the GATT and the WTO Agreement regarding provisions that deal with acceptance, accessions and successions. To understand those provisions, we placed

---

75   Document WT/L/93, Statement by the Chairman of the General Council, Decision-Making Procedures Under Articles IX and XII of the WTO Agreement (24 November 1995).

76   Document WT/L/429, Invocation by El Salvador of Article XIII of the WTO Agreement with respect to China (7 November 2001); and Document WT/L/501, Invocation by Turkey of Article XIII of the WTO Agreement with respect to Armenia (3 December 2002).

77   For more detail, see PL Hsieh, 'Facing China: Taiwan's Status as a Separate Customs Territory in the World Trade Organization' (2005) 39(6) *Journal of World Trade* 1195.

78   The accession happened at the same Ministerial Conference, for China first, and Taiwan one day later.

79   G van Grasstek, The History and Future of the World Trade Organization (WTO Publications, 2013) 140-43.

them in the broader context of other provisions in the GATT and the WTO Agreement that can help us define the term 'separate customs territory' for the purposes of WTO law.

Based on the analysis above, I submit the following argument. UN Members, themselves States, recognised the importance of including separate customs territories in the work of the Conference that negotiated the Havana Charter and the GATT, an importance that had to do with the reality, on the ground, of such territories' volume of international trade. They decided to adopt a pragmatic approach that was not tangled in intricate issues of sovereignty and to accept the full participation of such territories in the negotiations, so long as it could be shown that they – as a matter of *fact* – had full autonomy in the conduct of international trade. No requirements were put in place that their claims to autonomy had to be proven as a matter of international law or had to be endorsed by States. They also accepted that the governments of these separate customs territories had the capacity to accept and sign the GATT in their own right, their names appearing in the Preamble of the Agreement. They made sure to accommodate such territories' participation in the GATT and the Havana Charter by focusing on government capacity rather than international recognition.

Most importantly, despite their initial reservations, they accepted that the possibility of gaining full contracting party status should be available to *all* separate customs territories. In other words, their approach was framed as a reaction to the participation of Burma, Ceylon and Southern Rhodesia, but it was not limited to those three territories. It was not contingent on the three territories' special circumstances, i.e. of having been invited to the Conference, of having a sovereign colonial power that was sympathetic to their inclusion, of having a significant share of world trade that all States would stand to gain from by being included in the liberalising effort of the GATT project. Thus, they overcame their initial reservations towards 'hypothetical' separate customs territories that might join as contracting parties subsequent to the conclusion of the Agreement, albeit noting that their accession was contingent upon the unanimous acceptance of existing contracting parties to the GATT.[80] In fact, eventually, a few months after the text of the GATT was finalised, even the unanimity 'safeguard' was abandoned and accessions became

---

80   Document E/PC/T/198 (n 34) 4.

possible by a two thirds majority of the GATT contracting parties.[81] This spirit of pragmatism, together with the possibility for separate customs territories to be WTO Members, has been carried over to the WTO.

It could certainly be claimed that what I call 'pragmatism' is in fact simply a symptom of 'handling legal issues in a loose manner'.[82] Or perhaps it could be explained by separate customs territories not posing controversies regarding sovereignty, though that seems unlikely regarding all 63 territories that succeeded to the GATT.[83] It could also simply be the result of the GATT's conscious choice to follow UN practice on sensitive political matters, as had been also envisaged in the Havana Charter.[84] Yet, that does not answer satisfactorily *why* that choice was made. Finally, it could simply be a by-product of the GATT being for the entirety of its history only applied 'provisionally' by the contracting parties as a result of the failure of the Havana Charter to enter into force, meaning that rules and practices relating to acceptance, accessions and successions were less formalised and institutionalised than if ITO had been created. Yet the WTO *did* come into being, maintaining the same approach as the one adopted under the GATT.

Part of the explanation is of course that the GATT and the WTO allow for non-application between certain territories, through the invocation of Article XIII of the WTO Agreement. There is also the possibility of international mediation to resolve issues that arise between WTO Members. In the past this was done between Georgia and Russia, recently out of a conflict in South Ossetia, in relation to Russia's accession. It is also worth remembering that limited resources might mean that WTO Members choose to take the fight to some fora but not others. Choosing which one will depend on the suitability of the dispute settlement mechanism.[85] Thus, many potential disputes never materialise at the WTO to begin with.

---

81   Document ICITO I/8, Reports of Committees and Principal Sub-Committees (Havana Reports) (September 1948), 162, para. 7(a).

82   Kunugi (n 19) 290, presenting the opinions of others.

83   Even those that became States must have been in certain limbo for at least some period of time and many times GATT terms continued applying de facto even without a declaration that the new State had succeeded under Art XXVI:5(c) of the GATT. I cover the de facto application of GATT in the second article in the *Topoi of Ambiguity* series.

84   See Document SR.22/3, (March 1965) 1-2 and Art 86 of the Havana Charter.

85   E.g., there are four inter-state disputes brought by Cyprus against Turkey before the European Court of Human Rights but zero challenges in the WTO, despite Turkey not giving MFN treatment to Cyprus.

Yet the inclusion of separate customs territories as subjects of international trade law is also the result of something entirely different. In my opinion, that inclusion is not motivated by 'a desire to see that equity and fair play is given to the so-called self-governing customs territories' as the Burmese delegate to the Tariff Agreements Committee pleaded.[86] It is, instead, simply, that the GATT and the WTO are perceived as synallagmatic contracts whose system would suffer by dealing with politically sensitive and divisive matters. Since WTO Members consider that they have more to gain by being part of a system of trading that is not discredited, they have refrained from bringing claims on sanctions, embargoes, restrictions on trade of dual-use goods, territorial disputes, or issues of recognition.[87] Thus, a great deal of routine business carries on, irrespective of territorial or other disputes. In fact, much of what happens on a day-to-day basis at the WTO could not possibly affect the territorial claims of its Members.[88] Thus, day-to-day trade, economically important yet at the same time rather mundane, is probably considered by States not to be an indicium of recognition.

---

86   E/PC/T/TAC/PV/13 (n 23) 9.

87   E.g., the EU initiated consultations with the US on the latter's sanctions targeting Cuba, but in the end suspended the proceedings: Document WT/DS38/1, Request for Consultations by the European Communities, *United States – The Cuban Liberty and Democratic Solidarity Act* (13 May 1996) and Document WT/DS38/5, Communication from the Chairman of the Panel, *United States – The Cuban Liberty and Democratic Solidarity Act* (25 April 1997). The EU did engage the US on a related matter in *US – Section 211 Appropriations Act*, yet again, pursuant to an Understanding with the US, it has refrained from requesting authorisation from the DSB to suspend concessions under Art 22.2 of the DSU, although it has won the dispute: Document WT/DS176/16 Understanding between the European Communities and the United States, *United States – Section 211 Omnibus Appropriations Act of 1998* (1 July 2005). The item remains on the Agenda of the DSB, and the US provides monthly status reports. Cuba intervenes during the presentation of each status report to condemn the US measure. Cyprus has not brought any disputes against Turkey, nor has Israel brought any disputes as against any Arab States that boycott trade with it.

88   It seems, e.g., that Argentina's concerns on references to the Falkland Islands and implications that might have for its dispute on the islands' status with the United Kingdom were addressed by the WTO Secretariat quite unceremoniously, by issuing a corrigendum to an Annex, and ensuring that thenceforth the territory was named following the UN formula 'Falkland Islands (Islas Malvinas)': Document WT/COMTD/W/93/Corr.2, *Note by the Secretariat, Corrigendum to the Generalised System of Preferences: A preliminary analysis of the GSP schemes in the Quad* (25 March 2002).

Nowhere is this functional argument to the inclusion of de facto independent territories as subjects of international trade law better reflected than in the GATT contracting parties' response to the controversies surrounding China's regime change and the efforts of the exiled government in Taiwan to continue to represent mainland China in external relations. As the chairman of the contracting parties stated, 'it had been the policy of the contracting parties to avoid unproductive controversies over political questions which did not bear significantly on the many substantial questions with which the contracting parties were concerned.'[89] It is also present in Burma's (as Myanmar was then called) statement regarding specifically the status of separate customs territories that

> the general Agreement is primarily a tariff agreement, the general provisions serving only as safeguards for the effective application of tariff concessions. The proper and practical criterion is not who is the metropolitan territory in charge of Burma but where lies the power and authority competent to give effect to the various obligations laid down in the General Agreement.[90]

In other words, the question is simply who, on the ground, has the power to control trade. Realising that that is purely a question of fact ought to be a guiding principle for the treatment of de facto independent regimes, irrespective of statehood and recognition. That said, I recognise that States do not always see it that way and that they are often reluctant to accept the realities on the ground as they think that they may have implications for the territories' status under international law, just like they do, for instance, with regard to international humanitarian law. WTO law shows that the reluctance is in fact misguided.

7   **Implications for *Topoi* of Ambiguity**

If my argument – i.e. that GATT contracting parties before and WTO Members now have consciously adopted a pragmatic approach to the application of international trade rules to non-state entities and have refrained from bringing claims on sanctions, embargoes, restrictions on trade of dual-use goods, territorial disputes, or issues of recognition

---

89   Document SR.22/3 (n 83) 1-2.

90   E/PC/T/TAC/PV/13 (n 23) 11.

connected to territories whose status is ambiguous – is correct, it may have some significant implications for non-state entities that are more politically controversial than former colonies or overseas territories of metropolitan States.

As statehood and recognition are not connected to WTO Membership, at least in theory, there ought not to be any issues with States accepting that even politically controversial non-state entities can accede to the WTO. Places like South Ossetia, Abkhazia, Transnistria, Somaliland, Nagorno-Karabakh, Northern Cyprus, Kosovo, to name a few, could accede, so long as they would be, as a matter of fact, separate customs territories, and would manage to satisfy WTO Members to that effect. Kosovo is already treated as a 'customs territory' by the EU for the purposes of WTO concessions and this treatment was accepted by the WTO's General Council, which by Decision exempted the EU from the MFN requirement for the preferential treatment given to Kosovo.[91] Northern Cyprus is seen as 'temporarily outside the customs and fiscal territory of the [EU]'[92] but also as separate of Turkey's customs territory, meaning that de facto it could be considered as a separate customs territory. Taiwan's accession confirms that even powerful States will not react strongly, if they have enough to gain from the WTO. Of course, Taiwan's case is rather exceptional, as China became a Member only a day before Taiwan did. An existing Member might try to block the application of a separate customs territory with an ambiguous international law status. In such a case, that Member could be bypassed by calling, exceptionally, for a vote requiring a two thirds majority for the accession, in contravention of the typical consensus rule. Alternatively, that Member could choose to invoke Article XIII of the WTO Agreement to render WTO law inapplicable between it and the new Member, as for instance Turkey has done vis-à-vis Armenia. Finally, some issues could be dealt with under mediation between the existing Member and the acceding one, as was done by Russia and Georgia.

That said, accession may be considered undesirable for States that do not accept the legitimacy of such politically controversial non-state entities. The present analysis suggests that the real motive behind a reluc-

---

91 Decision of 28 July 2006, European Communities' preferences for Albania, Bosnia and Herzegovina, Croatia, Serbia and Montenegro, and the Former Yugoslav Republic of Macedonia, Document WT/L/654.

92 Council Regulation (EC) No 866/2004 of 29 April 2004 on a regime under Article 2 of Protocol 10 to the Act of Accession (the 'Green Line Regulation' (2004) OJ L 206/128, recital 4.

tance to accept such territories as Members cannot be a fear for recognition. Be that as it may, in reality many of those ambiguous territories conduct trade through a sympathetic State that is itself a Member. For instance, Northern Cyprus trades through Turkey, Nagorno-Karabakh through Armenia, Crimea through Russia, to name a few. In lieu of accession, non-State entities have yet another avenue open to them that would seem to be tolerated by States: to apply de facto WTO terms to their trade with States. That practice, which was quite common during the GATT years, is covered in the second article in this series.[93]

In any case, WTO law's (and the Membership's) treatment of 'separate customs territories' has hitherto been pragmatic, taking into account the reality that not only States engage in international trade and that State boundaries do not always overlap with customs boundaries. Ideally, this functional understanding of 'separate customs territories' could provide a realistic way to deal with non-state entities more generally under international law.

---

93   Iacovides (n 2).

5 International Courts and Contested Statehood

The ICJ and ICC in Palestine

*Alice Panepinto**

Abstract

Ambiguous and contested statehood under general international law can become a pretext for denying the reach and enforceability of specific treaty-based norms. This article explores how the ICJ and ICC have addressed this challenge through functional applications of their respective constitutive treaties. The first part highlights some of the difficulties posed by quasi-states, de facto states, and state-like entities for international law, and the ways the ICJ and ICC have dealt with such issues according to the parameters of their mandates. The second part investigates how these two international courts have asserted the object and purpose of their respective constitutive treaties in relation to Palestine. Proceeding on a basis of agnosticism as to whether Palestine is a state under general international law, this article argues that neither court is tasked to resolve complex questions of international law of statehood: this falls outside the boundaries of their respective mandates, and is evidenced in their jurisprudence to date. In *Wall* the ICJ discharged its advisory function as requested by the UNGA, which did not require a determination of statehood; no conclusions can yet be drawn in relation to ICJ jurisdiction in contentious proceedings (at the time of writing *Palestine v USA* is in its infancy). In *Situation in Palestine* the Pre-Trial Chamber confirmed the ICC's territorial jurisdiction regardless of Palestine's status under general international law, because Palestine's accession to the Rome Statute had followed the correct and ordinary procedure. The implication of becoming a State Party, therefore, is that treaty provisions apply to Palestine in the same manner as any other State Party.

---

* Lecturer in Law at Queen's University Belfast.

Keywords

Contested statehood – ICJ – ICC – jurisdiction – Palestine

1 Introduction

Contested statehood poses tangible challenges to international courts (ICs) seeking to enforce international law in all corners of the world. How can ICs ensure their reach – and that of public international law (PIL) – in relation to a wide variety of non-state actors (NSAs)? This grouping includes quasi-states, de facto states, entities approaching statehood, and contested states, which this article considers within the scope of de facto independent non-state territorial entities (DFINSTEs – understood as a category of NSAs).[1] The difficulties that ICs face in enforcing international law in DFINSTEs are evident in the accountability gaps for serious violations of norms within the specialised regimes of international humanitarian law (IHL), human rights (IHRL), and international criminal law (ICL) – only the latter of which has a dedicated international tribunal focusing on individual criminal responsibility (the International Criminal Court – ICC). This article builds on the paradox of state-centrism in PIL, whereby ambiguities and contestations of statehood can become pretexts for denying the reach of international law in relation to, and in

---

[1]   For the purposes of this article, the category of NSAs is considered a broad church, encompassing a wide variety of entities that operate on the international legal plane in different capacities and in subject-areas despite not being states, i.e. the primary actors ('subjects') of PIL. As the residual category of actors in PIL, NSAs include international organisations, NGOs, armed groups, buisnesses and many more. This contribution will not consider NSAs in general, as there is a rich and growing literature on the topic of NSAs in international law, which seeks to broaden the classic notion of 'subjects' and international legal personality in PIL to that of 'actors' (as informed by international relations), as presented by Andrea Bianchi, 'Introduction' in Andrea Bianchi (ed), *Non-State Actors and International Law* (Routledge 2017), xii, and many others, inter alia Math Noortmann *et al.* (eds), *Non-state Actors in International Law* (Hart 2015); Jean d'Aspremont (ed), *Participants in the International Legal System: Multiple Perspectives on Non-state Actors in International Law* (Routledge 2011). On the difficulties in asserting NSAs in a state-centric system, see Cedric Ryngaert, 'Non-state Actors: Carving Out a Space in a State-centred International Legal System' (2016) 63(2) *Netherlands International Law Review* 183.

INTERNATIONAL COURTS AND CONTESTED STATEHOOD 137

territories controlled by, NSAs, and thus impede its application, to the great detriment of its inhabitants.[2]

This contribution explores how ICs, and specifically the ICC and the International Court of Justice (ICJ), enforce international law in territories controlled by non-state actors, including DFINSTEs. The discussion on Palestine will provide a high-profile example of how the two ICs have sought to enforce international law in a contested state. The core argument posits that the extent to which ICs can and will enforce international law in DFINSTEs (and in relation to NSAs more broadly) rests on three elements: the parameters of their founding documents (generally, a treaty between states), their willingness to implement their mandate purposefully, and contextual case-by-case factors. Neither the ICJ nor the ICC have been oblivious to NSAs. In inter-state disputes (contentious cases), the ICJ has dealt with questions pertaining to NSAs, such as whether certain conduct of an armed group is attributable to a state (e.g. *Nicaragua*[3]). In its advisory function for organs of the United Nations (UN) the ICJ has already considered matters essentially concerning NSAs (e.g. *Chagos*[4]), and established its jurisdiction in occupied territories (e.g. *Wall*[5]) demonstrating a high degree of pragmatism within the parameters of its mandate to ensure the widest possible reach of international law. Similarly, the ICC has dealt with NSAs and DFINSTEs in various instances. Most recently, the Court has confirmed its territorial jurisdiction in Palestine by navigating complex questions of PIL before considering individual criminal responsibility.[6]

This article proceeds in two parts: the first part considers the challenges and jurisdictional hurdles posed by quasi-states, de facto states, and state-like entities in international law, and then analyses how the ICJ and ICC, respectively, have dealt with these complex entities within the parameters of their mandates. The second part addresses the ongoing engagement of these two courts with Palestine, as an example of how these

---

2 On the issue of statehood used as a pretence for politics, see Martti Koskenniemi, 'The Future of Statehood' (1991) 32 *Harv Int'l L J* 397, 409-410.

3 *Case Concerning Military and Paramilitary in and against Nicaragua (Nicaragua v United States of America)*, Judgment of 27 June 1986 [1986] ICJ Rep 14.

4 *Legal Consequences of the Separation of the Chagos Archipelago from Mauritius in 1965*, Advisory Opinion of 25 February 2019 [2019] ICJ Rep 95.

5 *Legal Consequences of the Construction of a Wall in the Occupied Palestinian Territory*, Advisory Opinion of 9 July 2004 [2004] ICJ Rep 136.

6 ICC PTC-I, *Decision on the Prosecution Request Pursuant to Article 19(3) for a Ruling on the Court's Territorial Jurisdiction in Palestine*, ICC-01/18-143 (5 February 2021).

ICs are reckoning with the challenge of DFINSTEs (and specifically contested states). As a high profile example of a well-defined entity whose statehood remains politically contested, Palestine is within reach of both the ICJ (*Wall* advisory opinion[7]) and the ICC (territorial jurisdiction in *Situation in Palestine*[8]) in line with their respective mandates, and the object and purpose of their constitutive treaties. As such, both courts have confirmed the reach of international law in 'territories occupied by Israel since 1967, namely Gaza and the West Bank, including East Jerusalem'.[9] Moreover, there is a contentious case pending before the ICJ (*Palestine v USA*[10]) which is in the very early stages of admissibility and jurisdiction. The evolution of these proceedings will illustrate the extent to which the Statute of the ICJ allows that court to enforce international law in inter-state disputes in Palestine.

2 International Courts and Contested Statehood

In order to consider the extent to which the ICJ and ICC can and will enforce international law in DFINSTEs, a brief discussion of statehood for the purposes of ICs is required. It is apparent that the application and enforcement of international law by ICs in relation to NSAs, including DFINSTEs and non-state armed groups (NSAGs), confronts the inherent state-centrism of the system. The vast majority of ICs, including the ICJ and ICC, are based on a treaty between states. Given international law is posited on states as primary subjects, entities falling short of the classic formalities (namely the Montevideo criteria) and recognition theories (declaratory and constitutive) of statehood pose conceptual as well as practical challenges to the field, notwisthanding the ambiguities

---

7   ICJ, *Wall Opinion* (n 5), para. 78, 101 (applicability of the Fourth Geneva Convention to occupied territories), 111 (applicability of ICCPR in respect to 'acts done by a State [i.e. Israel] in the exercise of its jurisdiction outside its own territory'), 112 (applicability of ICESCR in the same territory, binding on Israel qua occupying power an obliged 'not to raise any obstacle' where 'competence has been transferred to Palestinian authorities'), and 113 (applicability of the Convention on the Rights of the Child within the Occupied Palestinian Territory).

8   ICC PTC-I, *Decision on Territorial Jurisdiction in Palestine* (n 6).

9   *Ibid.*

10   ICJ Press Release 30th November 2018, *Relocation of the United States Embassy to Jerusalem (Palestine v. United States of America)*, available at <https://www.icj-cij .org/public/files/case-related/176/176-20181130-PRE-01-00-EN.pdf> accessed 26 May 2021.

INTERNATIONAL COURTS AND CONTESTED STATEHOOD

around the rules for ascertaining statehood.[11] ICs dealing with international law violations by, or in the territories of, DFINSTEs and persons who live under the control or influence of DFINSTEs may face the dilemma of how to pursue the object and purpose of the treaty that creates them when incidental questions of general international law emerge – such as whether they have jurisdiction in a contested state to apply and enforce international law.[12]

Building on the 'traditional' criteria of statehood (set out in the Montevideo Convention on Rights and Duties of States: defined territory, permanent population, government and capacity to enter into relations with other states), what constitutes a state remains a central question of international law.[13] Martti Koskenniemi has indicated that the 'most universally acclaimed principles of international law', listed as 'sovereignty, self-determination, territorial integrity, non-intervention, and consent', each reaffirm 'statehood as the law's creative center'.[14] Achieving the 'status of statehood can be associated with various sets of rights and duties', which give 'substance to statehood' politically and contextually.[15] And while 'statehood has long been the central organising idea in the international system', it is interesting that the notion of state carries 'multiple significance as a structuring concept' to account for the variety of forms and substance of states and other actors in international law.[16] Establishing statehood, therefore, remains the most straightforward way into international law, but it is not the only one: other actors may also have international legal personality.[17]

---

11   See *inter alia* Jure Vidmar, 'Territorial Integrity and the Law of Statehood' (2012) 44 *Geo Wash Int'l L Rev* 697; Rowan Nicholson, *Statehood and the State-Like in International Law* (OUP 2019), 5-6. On recognition specifically, see Tom Grant, 'How to Recognise a State (and Not)' in Christine Chinkin and Freya Baetens (eds), *Sovereignty, Statehood and State Responsibility: Essays in Honour of James Crawford* (CUP 2015).

12   For example, in ICC PTC-I, *Decision on Territorial Jurisdiction in Palestine* (n 6).

13   On the formal criteria for statehood, see James Crawford, 'The Criteria for Statehood in International Law' (1976-77) 48 *British Yearbook of International Law* 145; and more generally, Crawford, *The Creation of States in International Law* (2nd edn., OUP 2006).

14   Koskenniemi (n 2), 406.

15   *Ibid.* 408-409.

16   Karen Knop, 'Statehood, Territory, People, Government' in James Crawford and Martti Koskenniemi (eds) *The Cambridge Companion to International Law* (CUP 2012).

17   An early example is found in *Reparation for Injuries Suffered in the Service of the United Nations*, Advisory Opinion of 11 April 1949 [1949] ICJ Rep 174, confirming the

How statehood arises is varied and itself deeply contested; in reality 'international law continues to allow personality to take diverse forms'.[18] Doctrinal tensions remain between those who view statehood as a fact and those for whom it is a legal construction, and, in parallel, between 'those contending that statehood is objectively ascertained by international law and those arguing that international law accommodates intersubjectivity in the determination of statehood'.[19] Jean d'Aspremont suggests that competing approaches within the law of statehood point to its pluralistic nature and a 'social reality among those international lawyers who use its narratives and construct the world according to its cognitive paradigms'.[20] These debates and the inclusion or exclusion of a given entity from the club of states, however, can have practical effects on how ICs operate in respect to the realisation of the rights of certain groups and individuals in certain locations, as discussed in the second part. As Hyeyoung Lee pragmatically summarises:

> ... state-like entities exist, regardless of whether they receive recognition ... The lack of international recognition cannot vitiate the effective sovereignty of a claimant state that de facto controls people on certain territory, but the lack of recognition can prevent an entity from joining institutional "clubs" like the UN or the ICC.[21]

The examples of 'quasi-states' and 'de facto states' illustrate the variety of entities approaching statehood.[22] If statehood is considered a binary attribute, these descriptors illustrate how and why certain entities are

---

UN had capacity to bring an international claim against the State responsible with a view to obtaining reparation for damage caused to the Organization and to the victim (in the context of the killing of a Swedish national working for the UN by a paramilitary group in Jerusalem).

18   Nicholson (n 11), 5-6.

19   Jean d'Aspremont, 'The International Law of Statehood: Craftsmanship for the Elucidation and Regulation of Births and Deaths in the International Society' (2013) 29 *Connecticut J Int'l L* 201, 204.

20   *Ibid.* 224.

21   Hyeyoung Lee, 'Defining State for the Purpose of the International Criminal Court: The Problem ahead after the Palestine Decision' (2015) 77 *U Pitt L Rev* 345, 361-362.

22   On quasi-states, see Robert Jackson, 'Quasi-states, Dual Regimes and Neoclassical Theory: International Jurisprudence and the Third World' (1987) 41 *International Organization* 531; and on *de facto* states, Scott Pegg, 'De Facto States in the International System', Institute of International Relations The University of British Columbia Working Paper, No. 21, February 1998; Scott Pegg, *International Society and the De Facto State* (Routledge, 1998); and Scott Pegg, 'Twenty Years of de facto State

INTERNATIONAL COURTS AND CONTESTED STATEHOOD

not yet states. Conversely, if statehood is understood more broadly (and functionally), these labels indicate how and why certain entities act like a state, and thus should be considered states for a specific purpose. Quasi-states 'are internationally recognized as full juridical equals, possessing the same rights and privileges as any other state', but are 'generally incapable of delivering services to its population' and enjoy limited governance.[23] De facto states display 'an organized political leadership', 'popular support' and 'sufficient capacity to provide governmental services to a given population in a defined territorial area, over which effective control is maintained for an extended period of time'.[24] The de facto state 'views itself as capable of entering into relations with other states' and seeks 'international recognition as a sovereign state', although it is 'unable to achieve any degree of substantive recognition and therefore remains illegitimate in the eyes of international society'.[25] While they pose a challenge to international law, the international legal system has been able to accommodate de facto states, which enjoy 'a juridically significant existence'.[26]

As partial subjects of PIL, NSAs and DFINSTEs do possess certain obligations and rights, as evidenced in IHRL with regards to other entities,[27] and in IHL (and by extension, ICL) with regards to NSAGs.[28] However, some form of recognition of statehood has 'become crucial to triggering the jurisdiction' of some international courts.[29] Nonetheless, ICs have attempted to resolve the issue of defective or contested statehood them-

---

Studies: Progress, Problems, and Prospects' in *Oxford Research Encyclopedia of Politics* (2017).

23   Pegg (1998a) (n 22), 1.

24   *Ibid.*

25   *Ibid.*

26   *Ibid.* 12-15.

27   For instance, armed groups, see inter alia Amrei Müller, 'Can Armed Non-state Actors Exercise Jurisdiction and Thus Become Human Rights Duty-bearers?' (2020) 20(2) *Human Rights Law Review* 269; and businesses, see inter alia, Surya Deva and David Bilchitz (eds), *Human Rights Obligations of Business: Beyond the Corporate Responsibility to Respect?* (CUP 2013).

28   A prominent example is the role of NSAs, and in particular NSAGs, in IHL and through it, ICL. See inter alia Anthea Robertst and Sandesh Sivakumaran, 'Lawmaking by Nonstate Actors: Engaging Armed Groups in the Creation of International Humanitarian Law' (2012) 37(1) *Yale J of Int L* 107; John Cerone, 'Much Ado About Non-state Actors: The Vanishing Relevance of State Affiliation in International Criminal Law' (2008) 10 *San Diego Int'l LJ* 335.

29   Yael Ronen, 'Israel, Palestine and the ICC – Territory Uncharted but Not Unknown' (2014) 12 *Journal of International Criminal Justice* 7, 25.

selves to fulfil their mandates, as evidenced in the emerging 'jurisprudence of statehood'.[30] By acknowledging the 'tension between law and politics regarding the creation, modification and dissolution' of states, the debate is moving away from the 'largely mythological Westphalian international law of statehood' and towards what international courts actually do.[31] Comparing the ICJ and ICC, Amy Maguire and Katie Thompson have captured the differences between the former, with 'a broad subject-matter jurisdiction, enabling it to assess compliance with any number of international legal norms', and the latter with 'a narrow subject-matter jurisdiction, specifically focused on investigating and prosecuting violations of international criminal law'.[32] The following section will explore how these two ICs have dealt with NSAs, and specifically DFINSTEs, while ensuring their mandate and upholding the relevant parts of the international legal framework they oversee. In essence, and unsurprisingly, both rely on their constitutive treaty to enforce international law.

2.1 ICJ

Based on its Statute and mandate, the ICJ is set up to solve disputes between states and provide advisory opinions on 'legal questions submitted by the United Nations and its organs'.[33] The two procedures have different premises and different objectives: this helps explain why in advisory opinions the ICJ has been able to engage more substantively with NSAs compared with contentious proceedings. In contentious proceedings, Article 34(1) of the ICJ Statute is clear that 'only states may be parties in cases before the Court'. The following article asserts that 'the Court shall be open to the states parties to the present Statute' and provides access to other states which are not members of the UN.[34] In advisory opinions requested by UN organs, Article 66 allows states to furnish information

---

30 Samantha Besson, 'International Courts and the Jurisprudence of Statehood' (2019) 10(1) *Transnational Legal Theory* 30.

31 *Ibid.* 32-33.

32 Amy Maguire and Katie Thompson, 'Palestine, Self-determination and International Justice: Looking Back to the ICJ and Looking Forward to the ICC' (2017) 26(4) *Griffith Law Review* 532, 544.

33 Gleider Hernandez, 'Non-state Actors from the Perspective of the International Court of Justice' in Jean d'Aspremont (ed), *Participants in the International Legal System: Multiple Perspectives on Non-state Actors in International Law* (Routledge 2011), 140.

34 Statute of the International Court of Justice (1946) UKTS 67 (ICJ Statute), Art 35(2). See also comment available at <https://www.icj-cij.org/en/states-not-parties> accessed 26 May 2021.

INTERNATIONAL COURTS AND CONTESTED STATEHOOD   143

with regard to the question posed to the Court. As such, the Statute offers the Court limited scope for interactions with NSAs (including DFINSTEs) including 'entities striving towards statehood'.[35] And yet, on some occasions, the Court has pierced the veil of the state to engage issues pertaining to NSA and DFINSTEs, notably in the *Wall* and *Kosovo* advisory opinions, focusing on the specific circumstances of each without the emergence of a generalised rule.[36] In contentious proceedings, however, this opportunity has been much more limited.

Yael Ronen explains the Court's dual approach: on the one hand, NSAs are excluded from contentious proceedings in line with the ICJ's original purpose 'as a forum for adversarial inter-state dispute resolution'; while on the other, participation has been allowed 'in advisory opinions involving territorial entities aspiring to statehood or of otherwise indeterminate territorial status'.[37] With regards to advisory opinions, Article 66(2) allows states and international organisations (IOs) to provide the court with information relevant to the proceedings. The ICJ has allowed NSAs to participate in proceedings when they were 'directly involved in the disputes which triggered the advisory proceedings', in *Wall* (Palestinian Authority) and *Kosovo* (authors of the Declaration of Independence).[38] Neither entity, however, can be classified as IOs or states for the purposes of Art 66.[39] For Ronen, 'Palestine was invited on the basis of its quasi-state status reflected in its status in the General Assembly and its sponsorship of the request', whereas the drafters of the Kosovo Declaration of independence were invited to 'furnish information on the question' – though they were a governing body, and not an international organisation or a state.[40] She suggests that they were invited because they could contribute both procedurally and substantially as 'direct parties to the dispute underlying the request, and had a special interest in the outcome of the proceedings'.[41] Moreover, both NSAs were 'claimants to the disputed territory', and the issues revolved around the 'external right to self determination (...) within the territory under dispute'.[42] It is precisely

---

35   Hernandez (n 33), 150 151, 154.
36   *Ibid.* 151
37   Ronen, 'Participation of Non-State Actors in ICJ Proceedings' (2012) 11 *Law & Prac Int'l Cts & Tribunals* 77, 78, 85.
38   *Ibid.* 90-92.
39   *Ibid.* 94-95.
40   *Ibid.* 95-96.
41   *Ibid.*
42   Yael Ronen (n 37), 98.

the role of the principle and right to self-determination, she argues, that may have 'prompted the Court to permit their participation', given the 'tendency, in some contexts, to assimilate national liberation movements to states'.[43] But the Court's inclusive approach in *Wall* and *Kosovo* differs from the earlier exclusion of Polisario in the 1974 advisory proceedings in *Western Sahara*, which Ronen attributes to the timing and sequence of specific events (including UN recognition of Polisario as representative of the Western Saharan people only after the proceedings), and the fact that 'the right to self-determination was not affected by the request of an advisory opinion'.[44] She concludes, however, that if it were to reach the Court today, Polisario would likely be included in the proceedings.

This suggests that the ICJ has over time acknowledged that the right to self-determination attaches to specific groups of people, and not only or specifically to states, and has gradually widened its approach to interpreting the scope of its jurisdiction in relation to these NSAs (as evidenced more recently in *Chagos*, discussed below). If the ICJ were to relinquish its jurisdiction on territory and people whose legal status is contested or in flux, that would create legal black holes in which general international law (and the ICJ as its adjudicatory body) is absent. This would be extremely dangerous for international law as a whole, and paradoxical indeed for the ICJ to give up its ambitious mandate as a world court. The Court has been able to respond – albeit slowly and modestly – to the dramatic changes since 1945 regarding whom is considered a (partial) subject of international law (and indeed, since 1920, when the Statute of its predecessor, the Permanent Court of International Justice (PCIJ), was drafted). Despite being founded on a treaty between states, including imperial powers, the ICJ has not been oblivious to the reality of decolonisation and the influence of human rights on how PIL is understood today. The Court cannot (and indeed, should not) depart from its treaty-based foundations, but likewise, it cannot bury its head in the sand when NSAs, including contested states, appear on its horizon. No territory can exist beyond the pale of international law.

To date, the Court has managed to avoid the determination of whether a given entity is a state or not under general international law because its mandate, jurisdiction, and the cases and questions put to it, have not required such assessment. When dealing with DFINSTEs, the ICJ (and the PCIJ before it) gradually contributed to the development of the inter-

---

43   *Ibid.* 99.
44   *Ibid.* 102-104.

INTERNATIONAL COURTS AND CONTESTED STATEHOOD 145

national law of statehood consolidating a particular Western notion of what constitutes a state (despite diverging views of individual judges).[45] Early jurisprudence focused on the (classic) 'identification and inter-pretation of the criteria for statehood', including issues of territoriality, self-determination and jurisdiction; but this carried imperialist legacies and the risk of creating 'empty shells' under the guise of states.[46] In later years, as seen in *Kosovo*, the Court has tended towards 'judicial economy and pragmatism' in answering the questions put to it, even when it is 'elevated into the role of the arbitrator of a universal multilateral politi-cal dispute that the international community had not been able to settle itself'.[47] The Court's timidity, exemplified in its reluctance to engage di-rectly with the popular and political dimension of self-determination in *Kosovo* and *Wall*,[48] reveal a somewhat conservative approach in relation to DFINSTEs, but not complete avoidance.

Over the years, the ICJ has given several advisory opinions – which are not limited by jurisdiction over disputes between states – piercing the veil of states to engage with the rights under international law of indig-enous populations (*Namibia, Western Sahara, Wall, Kosovo*). It should be stressed, however, that when the ICJ deals with NSAs through advisory opinions this is not driven by a formal request by the NSA. Advisory opin-ions are requested by UN organs (such as the General Assembly) posing a question of international law that happens to engage issues related to NSAs and DFINSTEs. What is interesting, however, is that some requests for an advisory opinion look like contentious cases in disguise, because such a case could not be brought for procedural reasons. The fact that the ICJ does not exercise its right to refuse to give an advisory opinion in such situations illustrates its receptiveness to NSA and DFINSTE con-texts – ensuring international law is enforced broadly, and the Court it-self remains relevant. A recent example is the *Chagos* advisory opinion, which considered ongoing legacies of (British) colonialism.[49] Despite the request displaying some of the features of a dispute in disguise (which could have enabled the ICJ to refuse to give an opinion), the Court was able to look beyond the UK's lack of consent, the fact that Chagos is not

---

45   Besson (n 30), 40, 43-44.

46   *Ibid.* 45, and 55-59.

47   Jean d'Aspremont, 'The Creation of States Before the International Court of Justice: Which (Il)Legality?' (2010) *Hague Justice Portal* 1, 2-3.

48   Besson (n 30), 59, also discussing ICJ Advisory Opinions on *Kosovo* and *Wall* and distinguishing *Chagos*.

49   ICJ, *Chagos* (n 4).

a state and the ambiguous relationship between Chagossians and Mauritius, since this was not a contentious case. The ICJ used its discretion to exercise jurisdiction given the 'issues raised by the request [were] located in the broader frame of reference of decolonization', a matter 'of particular concern to the United Nations'.[50] For the ICJ in 2019, 'the emergence of the right to self-determination deprived colonial powers of the prerogative to dispose of colonial territories', reaffirming its erga omnes character requiring that 'all UN Member States must cooperate with the UN in completing the decolonisation of Mauritius'.[51] This advisory opinion demonstrates the Court's ability and willingness to use its mandate under international law more holistically, taking stock of cross-cutting human rights imperatives to hear claims of indigenous groups. Notwithstanding the limitations faced by the Court in addressing international law violations in DFINSTEs and colonial territories claimed by indigenous groups, in *Chagos* it traced a clear correlation between international law violations by states and the suffering and human rights of a group of people with a clear cultural and political identity.

While it is unlikely that *Chagos* will mark a new beginning for the Court's proactivity in extending international law protections wholesale to NSAs and DFINSTEs, this advisory opinion signals a greater self-awareness of its global role in reaffirming the broad reach of international legal standards regardless of the type of actors affected or the ambiguity of the territory in which violations are committed. Never for one moment does the Court suggest that international law does not apply to this case because of the contested nature of the Chagos islands as a colonial (non-self-governing) territory. In recognising the right to territorial integrity to groups that are bearers of the right to self-determination but are clearly not a state, the Court reaffirmed that customary international law (and specifically, the right to self-determination) applies beyond states.[52] The Court was timid in addressing the plight of the Chagossians directly by ruling on their human rights, but this is unsurprising, as it is not a hu-

---

50 *Ibid.* at 88, discussed in Fernando Bordin 'Reckoning with British Colonialism: The Chagos Advisory Opinion' (2019) 78(2) *Cambridge Law Journal* 253, 254; Stephen Allen, 'Self-determination, the Chagos Advisory Opinion and the Chagossians' (2020) 69(1) *International & Comparative Law Quarterly* 203; Robert McCorquodale *et al.*, 'Territorial Integrity and Consent in the Chagos Advisory Opinion' (2020) 69(1) *Int'l & Comp L Q* 221; Victor Kattan, 'The Chagos Advisory Opinion and the Law of Self-Determination' (2020) 10(1) *Asian Journal of International Law* 12.

51 Bordin (n 50), 255.

52 See McCorquodale *et al.* (n 50) for more detailed discussion.

INTERNATIONAL COURTS AND CONTESTED STATEHOOD   147

man rights court. Nonetheless, the fact that it recognised that the plight of the islanders was a direct consequence of British colonial legacies and ongoing violations of international law is remarkable. Within the boundaries of its mandate, the Court chose to position itself on the right side of history by rejecting the remnants of colonialism. By clarifying the responsibilities under international law of the colonial state, it also acknowledged that the customary international law of self-determination applies to groups (i.e. NSAs) claiming the right to return to colonial (non-self-governing) territories.

2.2   ICC

Unlike the ICJ, the ICC 'cannot rule on inter-states disputes as it does not have jurisdiction over States, but exercises its jurisdiction solely over natural persons' – as reaffirmed in the recent Pre-Trial Chamber I decision confirming territorial jurisdiction in the *Situation in Palestine*.[53] Nonetheless, the ICC's focus on individual criminal responsibility operates within the framework of the Rome Statute, a treaty of international law ratified by states to set up the Court.[54] As such, while the Court is set up to look beyond the state, it remains premised on the ordinary state-centric paradigm of PIL. Therefore, the ICC's reach over 'natural persons' (which include members of NSAs, or individuals committing alleged crimes in the jurisdiction of DFINSTEs) does not operate in a vacuum: sometimes the Court must face complex questions of general international law premised on the state-centric framework before proceeding with investigations.

In line with the general rules of international treaty law, the ICC's 'authority is grounded in state consent' and the Rome Statute is 'designed to strengthen domestic jurisdiction'.[55] The Court may only intervene when

---

53   ICC PTC-I, *Decision on Territorial Jurisdiction in Palestine* (n 6), para. 59.

54   The Rome Statute does not provide a definition of the term 'State', though it refers to states more than 400 times, in four contexts: (1) state-party, (2) state eligible to make a declaration accepting the Court's jurisdiction, (3) a state 'whose wrongful policy enables an individual to commit genocide and/or crimes against humanity', and (4) a state 'that constitutes contextual legal elements of war crimes and the crime of aggression' – see Lee (n 21), 348, 366; Rome Statute of the International Criminal Court 2187 UNTS 38544 (Rome Statute).

55   Discussed inter alia in Carsten Stahn, 'The ICC, Pre-Existing Jurisdictional Treaty Regimes, and the Limits of the *Nemo Dat Quod Non Habet* Doctrine – A Reply to Michael Newton' (2016) 49 *Vand J Transnat'l L* 443, 446, responding to Michael Newton, 'How the International Criminal Court Threatens Treaty Norms' (2016) 49 *Vand J Transnat'l L* 371. On related topics, see also: Frédéric Mégret, 'The Inter-

domestic courts are unable or unwilling to hold alleged perpetrators to account.[56] Under Article 12(2) 'the Court may exercise its jurisdiction' if the state on whose territory the alleged crime occurred, or the state of nationality of the accused, is a State Party to the Statute or has accepted ICC jurisdiction. Two of the three jurisdictional triggers (state referral and *propio motu*) require the atrocities to have been committed on the territory or by a national of a state party or non-state party that has accepted the Court's jurisdiction. The residual category of UN Security Council referral does enable the ICC to investigate in any country (but these are rare and subject to the political whims of the P5).[57] In dealing with NSAs, including DFINSTEs, the Court must find ways to fulfil the 'individual criminal responsibility' mandate of the Rome Statute within the parameters of general international law – two regimes with different, but not necessarily clashing, foci.

Notwithstanding the centrality of state consent in international law contained in Article 2 of the Vienna Convention on the Law of Treaties (VCLT), it is important to consider the exceptional nature of the mandate of the Court as 'a permanent institution' with 'the power to exercise its jurisdiction over persons for the most serious crimes of international concern' (Article 1, Rome Statute). Considering the universalist versus delegation-based foundations of ICC jurisdiction, Carsten Stahn explains that the 'ICC Statute is a special type of multilateral treaty', because the 'fundamental premise of the Statute goes beyond protection of sovereignty and state interests' and, instead, is 'geared at the protection of individuals and the establishment of a system of justice'.[58] Thus, its 'normative justification' is supported by 'the fact that individuals face direct individual criminal responsibility under international law for interna-

---

national Criminal Court: Between International *Ius Puniendi* and State Delegation' (2020) 23(1) *Max Planck Yearbook of United Nations Law Online* 161.

56   On the compliexities of the principle of complementarity set out in Article 17 of the Rome Statue and its applications, see inter alia Mohamed El Zeidy, 'The Principle of Complementarity: A New Machinery to Implement International Criminal Law' (2001) 23 *Mich J Int'l L* 869; Thomas Obel Hansen, 'A Critical Review of the ICC's Recent Practice Concerning Admissibility Challenges and Complementarity' (2012) 13 *Melb J Int'l L* 217; Rod Rastan, 'What is 'Substantially the Same Conduct'? Unpacking the ICC's 'First Limb' Complementarity Jurisprudence' (2017) 15(1) *Journal of International Criminal Justice* 1.

57   On UN Security Council referrals to the ICC see inter alia Dapo Akande, 'The Legal Nature of Security Council Referrals to the ICC and its Impact on Al Bashir's Immunities' (2009) 7(2) *Journal of International Criminal Justice* 333.

58   Stahn (n 55), 446-448.

tional crimes'.[59] As such, he argues that 'accession to the Statute merely activates the power of the ICC to exercise a jurisdiction grounded in international law. Jurisdictional constraints encountered by the acceding state do not necessarily affect the jurisdictional title of the ICC'.[60] This is relevant to the question of how NSAs, such as DFINSTEs, can activate the Court's jurisdiction – i.e. initiate an investigation into alleged violations of ICL into a territory controlled by a NSA.

As the rationale of the ICC, individual criminal responsibility informs the possible treatment of NSAs in that Court. Hyeyoung Lee argues that given that international criminal law does not 'automatically exclude unrecognized state-like entities as a possible perpetrator of crimes or a victim to a group of crimes', and given the ICC's purpose, it could be possible for the Court to 'embrace those entities within its jurisdictional scope' in order to uphold its Statute.[61] Moreover, the Rome Statute (Art 8(2)(f), on war crimes) explicitly mentions 'organized armed groups' participating in armed conflicts with governmental authorities and between themselves 'in the territory of a State', acknowledging the role of NSAGs as a category of NSAs in armed conflicts not of an international character.[62] This, however, poses challenges to the operations of the contractual principle underpinning international law and the principle of complementarity (and jurisdictional delegation).

The principle of state-based 'consent to be bound by a treaty' is challenged by NSAs, including DFINSTEs, such as territories approaching statehood (for example when a quasi state or a de facto state attempts to accede to the Rome Statute), or whose statehood is somehow contested or deficient (for example when protracted belligerent occupation impedes the judicial functions of DFINSTEs). For example, as discussed again later in this article, Palestine joined the ICC by following 'the correct and ordinary procedure' of article 125(3) of the Rome Statute, despite ambiguities around its statehood, and regardless of its status under general international law.[63] On that basis, it consented to be bound by a

---

59   *Ibid.*

60   *Ibid.*

61   Hyeyoung Lee (n 21), 383.

62   On NSAs and the ICC, see inter alia Frédéric Mégret 'Is the ICC Focusing Too Much on Non-State Actors?' in Margaret de Guzman and Diane Amann (eds), *Arcs of Global Justice: Essays in Honour of William A. Schabas* (OUP 2018); and William Schabas, 'Punishment of Non-state Actors in Non-international Armed Conflict' (2002) 26 *Fordham Int'l L J* 907.

63   ICC PTC-I, *Decision on Territorial Jurisdiction in Palestine*, paras. 101-102.

treaty, and the ICC Pre-Trial Chamber I confirmed its territorial jurisdiction over its territory.[64] As such, it affirmed that

> In view of its accession, Palestine shall thus have the right to exercise its prerogatives under the Statute and be treated as any other State Party would...
>   ...Palestine is therefore a State Party to the Statute, and, as a result, a 'State' for the purposes of article 12(2)(a) of the Statute. These issues have been settled by Palestine's accession to the Statute.[65]

This echoes Hyeyoung Lee's context-dependent approach that allows for 'the term "state" for the specific purpose of the Rome Statute [to] be defined differently from the definition of "state" used for the general purposes of international law'.[66] Therefore, given the ICC's purpose, it would be paradoxical if the contractual nature of international law invalidated the Court's core mandate to hold individuals to account for international crimes committed in (or by) DFINSTEs *qua* entities falling short of statehood who are able to consent to join a treaty.

In parallel, NSAs challenge the operation of the principle of complementarity set out in Article 1 of the Rome Statute, establishing that the Court's jurisdiction 'shall be complementary to national criminal jurisdictions'. This raises the question of how the Court might consider courts run by NSAs (including NSAGs and DFINSTEs) in determining whether the complementarity requirements are met.[67] In particular, 'Article 17(1)(c) and Article 20(3) require the ICC to give legal recognition to decision from courts of NSAG providing that the requirements in Article 20(3) are met'.[68] In principle, the 'straightforward meaning' of the wording of Article 20(3) ('another court') may extend to 'not only a court of a State party to the Rome Statute but also a court of a non-party State, an international court, and a court established by a non-State entity, such as an organized armed group or some other insurrectional or similar movement exercis-

---

64   *Ibid.* 109-113, and 118.

65   *Ibid.* 112.

66   Lee (n 21), 376, 379-380.

67   See paper (unpublished) by Joanna Nicholson, 'The International Criminal Court and Courts of Non-State Armed Groups: Always uncomplimentary?' as circulated in 'Workshop: Non-state Armed Groups (NSAGs) and De Facto Independent Non-state Territorial Entities (DFINSTE) in International Law', 11 April 2019, Belfast.

68   *Ibid.* 3-4.

ing *de facto* authority over part of the territory of a State'.[69] Gaiane Nuridzhanian offers a narrow reading: there are limited circumstances in which article 20(3) can apply to non-state courts, that is, 'where the trial before such a court is attributable to a State under the customary international rules of attribution of conduct to a State', depending on the facts.[70] She offers two examples in which the ICC did not consider proceedings of non-state courts relevant for its complementarity rule, in the situation in Georgia and *Al-Werfalli* (Libya). Other commentators have evaluated the procedural and substantive significance of criminal proceedings before the courts of NSAs, including non-state armed groups (NSAGs), more broadly. Frédéric Mégret has suggested that complementarity is more than deference to state sovereignty, and should accommodate diversity.[71] Indeed, there are a number of arguments 'in support of the inclusion of NSAG criminal prosecutions in the ICC's complementarity test'.[72] Reflecting on the complex political and military situation in Libya, the 2018 arrest warrant for Al-Werfalli (in which the Pre-Trial Chamber considered that proceedings initiated by General Haftar's Libyan National Army did not satisfy the ICC's complementarity test), Alessandro Amoroso argues that the ICC should assess its complementarity in relation to criminal proceedings instigated by NSAGs based on whether 'NSAGs armed groups that control a territory are capable of exercising criminal jurisdiction and have a legal basis in international law to do so'.[73] Moreover, focusing on the 'ultimate purpose of the ICC', that is 'filling the impunity gap', Amoroso argues that 'a blunt denial of relevance for criminal trials by NSAGs would discourage prosecution of cases that neither states (who no longer

---

69   Gaiane Nuridzhanian, '*Ne Bis In Idem* in Article 20(3) of the Rome Statute and Non-State Courts' (2019) 18(2) *The Law & Practice of International Courts and Tribunals* 219, discussing Georgia and Libya.

70   *Ibid.* 230.

71   Frédéric Mégret, 'Too Much of a Good Thing? ICC Implementation and the Uses of Complementarity' in Carsten Stahn and Mohamed El Zeidy (eds), *The International Criminal Court and Complementarity: From Theory to Practice* (CUP 2010).

72   Alessandro Amoroso, 'Should the ICC Assess Complementarity with Respect to Non-state Armed Groups? Hidden Questions in the Second *Al-Werfalli* Arrest Warrant' (2018) 16(5) *Journal of International Criminal Justice* 1063, 1083. These are listed as '(1) the text of the relevant provisions; (2) the rationale of the ICC's admissibility regime; (3) the mechanism and implications of command responsibility under the Rome Statute; (4) the rationale underlying ne bis in idem and its protected interests; and (5) the necessity to foster compliance with IHL by NSAGs while at the same time upholding the respect of fair trial guarantees'.

73   *Ibid.*

control the territory in question) nor the ICC (whose limited resources do not permit to reach most perpetrators) can cover, thereby widening the impunity gap'.[74] According to this view, direct engagement with NSAs (and specifically, NSAGs) can help overcome 'the obstructionist limitations of the state', and at the same time operate as a reward to increase IHL compliance of NSAGs.[75] So, if courts established by NSAGs were considered under the ICC complementarity test, this 'would help recognize that NSAGs are (...) also actors that potentially promote order in the fragile contexts where they represent the only authority upon which the lives and rights of entire populations depend'.[76] Given the unique context of each situation brought before the ICC, evaluating the relevance of proceedings before the courts of NSAs for Article 17(1)(c) and Article 20(3) should be conducted on a case-by-case basis.

There is a further question as to the ability of NSAs, and in particular DFINSTEs, to delegate jurisdiction to the ICC. In contexts where for different contextual reasons DFINSTEs do not possess or exercise full jurisdictional title over their territory, some may argue that the *nemo dat quod non habet* doctrine might limit the ability to delegate jurisdiction to the ICC.[77] A narrow reading, however, is unwarranted. Considering instances in which bilateral treaty regimes affect jurisdiction, Stahn distinguishes between prescriptive jurisdiction and enforcement jurisdiction:

> If a state has conferred jurisdiction to the ICC, despite a previous bilateral treaty arrangement limiting domestic jurisdiction, the resolution of conflicting obligations becomes an issue of complementarity and cooperation. The ICC is not bound by the agreement of the State Party.[78]

So while the jurisdiction to prescribe is not limited, the jurisdiction to enforce is: the Court will have to consider whether there are any domestic investigations before proceeding with its own investigation.[79] Enforcement, therefore, will 'depend on the interpretation of the scope of Article 98 (2), which limits the ability of the Court to request the arrest and

---

74   *Ibid.* 1087.

75   *Ibid.* 1089.

76   *Ibid.* 1091.

77   E.g. Newton (n 55).

78   Stahn (n 55), 450-452.

79   *Ibid.*

surrender of a person'.[80] This is relevant to DFINSTEs inasmuch as their capacity to enforce might be reduced in practice (but not necessarily *de jure*) by the circumstances, or bilateral arrangements (including treaties), which do not however result in a permanent surrender of jurisdiction under international law. Moreover, in contexts where DFINSTEs are approaching statehood in a (post)colonial setting, the relevance of the right to self-determination cannot be overlooked. This principle is enshrined in Article 1(2) of the UN Charter and as such can offer a useful normative reference point for the entire system of international law.[81] Indeed, to the extent that governing authorities of a non-state / quasi-state entity exercise that right on behalf of the people and in line with the will of the people seeking self-determination, the legal and political actions of those authorities become significant. Thus, if the representatives of a people delegate jurisdiction to the ICC through the ordinary routes set out in the Rome Statute, those (political) acts may be interpreted also through the (legal) lens of the right to self-determination. The importance of the principle of self-determination in relation to the ICC *Situation in Palestine* has been widely discussed in light of broad human rights concerns as well as in relation to the specific role the Court might play in furthering Palestinian self-determination *through* statehood.[82] However, a more holistic understanding of self-determination suggests that it should be understood *regardless* of claims to statehood: the very notion of 'the state' and the 'traditional notion of sovereignty carries the unpleasant traits of colonialism'.[83] Instead, as Rashwet Shrinkhal suggests, 'self-determination should be understood as power of "peoples" to control their own destiny', a tool to protect human rights and struggle for self-governance.[84]

---

80   *Ibid.* Rome Statute Art 98 reads: The Court may not proceed with a request for surrender which would require the requested State to act inconsistently with its obligations under international agreements pursuant to which the consent of a sending State is required to surrender a person of that State to the Court, unless the Court can first obtain the cooperation of the sending State for the giving of consent for the surrender.

81   On self-determination in international law, see inter alia Milena Sterio, *The Right to Self-determination Under International Law: "Selfistans", Secession and the Rule of the Great Powers* (Routledge 2013).

82   Inter alia, Maguire and Thompson (n 32), 532.

83   Rashwet Shrinkhal, '"Indigenous Sovereignty" and Right to Self-determination in International Law: A Critical Appraisal' (2021) 17(1) *AlterNative: An International Journal of Indigenous Peoples* 71. See also Vasuki Nesiah, 'Placing international law: White spaces on a map' (2003) 16 *Leiden Journal of International Law* 1.

84   Shrinkhal (n 83), 79.

If we consider the example of Palestine discussed again later, the *de facto* ability to delegate jurisdiction to the ICC is hindered by the continuing effects and entrenchment beyond the original timeframe of the Oslo Accords (in particular, *Oslo II*[85]) that place large areas of the West Bank under temporary Israeli control.[86] For a minority of commentators, who fail to fully appreciate the framework of protracted belligerent occupation in the context of settler-colonialism, the rules of IHL and the right to self-determination, Palestine cannot delegate jurisdiction to the ICC because under the terms of *Oslo II* it does not exercise criminal jurisdiction in Area C (over 65% of the West Bank).[87] This narrow and decontextualised reading on the issue of competence transfer in Area C was adopted in Judge Péter Kovács' Partly Dissenting Opinion in the 2021 PTC-I decision on territorial jurisdiction in *Palestine*.[88] But, as many other scholars have amply demonstrated, context matters in such a complex scenario: in *Oslo II* Palestine did not relinquish jurisdiction in Area C, but agreed to a temporary arrangement with an expiry date which Israel has not respected.[89] As a bilateral treaty between Israel (qua occupying power un-

---

85   Peace Agreements & Related, *Israeli-Palestinian Interim Agreement on the West Bank and the Gaza Strip* (Oslo II), 28 September 1995, available at https://www .refworld.org/docid/3de5ebbco.html accessed 27 May 2021.

86   On the broader context, see Robert Heinsch and Giulia Pinzauti, 'To Be (a State) or Not to Be? The Relevance of the Law of Belligerent Occupation with Regard to Palestine's Statehood Before the ICC' (2020) 18(4) *Journal of International Criminal Justice* 927. On the denial of Palestinian jurisdiction in some parts of the West Bank due to *Oslo II* and the annexationist effects of Israeli extraterritorial jurisdiction through military and civilian courts in Palestine, see Panepinto, 'From Extraterritorial Jurisdiction to Sovereignty: The Annexation of Palestine' in Daniel Margolies *et al.* (eds), *The Extraterritoriality of Law* (Routledge 2019).

87   E.g. Eugene Kontorovich, 'Israel/Palestine – The ICC's Uncharted Territory' (2013) 11 *Journal of International Criminal Justice* 979.

88   ICC PTC-I, Decision on the Prosecution Request Pursuant to article 19(3) for a Ruling on the Court's Territorial Jurisdiction in Palestine, Partly Dissenting Opinion by Judge Péter Kovács, 5 February 2021, ICC-01/18-143-Anx1, in particular 372.

89   Inter alia, Ronen (n 29), 7; Stahn (n 55), 443; Yassir Al-Khudayri, 'Procedural Haze: The ICC's Jurisdiction over the Situation in Palestine' (2020) 20(1) *The Palestine Yearbook of International Law* 117; Jeff Handmaker and Alaa Tartir, 'ICC and Palestine Symposium: The (Non) Effects of Oslo on Rights and Status' *Opinio Juris* 06.02.20, available at <http://opiniojuris.org/2020/02/06/icc-and-palestine-symposium-the -non-effects-of-oslo-on-rights-and-status/> accessed 26 May 2021; and Yassir Al-Khudayri, 'Are the Oslo Accords Still Valid? For the ICC and Palestine, It Should Not Matter' *Opinio Juris* 10.06.20, available at <http://opiniojuris.org/2020/06/10/ are-the-oslo-accords-still-valid-for-the-icc-and-palestine-it-should-not-matter/> accessed 26 May 2021.

der IHL) and the Palestinian Authority in the occupied territory, in *Oslo II* Palestinians conceded some of their powers to the occupying power for a specific time frame; therefore, Palestine did not voluntarily waive its right to exercise jurisdiction indefinitely, but as the 5-year period ended it was 'denied this power by the occupant of its territory'.[90] As such, the Oslo Accords do not bar 'the ICC's jurisdiction in Palestine' because, first, they 'did not strip Palestinians of their *prescriptive* jurisdiction over acts committed in their territory, but rather of their ability to *enforce* jurisdiction'; and second, 'the Fourth Geneva Convention prevents Palestinians from renouncing criminal jurisdiction over their territory in favor of Israel as the occupying power'.[91] There is a further argument in support of the limited effects of *Oslo II* on Palestine's ability to delegate jurisdiction in the territories occupied by Israel in 1967: the right to self-determination of the Palestinian people, including their right to an independent State of Palestine, as reaffirmed in numerous UN Resolutions.[92] As such, the only way for the Palestinian people to relinquish their sovereignty claims in 'Area C' is through their official representatives excluding that part from the territory upon which they seek to exercise self-determination. Otherwise, as recognised in multiple UN resolutions and the *Wall* Advisory Opinion, the presumption remains that the land upon which Palestinians exercise the right to self-determination (and free state) is taken as an indivisible whole.[93] As the military occupier, Israel may not unilaterally assume permanent jurisdiction over any part of occupied Palestine, because 'there is not an atom of sovereignty in the authority of the occupying power'.[94] Under international law, therefore, Israeli jurisdiction in Area C based on the *Oslo Accords* is merely a temporary, extraterritorial, administrative measure in the frame of its belligerent occupation of those parts. The fact that this protracted occupation has no end in sight, and that Israel

---

90   Ronen (n 29), 23.

91   Al-Khudayri (n 89).

92   These include: UNGA Resolution 73/150, Right of the Palestinian People to Self-determination, 9 January 2019 (A/RES/73/158); UNGA Resolution 73/18, Committee on Exercise of Inalienable Rights of Palestinian People, 4 December 2018 (A/RES/73/18), and many more. Moreover, the right of the Palestinian people to self-determination has been confirmed by the ICJ, *Wall Opinion* (n 5).

93   See also PLO Declaration of Independence of 15 November 1988, communicated by UNSC-UNGA letter of 18 November 1988, UN Docs A/43/827 and S/20278, insists on Israel's withdrawal from territories occupied since 1967.

94   Discussed in more detail in Panepinto (n 86), 201, citing Oppenheim 1917; and Aeyal Gross, *The Writing on the Wall: Rethinking the International Law of Occupation* (CUP 2017).

has not relinquished its temporary assumption of jurisdiction in Area C (despite the formal expiration of that provision of the *Oslo Accords*) does not constitute an exception to the IHL rule that occupation does not transfer sovereignty. A *de facto* situation of continuing Israeli jurisdiction exercised in Area C within the framework of the Fourth Geneva Convention does not transform the occupying power's jurisdictional reach into a permanent *de jure* transfer of jurisdiction away from Palestine.

A further issue to consider is the ICC's ability to prosecute nationals of a state (or DFINSTE) not party to the Rome Statute when crimes are committed on the territory of a state party. While the general rule in Article 34 of the VCLT provides that treaties cannot create rights and obligations for third parties in PIL (though this rule has many exceptions, for instance in specialised regimes such as IHRL), Yael Ronen explains that 'States do not have a right that their nationals not be prosecuted without their consent'.[95] Citing the 2017 preliminary examination activities on the Rohingya deportation to Bangladesh (a party to the Rome Statute) from Myanmar (not a state party), she reports that the ICC reaffirmed the 'primacy of peremptory norms' (Article 38 VCLT) and 'the customary character of the norms it enforces'.[96] When the ICC Pre-Trial Chamber III (PTC-III) authorised the opening of an investigation into the situation in Bangladesh/Myanmar in November 2019, it concluded that the Court may exercise jurisdiction over crimes when part of the criminal conduct (specifically, the crime against humanity of deportation) takes place on the territory of a State Party.[97] The judges therefore authorised

> investigation in relation to any crime, including any future crime, as long as: a) it is within the jurisdiction of the Court, b) it is allegedly committed at least in part on the territory of Bangladesh, or on the territory of any other State Party or State accepting the ICC jurisdiction, c) it is sufficiently linked to the situation as described in the present decision, and d) it was allegedly committed on or after the

---

95 Yael Ronen, 'The ICC and Nationals of Non-party States', in Gerhard Werle and Andreas Zimmermann (eds) *The ICC in Turbulent Times* (T.M.C. Asser Press, 2019) (Advance version consulted on SSRN), 19.

96 *Ibid.* 18.

97 ICC PTC-III, *Decision Pursuant to Article 15 of the Rome Statute on the Authorisation of an Investigation into the Situation in the People's Republic of Bangladesh/Republic of the Union of Myanmar*, 14 November 2019, ICC-01/19-27, summarised at <https:// www.icc-cpi.int/Pages/item.aspx?name=pr1495> accessed 26 May 2021.

INTERNATIONAL COURTS AND CONTESTED STATEHOOD

date of entry into force of the Rome Statute for Bangladesh or other relevant State Party.[98]

When crimes occur 'partially on the territory of a State Party and partially on the territory of a non-State party',[99] it would be paradoxical indeed if the Court's jurisdiction were barred because, as the PTC-III found, 'this would mean that the Court could not hear cases involving war crimes committed in international armed conflicts involving non-States Parties', a limitation which was not intended by the drafters of the Rome Statute.[100] Ronen goes a step further in clarifying that, given that some crimes are carried out in an official capacity or as state policy of the non-party state (or DFINSTEs), the fact that the ICC pursues individual criminal responsibility means that even state officials can be tried individually for crimes committed on the territory of a party to the ICC.[101] The decision in Myanmar illustrates the broad jurisdictional reach of the ICC in light of its constitutive treaty.

The discussion of the ICC's exceptional nature as an IC set up to prosecute individuals responsible for the most serious crimes of international concern and the tension with the principle of consent demonstrates that it is, in principle, better equipped than the ICJ in dealing with NSAs, in particular NSAGs and DFINSTEs, because of its focus on individual criminal responsibility and not the state. The recent decision in Myanmar illustrates the ICC's ability to honour its object and purpose as a global international court with a specific mandate accommodated by the traditional contractual nature of international law; specifically, that Court is able to hold to account individual nationals of states (or potentially NSAs) that are not ICC members, if there is a clear link with the territory of a state party of the Rome Statute. As such, in principle the ICC can go further than the ICJ in engaging NSAs, including DFINSTEs, given the latter's focus on violations of international law by states which prima facie poses greater barriers under the contractual principle.

On closer reading, however, both ICs have the ability to engage effectively with NSAs within the parameters of their respective mandates. By virtue of their Statutes, both the ICC and the ICJ possess

---

98   *Ibid.*
99   *Ibid.* 45.
100 *Ibid.* 60.
101 Ronen (n 95), 14, 20, recalling the exceptions posed by the crime of aggression and the 'transfer by an occupying power of its civilian population into occupied territory (Article 8(2)(b)(viii)' (which indicate state policy).

a special international character with universalising traits, and a broad jurisdictional reach beyond a strict reading of the contractualism principle. It would be paradoxical if these courts were set up to 'unsee' actors of international law outside the confines of states as subjects of international law: that would be inconsistent with the underpinning treaties that created them, their object and purpose. Moreover, to create 'legal black holes' would negate the purpose of both courts and the vision of international law as a system of norms applicable globally, as articulated in the UN Charter Article 1(1). As evidenced in the recent jurisprudence in both courts (*Chagos* and *Myanmar*), both the ICJ and the ICC can exercise discretion within their mandates to attempt to bring violations in territories controlled by, and by, NSAs within their jurisdictional fold. The ways in which these two ICs may activate their jurisdiction with respect to NSAs (including DFINSTEs) rests on the parameters of their statutes and how a case reaches them. The ICJ, procedurally, can give advisory opinions pertaining to DFINSTEs as requested by UN organs; it is much less likely for a NSA to attempt to instigate contentious proceedings given the constraints of the statute. On the other hand, procedurally, the ICC may claim jurisdiction over individual perpetrators with a personal or territorial link to a state party to the Rome Statute – regardless of their statehood status under general international law. The following section discusses these considerations in relation to Palestine, as an example of how both courts have shown pragmatism in fulfilling their mandates within the letter and spirit of their respective constitutive documents.

3 Palestine and the International Courts

The second part of this article considers how the two ICs discussed above have dealt with international law questions in Palestine. Despite different objects and purposes, both the ICJ and the ICC have carefully considered the legal questions put to them in light of the contemporary demands of international justice. Before continuing with the analysis, it is important to clarify that this discussion proceeds on the basis of agnosticism on whether Palestine is a state under general international law. There are some excellent studies that articulate the arguments for statehood convincingly, providing the foundation for full inclusion of Palestine within the scope of international law and the jurisdiction of ICs understood through the classic contractual lens, which would solve much of the controversy around whether international law not only applies, but can also be enforced there.[102] However, the present article engages with the competing view, and argues that even if Palestine is not a state under general international law, its territory and its inhabitants are not in principle excluded from the protections of international law. As such, it will demonstrate that the ICJ and ICC have ample scope to exercise their jurisdiction in relation to Palestine *regardless* of its formal status as a state, given both Courts' ability to consider NSAs, such as DFINSTEs, as partial subjects of international law.

Much has been written about the status of Palestine's statehood and the significance of its membership in the UN and other international organisations.[103] In its capacity as a national liberation movement, the PLO was granted UN Observer status in 1974, and in 1988 the General Assembly acknowledged the sovereignty of the Palestinian people over territory occupied in 1967 by adopting the designation of 'Palestine' instead of the former designation of 'PLO'.[104] Over the past 10 years a number of symbolic events have indicated an acceleration of the process, despite the continuing doctrinal (and political) debates. Mahmoud Abbas, Palestinian President and Chairman of the PLO, applied for full UN membership on behalf of the State of Palestine on 23rd September 2011.[105] While the matter was under consideration by the UN Security Council and the Committee on the Admission of New members, UNESCO's General Conference voted to admit Palestine as a member on 31st October 2011.[106]

---

102 Most recently, Mutaz Qafisheh, 'What is Palestine? The *De Jure* Demarcation of Boundaries for the ICC's *Ratione Loci* Jurisdiction and Beyond' (2020) 20 *International Criminal Law Review* 908.

103 Inter alia, John Quigley, *The Statehood of Palestine: International Law in the Middle East Conflict* (CUP 2010); Valentina Azarov, 'An International Legal Demarche for Human Rights? Perils and Prospects of the Palestinian UN Bid' (2014) 18(4) *The International Journal of Human Rights* 527; Mutaz Qafisheh (ed), *Palestine Membership in the United Nations: Legal and Practical Implications* (Cambridge Scholars Publishing, 2014).

104 Paul Eden, 'Palestinian Statehood: Trapped between Rhetoric and Realpolitik' (2013) 62(1) *International and Comparative Law Quarterly* 225, discussing 'Observer Status for the Palestine Liberation Organization', UNGA Res 3237 (XXIX) (22 November 1974) and 'Question of Palestine', UNGA Res 43/177 (15 December 1988).

105 See *Application of the State of Palestine for Admission to Membership in the United Nations*, presented by Mahmoud Abbas to UNSG Ban Ki Moon, 23rd September 2011, and summary in Eden (n 104).

106 See *Address by Ms Irina Bokova, Director-General of UNESCO, on the occasion of the agenda item concerning the admission of Palestine as UNESCO State Member*, Plenary session of the 36th session of the General Conference of UNESCO, Paris, 31 October 2011, and discussion in Eden (n 104). See also discussion in Larry Johnson,

On 29th November 2012 the UN General Assembly accorded Palestine 'non-member observer State status in the United Nations' in Resolution 67/19.[107] The ambiguity of that resolution on the issue of statehood, according to Yael Ronen, has been intentional.[108] Jure Vidmar has argued that the UNGA vote has 'neither confirmed nor altered the legal status of Palestine', because 'State creation cannot be an implicit side-effect of international treaties or voting procedures in international organizations'.[109] Instead, he suggests, in light of its UNESCO membership, Palestine 'has a previously acquired international capacity to act like a State and can, inter alia, become a party to the ICC Statute and possibly bring a case to the ICJ' (even without ratifying its Statute), but neither the GA resolution nor UNESCO membership are conclusive on the question of statehood under general international law.[110] Indeed, 'the "Vienna formula" and its application suggests that the term "State party" in international treaties needs to be understood broadly and in the context of a certain treaty, not as having implications for the general legal status of an entity'.[111] Given Palestinian statehood under general international law remains politically contested, that fact that in many forums (notably in the UN) it is treated like a state becomes legally relevant; as such, even if Palestine were only a DFINSTE, the ICJ and the ICC cannot justifiably deny the extension of international law in that territory and to its people.

The uncertainties around the establishment or recognition of statehood through the UNSC or UNGA have shifted the attention towards the ICJ and ICC.[112] Adam Yoffie argues that 'international courts provide an unconventional path to statehood', but considers that 'the mere spectre of a case before the ICC could (...) advance the international legal sovereignty of Palestine through the Israeli Supreme Court's judicial recognition of Palestinian grievances'.[113] In light of the structural impossibility

---

'Palestine's Admission to UNESCO: Consequences within the United Nations' (2020) 40(1) *Denver Journal of International Law & Policy* 12.

107 UNGA Res 67/19, Status of Palestine in the United Nations, UN Doc A/RES/67/19 (4 December 2012).

108 Yael Ronen, 'Recognition of the State of Palestine' in Christine Chinkin and Freya Baetens (eds), *Sovereignty, Statehood and State Responsibility* (CUP 2015), 242.

109 Jure Vidmar, 'Palestine and the conceptual problem of implicit statehood' (2013) 12(1) *Chinese Journal of International Law* 19.

110 *Ibid.*

111 *Ibid.* 37.

112 Adam Yoffie, 'Palestine Problem: The Search for Statehood and the Benefits of International Law' (2011) 36 *Yale J Int'l L* 497, 499.

113 *Ibid.* 505, 510.

INTERNATIONAL COURTS AND CONTESTED STATEHOOD

of the legal system of the occupying power to deliver justice for Palestine and Palestinians,[114] there is merit in pursuing cases before the ICJ and ICC to confirm that international law applies to its territory and inhabitants in specific contexts regardless of its statehood.

The growing recognition of international law's reach in Palestine is evidenced in its joining numerous human rights treaties in the last few years,[115] accepted by the Secretary-General as depositary.[116] Palestine acceded to the Vienna Convention on the Law of Treaties (2 April 2014) and to the Optional Protocol (22 March 2018), the four Geneva Conventions of 1949 (2 April 2014) and Additional Protocols I, II and III, and the Rome Statute (2 January 2015, entered into force 1 April 2015).[117] Over time, Palestine has sought the jurisdiction of both the ICJ and the ICC for international law violations committed on its territory and against its nationals. The sections that follow will explore how the ICJ and the ICC have dealt with Palestinian claims, suggesting that even if Palestine does fall short of being a state for general purposes under international law, the two courts may still exercise their jurisdiction over its territory as a DFINSTE.

3.1   Palestine and the ICJ

Despite the unresolved question of Palestinian statehood, the ICJ has had meaningful engagements with Palestine for some time. Most notably, in 2004 the Court issued an Advisory Opinion (*Wall*) requested by the UN General Assembly on issues pertaining to (responsibility for violations of) international peace and security law in Palestine to counter inaction by the UN Security Council.[118] Unlike contentious cases, advisory opin-

---

114   Discussed in more detail in Panepinto (n 86). See more generally, David Kretzmer, *The Occupation of Justice* (SUNY Press, 2002).

115   For an updated list, see UN OHCHR, *UN Treaty Body Database*, State of Palestine available at <https://tbinternet.ohchr.org/_layouts/15/TreatyBodyExternal/Treaty .aspx?CountryID=217&Lang=en> accessed 26 May 2021.

116   Office of the UN Secretary General, Note to Correspondents – Accession of Palestine to Multilateral Treaties (7 January 2015) available at <https://www .un.org/sg/en/content/sg/note-correspondents/2015-01-07/note-correspondents accession-palestine-multilateral> accessed 26 May 2021.

117   Full lists available at UN Treaty Collection, <https://treaties.un.org/Pages/CNs .aspx?cnTab=tab2&clang=_en> accessed 26 May 2021, and ICRC Treaties, State Parties and Commentaries, <https://ihl-databases.icrc.org/applic/ihl/ihl.nsf/vw TreatiesByCountrySelected.xsp?xp_countrySelected=PS> accessed 26 May 2021.

118   Charles Whitman, 'Palestine's Statehood and Ability to Litigate in the International Court of Justice' (2013) 44 *California Western International L J* 73, 106. There has been much commentary around the *Wall* advisory opinion, inter alia Andrea Bi-

ions do not require state consent to jurisdiction, as they are requested by and given to a UN organ, in addition to not having binding force.[119] The Court plainly observed

> that the lack of consent to the Court's contentious jurisdiction by interested States has no bearing on the Court's jurisdiction to give an advisory opinion.[120]

In that Advisory Opinion, the ICJ did not address the issue of statehood, as it was not asked to do so in the question put to it by the General Assembly.[121] The 2004 Advisory Opinion illustrates the tangible possibility for Palestine to use its broad political support in the General Assembly to put questions to the ICJ on issues pertaining to responsibility for international law violations in its territory (and potentially, by its nationals) – regardless of whether its territory meets the formal criteria and threshold of statehood.

Building on the discussion in the first part of this article, for a long time the possibilities for Palestine to successfully bring a contentious case before the Court seemed limited by its ambiguous statehood status and other procedural and political barriers. Writing prior to Palestine's declaration accepting the jurisdiction of the ICJ in 2018 (discussed below), Whitman identified three avenues for Palestine to bring a case before that Court: (1) by 'join[ing] the ICJ Statute without becoming a UN Member State';[122] (2) by 'bring[ing] a proceeding before the ICJ pursuant to Article 35(2) of the ICJ Statute'; (3) via 'a treaty [that] may have a provision that gives the ICJ jurisdiction to settle disputes between State Parties to the treaty'.[123] The second option was eventually adopted by Palestine,

---

anchi, 'Dismantling the Wall: The ICJ's Advisory Opinion and Its Likely Impact on International Law' (2004) 47 *German YB Int'l L* 343.

119   *Ibid.* 108.

120   ICJ, *Wall Opinion* (n 7), para. 47.

121   The question was as follows: 'What are the legal consequences arising from the construction of the wall being built by Israel, the occupying Power, in the Occupied Palestinian Territory, including in and around East Jerusalem, as described in the report of the Secretary-General, considering the rules and principles of international law, including the Fourth Geneva Convention of 1949, and relevant Security Council and General Assembly resolutions?' as reported in the text of the Advisory Opinion.

122   Under Charter of the United Nations (1945) 1 UNTS XVI (UN Charter) Art 93 and ICJ Statute Art 35(1).

123   Whitman (n 118), 89-90 *et seq.*

INTERNATIONAL COURTS AND CONTESTED STATEHOOD 163

and on 4 July 2018 it deposited in the Registry of the Court a declaration accepting the jurisdiction of the ICJ.[124]

After accepting the ICJ's jurisdiction, Palestine responded to the Trump administration decision to move the US embassy from Tel Aviv to Jerusalem (in May 2018) by issuing proceedings against the US on 28th September 2018, alleging a violation of the Vienna Convention on Diplomatic Relations (VCDR) (1961).[125] Palestine invoked Article 1 of the Optional Protocol to the Vienna Convention concerning the Compulsory Settlement of Disputes as a basis for the Court's jurisdiction. Its application requested that the Court declare the embassy move as a breach of the Vienna Convention, and order the US to withdraw its diplomatic mission in Jerusalem; this is because the city enjoys special status under international law by virtue of General Assembly Resolution 181 of 29th November 1947 (and under international law is thus not considered to be either Israeli or Palestinian – both of whom claim it as their capital). In his summary of the claim, Marko Milanovic recalls Palestine's position:

> Palestine argues that various articles of the VCDR, especially Article 3 thereof, require that the functions of the diplomatic mission be performed 'in the receiving state,' which means that the mission must be established in the receiving state. Jerusalem is not Israeli territory, and therefore moving the embassy there meant that it was

---

124   Declaration of the State of Palestine to the ICJ of 4 July 2018, accepting the competence of the Court 'Pursuant to Security Council Resolution 9 (1946) of 15 October 1946, which provides the conditions under which the Court shall be open to States not parties to the Statute of the International Court of Justice, adopted by virtue of its powers under Article 35 (2) of the Statute of International Court of Justice', available at <https://www.icj-cij.org/en/states-not-parties> accessed 26 May 2021.

125   For the full text of the *Application Instituting Proceedings: Relocation of the United States Embassy* (*Palestine v United States of America*) of 28 September 2018, see <https://www.icj-cij.org/files/case-related/176/176-20180928-APP-01-00-EN.pdf> accessed 26 May 2021. See also ICJ Press Release of 28 September 2018 <https://www.icj-cij.org/files/case-related/176/176-20180928-PRE-01-00-EN.pdf> accessed 26 May 2021. For a summary of the background and the facts, see inter alia: Jean Galbraith, 'Palestine Brings a Case Against the United States in the International Court of Justice at a Fraught Time for U.S.-Palestinian Relations' (2019) 113(1) *American Journal of International Law* 143; Basheer Alzoughbi, 'The Relocation of the US Embassy from Tel Aviv to Jerusalem (*Palestine v. United States of America*): a Commentary on the Merits of the Case, Jurisdiction of the International Court of Justice and Admissibility of Palestine's Application' (2019) 4 *U Bologna L Rev* 114; Will O'Connor, 'ICJ Jurisdiction and Necessary Parties in State of Palestine v. United States of America' (2020) 29 *Minn J Int'l L* 211.

164   5 – PANEPINTO

not established in the receiving state. Ergo, there was a violation of
the VCDR.[126]

Following that application, on 15th November 2018 the Court issued an
Order establishing the timeline for written pleadings on the question of
jurisdiction (which at the time of writing, have not been published on the
ICJ website), separated from the merits of the case.[127] The order reports
that after Palestine's accession to the Optional Protocol of the Vienna
Convention the US had submitted a 'communication to the Secretary-
General of the United Nations, declaring that the United States did not
consider itself to be in a treaty relationship with the Applicant under the
Optional Protocol', and according to the US, 'the Court ha[d] no jurisdiction in respect of the Application' and that 'the case ought to be removed
from the list'.[128]

Scholarly reception of the significance and possibilities of Palestine's
2018 application to the Court focused on initial questions of jurisdiction
(and admissibility), specifically through the consent principle (*Monetary
Gold* doctrine[129]) and relatedly, the issue of Palestinian statehood. In essence, 'the principle of consent requires [the Court] to abstain from deciding the case where the legal interests of a non-consenting third State
formed "the very subject matter" of the case' (in this case, Israel is the
third party allegedly excluded in the proceedings).[130] In light of the im-

---

126   Milanovic, Marko, 'Palestine Sues the United States in the ICJ re Jerusalem
       Embassy' *EJIL: Talk!*, 30 September 2018, available at <https://www.ejiltalk.org/
       palestine-sues-the-united-states-in-the-icj-re-jerusalem-embassy/> accessed 26
       May 2021.

127   ICJ Order of 15th November 2018 available at <https://www.icj-cij.org/files/case
       -related/176/176-20181115-ORD-01-00-EN.pdf> accessed 26 May 2021.

128   *Ibid.* It is worth recalling that 'Palestine acceded to the Vienna Convention on 2
       April 2014 and to the Optional Protocol on 22 March 2018, whereas the United
       States of America is a party to both these instruments since 13 November 1972' as
       stated in the ICJ Press release of September 2018 (n 125).

129   For an overview of different perspectives on the Monetary Gold principle emanat-
       ing from *Case of the Monetary Gold Removed from Rome in 1943* (*Italy v. France and
       Others*) [1954] ICJ Rep 19, see Alexander Orakhelashvili, 'The Competence of the
       International Court of Justice and the Doctrine of the Indispensable Party: from
       Monetary Gold to East Timor and Beyond' (2011) 2(2) *Journal of International Dis-
       pute Settlement* 373; Ori Pomson, 'Does the Monetary Gold Principle Apply to In-
       ternational Courts and Tribunals Generally?' (2019) 10(1) *Journal of International
       Dispute Settlement* 88.

130   A clear summary of the Monetary Gold principle in relation to ICC proceedings
       (not the ICJ, but with some parallels) is offered by Dapo Akande, 'The Monetary

INTERNATIONAL COURTS AND CONTESTED STATEHOOD 165

plicit question of territorial sovereignty, Milanovic (writing before the Order of 15th November 2018) discusses the limiting effect of the *Monetary Gold* principle, according to which the Court 'will not adjudicate on claims that involve the legal interests of third parties without the consent of these parties' who are not part of the proceedings (in *Palestine v US*, the third party in question is Israel).[131] In contrast, Alina Miron clarifies that 'the *Monetary Gold* principle is not about affecting the legal interests of the third State, but about protecting its rights and obligations from international adjudication without its consent'.[132] In light of this, she argues that the Court could answer the claims without 'determining the extent of Israel's territory', or adjudicating over any alleged Israeli violation of international law in those parts. Therefore, the *Monetary Gold* principle 'can be overridden' and, cautions Miron, 'should not be used as a pretext to evade highly debated issues'. Supporting this position, Victor Kattan suggests that Israel (whose position the US is likely to follow) may have 'consented to the jurisdiction of the ICJ when it accepted the 1947 UN Partition Plan', which contained a dispute resolution clause on the application or interpretation of the declaration by the ICJ 'unless the parties agree to another mode of settlement'.[133]

Moving on to the second issue: the US has made it clear that it does not recognise Palestine as a state. So, according to Kattan, the Court will have to address the challenge of statehood, at least for the purposes of the ICJ Statute, before considering issues of jurisdiction, admissibility and merits.[134] Nonetheless, considering Art 35 of the ICJ Statute, Miron notes

---

Gold Doctrine and the ICC: Can the ICC determine the Territorial Boundaries of Israel and Palestine?' *EJIL: Talk!* 16th June 2020, available at <https://www.ejiltalk.org/the-monetary-gold-doctrine-and-the-icc-can-the-icc-determine-the-territorial-boundaries-of-israel-and-palestine/> accessed 26 May 2021.

131   Milanovic (n 126).

132   Alina Miron, 'Palestine's Application to the ICJ, Neither Groundless nor Hopeless. A Reply to Marko Milanovic' *EJIL: Talk!*, 8 October 2018, available at <https://www.ejiltalk.org/palestines-application-the-icj-neither groundless nor-hopeless-a-reply-to-marko-milanovic/> accessed 26 May 2021.

133   Victor Kattan, 'Palestine Declares (Legal) War on the United States of America' *Haaretz* 4 October 2018, available at <https://www.haaretz.com/middle-east-news/.premium-palestine-declares-legal-war-on-the-united-states-of-america-1.6527711> accessed 26 May 2021, citing UNGA Res 181 (II), Future government of Palestine, 29 November 1947, at section C, Chapter 4, para. 2. See also Kattan, 'It's Time to Take Palestine v United States of America Seriously', *Opinio Juris*, 16 October 2018 available at <http://opiniojuris.org/2018/10/16/its-time-to-take-palestine-v-united-states-of-america-seriously/> accessed 26 May 2021.

134   Kattan (n 133).

that 'the Court could simply defer to the general recognition of Palestine as a state' both through 'its admission to the United Nations as a non-member observer State' (per resolution 67/19 of 4th December 2012), as well as by following the ICC Prosecutor's approach based on Palestine's admission to the UN as an observer state.[135] While undoubtedly relevant to the broader political context of the case, solving the issue of statehood is not required in order for the court to recognise its reach in Jerusalem and reaffirm the extension of international law there.

The question of statehood under general international could be eschewed by the Court in its entirety, much like the ICC PTC-I did in its decision confirming territorial jurisdiction in Palestine discussed elsewhere in this article. Jure Vidmar argues that 'for the purposes of Article 34(1) the ICJ does not need to decide whether Palestine is a state, let alone weigh the Montevideo criteria' because it 'may be a "state" for the functional purposes of certain treaties' without implications for general international law.[136] In support of this claim, he argues that the Vienna Convention on the Law of Treaties (VCLT) Article 81 (summarised as the 'Vienna formula') adopts 'a purely functional approach for the purposes of treaty participation and without any discussion about the entity's legal status under the law of statehood'.[137] As such, 'the question is not whether Palestine can become a party to the ICJ Statute but whether it can bring this case as a state non-party to the Statute'.[138] Supposing the Vienna formula can be used functionally outside the VCLT, this would enable Palestine to 'still be participating in the treaty-established procedures' without joining a treaty.[139] By invoking UNESCO membership as a 'window into the Vienna formula', Palestine could participate in inter-

---

135   Miron (n 132), quoting ICC Press Release of 16 January 2015, '[f]or the Office, the focus of the inquiry into Palestine's ability to accede to the Rome Statute has consistently been the question of Palestine's status in the UN (...). The UNGA Resolution 67/19 is therefore determinative of Palestine's ability to accede to the Statute pursuant to article 125, and equally, its ability to lodge an article 12(3) declaration.'

136   Jure Vidmar, 'Palestine v United States: Why the ICJ Does Not Need to Decide whether Palestine is a State' *EJIL: Talk!*, 22 November 2018, available at <https://www.ejiltalk.org/palestine-v-united-states-why-the-icj-does-not-need-to-decide-whether-palestine-is-a-state/> accessed 26 May 2021.

137   *Ibid.* Following Vidmar, *ibid.*, for a discussion of Art 81 VCLT in relation to this case, see also Islam Md Rizwanul 'The Case of Palestine Against the USA at the ICJ: A Non-Starter or Precedent Setter?' (2019) 48(1) *Georgia Journal of International and Comparative Law* 1.

138   Vidmar (n 136). Some of this had also been discussed earlier in Vidmar (n 109).

139   *Ibid.*

INTERNATIONAL COURTS AND CONTESTED STATEHOOD

national treaties, including bringing a case before the ICJ – without the Court needing to consider the general issue of statehood.[140] While this approach is both legally sound and politically sensible, it remains to be seen if the Court will adopt this solution to exercise some form of independent and impartial judicial oversight over violations of international law occurring in Palestine, regardless of its characterisation as a state under general international law.

The evolution of these proceedings before the ICJ could inform the parallel investigations at the ICC, and developments elsewhere in the UN family's dealings with Palestine. As Andrea Bianchi remarked in relation to the Wall advisory opinion, the ICJ may find itself exercising a judicial review of sorts on the actions (or inaction) of other organs of the UN.[141] Whatever the Court decides in due course, however, will have consequences not only for Palestine, but also for other contexts of contested statehood where international law faces DFINSTEs. The potential ripple effect of allowing legal black holes in the Middle East and elsewhere around the globe is perhaps the strongest argument for the ICJ to ensure that Palestine – even if it is a DFINSTE or NSA – is situated squarely within the fold of international law.

3.2 *Palestine and the ICC*

The evolution of the *Situation in Palestine* before the ICC reveals a functional approach in determining jurisdiction in relation to entities whose statehood is contested and might still be considered DFINSTE. Despite its focus on individual criminal responsibility and not on states, the ICC has grappled with the question of whether Palestine can be considered a state for the purpose of the Rome Statute and/or general international law for over a decade. The procedural background to the Pre-Trial Chamber I (PTC-I) decision confirming territorial jurisdiction on 5th February 2021 is well-known.[142] On 16th January 2015 the Prosecutor opened a pre-

---

140   Rizwanul (n 137).

141   Bianchi (n 118), 363-365.

142   For an overview of the various stages of the relationship between Palestine and the ICC, including the initial Palestinian declaration recognising jurisdiction of the ICC lodged on 21st January 2009 and the milestone formal accession to the Court on 2 January 2015, see inter alia Valentina Azarova and Triestino Mariniello 'Why the ICC Needs a "Palestine Situation" (More than Palestine Needs the ICC): On the Court's Potential Role (s) in the Israeli-Palestinian Context' (2017) 1 *Diritti Umani e Diritto Internazionale* 115; and Thomas Obel Hansen 'Opportunities and Challenges Seeking Accountability for War Crimes in Palestine under the International Criminal Court's Complementarity Regime' (2019) 9(2) *Notre Dame Journal of In-*

liminary examination into the situation in Palestine. On 22 May 2018, the State of Palestine referred the situation in Palestine for investigation to the ICC and specifically requested the Prosecutor 'to investigate, in accordance with the temporal jurisdiction of the Court, past, ongoing and future crimes within the court's jurisdiction, committed in all parts of the territory of the State of Palestine' (sic). [143] In December 2019 the Prosecutor concluded the preliminary examination and sought a ruling on the scope of the Court's territorial jurisdiction.[144] In that document, the Prosecutor was

> satisfied that there is a reasonable basis to initiate an investigation into the situation in Palestine, pursuant to article 53(1) of the Statute. There is a reasonable basis to believe that war crimes have been or are being committed in the West Bank, including East Jerusalem, and the Gaza Strip ("Gaza" or "Gaza Strip"), and the Prosecution has identified potential cases arising from the situation which would be admissible. There are no substantial reasons to believe that an investigation would not serve the interests of justice.[145]

The Prosecutor's decision to seek confirmation that the territory over which the Court has jurisdiction comprises the occupied Palestinian territory in its entirety attempts to resolve *ex ante* contentious preliminary issues around Palestine's status under the Rome Statute.[146] Her request did not include elucidating whether Palestine is a state under general international law: territorial jurisdiction for the purposes of the ICC can be ascertained specifically, and functionally, in relation to the object and

---

ternational and Comparative Law 3; John Dugard, 'Palestine and the International Criminal Court: Institutional Failure or Bias?' (2013) 11(3) *Journal of International Criminal Justice* 563.

143 See ICC Prosecutor's Annual Report on Preliminary Examination Activities (2018) – Situation in Palestine, paras. 251-254, available at <https://www.un.org/unispal/document/icc-prosecutors-annual-report-on-preliminary-examination-activities-2018-situation-in-palestine/> accessed 26 May 2021.

144 Statement of ICC Prosecutor, Fatou Bensouda, on the Conclusion of the Preliminary Examination of the Situation in Palestine, and Seeking a Ruling on the Scope of the Court's Territorial Jurisdiction, 20 December 2019, available at <https://www.icc-cpi.int/Pages/item.aspx?name=20191220-otp-statement-palestine> accessed 26 May 2021.

145 OTP, *Prosecution Request Pursuant to Article 19(3) for a Ruling on the Court's Territorial Jurisdiction in Palestine*, ICC-01/18 (22 January 2020), 2.

146 *Ibid.* 5-6.

INTERNATIONAL COURTS AND CONTESTED STATEHOOD 169

purpose of the Rome Statute. Nonetheless, she was 'mindful of the unique history and circumstances of the Occupied Palestinian Territory' and 'the fact that the question of Palestine's statehood under international law does not appear to have been definitively resolved'.[147]

The general question of Palestinian statehood – and depending on the assessment, the ICC's jurisdiction – resurfaced in numerous amicus curiae submissions deposited in March 2020. At one end of the spectrum, some argued that the Court has no jurisdiction because (in their view) Palestine is not a state under general international law;[148] at the other end of the spectrum, some others argued that Palestine is a state for both the purpose of the ICC as well as under general international law.[149] The PTC-I eventually clarified that 'regardless of Palestine's status under general international law, its accession to the Statute followed the correct and ordinary procedure', and as such it became a State Party. Thus, it agreed 'to subject itself to the terms of the Statute and, as such, all the provisions [in the Rome Statute] shall be applied to it in the same manner than to any other State Party'.[150] In answering the Prosecutor's request the PTC-I confirmed that 'the Court's territorial jurisdiction in the *Situation in Palestine* extends to the territories occupied by Israel since 1967, namely Gaza and the West Bank, including East Jerusalem'.[151]

What is significant about this decision confirming territorial jurisdiction is (as briefly discussed in the first part of this article) that the Chamber clarified it did not need to consider statehood requirements in general international law to determine whether Palestine is a state for the purposes of the Rome Statute. In assessing 'whether Palestine can be considered 'the State on the territory of which the conduct in ques-

---

147   *Ibid.* 5, cited also in ICC PTC-I, *Decision on Territorial Jurisdiction in Palestine* (n 6), para. 22.

148   In particular, Australia, Austria, Brazil, Canada, Czech Republic, Germany, Hungary and Uganda contended that Palestine is not a state, and as such the ICC would have no jurisdiction over its territory, analysed in detail in Ardi Imseis, 'State of Exception: Critical Reflections on the Amici Curiae Observations and Other Communications of States Parties to the Rome Statute in the Palestine Situation' (2020) 18(4) *JICJ* 905. In its decision, PTC-I also noted that these states 'remained silent during the accession period' and did not challenge 'Palestine's accession before the Assembly of States Parties at that time or later' (para. 101).

149   See in particular, *Amicus Curiae* Observations of the Palestinian Bar Association ICC-01/18 (14 February 2020) available at <https://www.icc-cpi.int/CourtRecords/CR2020_00469.PDF> accessed 26 May 2021.

150   ICC PTC-I *Decision on Territorial Jurisdiction in Palestine* (n 6), para. 102.

151   *Ibid.* para. 118.

tion occurred' within the meaning of article 12(2)(a) of the Statute', the PTC-I invoked article 31(1) of the Vienna Convention; on that basis, it interpreted the provision 'in good faith in accordance with the ordinary meaning to be given to its terms in their context and in the light of the object and purpose of the Statute'.[152] It continued by explaining that the provision 'does not, however, require a determination as to whether that entity fulfils the prerequisites of statehood under general international law'.[153] The Chamber then proceeded to analyse whether Palestine had followed the ordinary and correct procedures under article 125(3) to accede to the Rome Statute, which it answered affirmatively.[154] It further explained that 'the United Nations Secretary-General circulated Palestine's instrument of accession among the States Parties before accepting it and no State Party, except for Canada, manifested any opposition at the time', after which the accession was accepted by the UNSG and the 'President of the Assembly of States Parties to the Rome Statute (...) greeted Palestine in a welcoming ceremony, which 'marked the entry into force of the Rome Statute for the State of Palestine [...] thereby becoming the 123rd State Party".[155] Its active participation as a member of the Assembly of State Parties, its election to the Bureau, the participation of its representative in the discussions on the crime of aggression and indeed its budgetary contributions are all listed as evidence that, for the purposes of the Rome Statute, Palestine was acting, and being accepted by others, as a state party.[156] As such, continues the Chamber, 'by becoming a State Party, Palestine has agreed to subject itself to the terms of the Statute and, as such, all the provisions therein shall be applied to it in the same manner than to any other State party'.[157] This outcome of the accession procedure, therefore, is binding, and 'the Chamber has no authority to review that procedure' which would be *ultra vires* as regards its authority under the Rome Statute'.[158] Thus, the Chamber excluded that the 'interpretation of '[t]he State on the territory of which the conduct in question occurred' in article 12(2)(a) of the Statute' refers 'to a State within the meaning of general international law'.[159] Therefore, the Chamber states clearly that

---

152   *Ibid.* para. 91.
153   *Ibid.* para. 93.
154   *Ibid.* para. 102.
155   *Ibid.* para. 100.
156   *Ibid.*
157   *Ibid.* para. 102.
158   *Ibid.*
159   *Ibid.* para. 103.

INTERNATIONAL COURTS AND CONTESTED STATEHOOD 171

for the Court to consider whether a state fulfils the criteria for statehood under general international law would 'exceed the object and purpose of the Statute and, more specifically, the judicial functions of the Chamber to rule on the individual criminal responsibility of the persons brought before it'.[160]

Relatedly, the Chamber considered the 'delimitation of the territory of Palestine for the sole purpose of defining the Court's territorial jurisdiction'.[161] It drew on numerous UN documents, notably UN General Assembly Resolution 67/19 reaffirming 'the right of the Palestinian people to self-determination and to independence in their State of Palestine *on the Palestinian territory occupied since 1967*' to establish that 'the Court's territorial jurisdiction in the *Situation in Palestine* extends to the territories occupied by Israel since 1967, namely Gaza and the West Bank, including East Jerusalem'.[162] Essentially, the Chamber followed the UN position on what constitutes the Palestinian territory, much like the ICJ did in its *Wall* Advisory Opinion. It then offered further analysis on the right to self-determination, citing various UN sources, the *Wall* Advisory Opinion, and Security Council resolution 2334.[163] Finally, it considered the Oslo Accords (discussed earlier in this article), concluding that they are 'not pertinent to the resolution of the issue under consideration, namely the scope of the Court's territorial jurisdiction in Palestine'.[164]

The two opinions appended to the PTC-I Decision illustrate the rich debates surrounding this situation. Nonetheless, even the lengthy Partly Dissenting Opinion of Judge Péter Kovács (cited above) analysing the issue of statehood concluded – like the majority – that:

> The geographical scope of application of the Prosecutor's competence to investigate covers the territories of the West-Bank, East-Jerusalem and the Gaza strip.

His departure from the majority is the view that the Oslo Accords (discussed earlier) limit the Court's jurisdiction In 'consideration of the dif-

---

160   *Ibid.* para. 106.

161   *Ibid.* para. 114.

162   *Ibid.* paras. 116-118, citing UNGA Res 67/19, Status of Palestine in the United Nations, 29 November 2012, UN Doc A/RES/67/19, para. 1.

163   PTC-I *Decision on Territorial Jurisdiction in Palestine*, (n 6) paras. 120-122, citing UNSC, Resolution 2334 (2016), 13 December 2016, UN Doc S/RES/2334.

164   *Ibid.* paras. 124-129.

ferent legal regimes applied in areas A, B, C and East Jerusalem'. [165] Despite this differentiation, Kovács adopts a pragmatic interpretation of the Montevideo criteria, indicating that 'the fact that an entity is a State (because it has a population, a territory and sovereignty) does not mean that its borders are absolutely settled', and it is clearly not the task of the ICC to define Palestine's boundaries.[166] As such, the three judges (and indeed, the Prosecutor) are unanimous as regards the fact that the ICC should not concern itself with the ascertainment of Palestinian statehood in general international law.

The Partly Dissenting Opinion is particularly interesting for the purposes of understanding how the ICC might extend its reach to NSAs: Kovács describes Palestine 'a State in statu nascendi', considering that 'all the indicia show that it is premature to speak of a full-fledged 'State".[167] So, although he places Palestine within the category of DFINSTEs, Kovács adopts a functional interpetation of the Rome Statute and affirms that 'Palestine is a State Party, despite its current and perhaps peculiar international legal situation' and as such 'may also perform its rights and obligations'.[168] Coming from the most politically conservative of the three judges in the PTC-I decision, this statement is of particular significance: on this set of facts, it illustrates that even when an entity is somewhere between statehood and a DFINSTE under general international law, the Rome Statute and the accession route to the Court is inclusive, in the interest of its mandate, and the letter and spirit of the law. The unique context in which Palestine exists in international law cannot be overlooked, but to the extent it is a State Party to the ICC it – like others – has rights and obligations under the Rome Statute and indeed under international law. In other words, the fact that Palestine may or may not be a state under general international law is not a question the Court needs to assess; Palestinian accession to the Rome Statute and its participation in the Assembly of State Parties gives it access to the Court's jurisdiction as a State Party – regardless of whether or not it is a state outside that context.

Based on the PTC-I decision, on 3rd March 2021 the Prosecutor opened her official investigation in Palestine.[169] Her 2020 summary of Preliminary Examination Findings indicates four main foci of the investigations:

---

165   Judge Péter Kovács' Partly Dissenting Opinion (n 88), para. 372.

166   *Ibid.* para. 189.

167   *Ibid.* paras. 10-11.

168   *Ibid.* para. 267.

169   OTP, Statement of ICC Prosecutor, Fatou Bensouda, respecting an investigation of the Situation in Palestine (3 March 2021) available at <https://www.icc-cpi.int/

alleged war crimes committed by members of the Israeli Defence Forces (IDF) in the 2014 hostilities in Gaza; alleged war crimes committed by members of Hamas and Palestinian Armed Groups – which fall under the category of NSAs; alleged war crimes committed by members of the Israeli authorities in the context of the transfer of Israeli civilians in the context of the occupation of the West Bank, including East Jerusalem (i.e. the settlement enterprise); and alleged crimes committed by members of the IDF against persons participating in demonstrations on the border between Gaza and Israel in 2018 (the Great March of Return).[170] The preliminary list – which may change as the investigations proceed – includes alleged crimes committed by a range of individuals: members of the official army of a state non-party to the Rome Statute; members of the armed wing of a political group within a state party; members of (currently unspecified) armed groups operating within the territorial jurisdiction of a state party; members of the authorities (military and civilian) of a non-party state; and possibly more. For the sake of the victims of crimes within the jurisdiction of the ICC, however, the identity of the perpetrators does not change the fact of the harm suffered, less still the formal or informal affiliation to a state, a DFINSTE or a NSA.

4   Conclusion

To ensure grey areas of contested statehood do not become legal black holes of impunity for international law violations occurring in, or committed by, DFINSTEs and persons under the control of DFINSTEs, ICs routinely look under the veil of states as subjects of international law to include NSAs. This article argued that both ICJ and ICC find a balance between the contractual requirements of a state-centric legal order and the ambitious mandates set out in their constitutive treaties to deal with NSAs as well as states within the fold of international law. As illustrated in the discussion, how these ICs enforce international law in DFINSTEs (and in relation to NSAs more broadly) rests on the parameters of their founding treaties, their willingness to implement their mandate

---

Pages/item.aspx?name=210303-prosecutor-statement-investigation-palestine> accessed 26 May 2021.

170 The detail is contained in OTP, Situation in Palestine, Summary of Preliminary Examination Findings, available at <https://www.icc-cpi.int/itemsDocuments/210303 -office-of-the-prosecutor-palestine-summary-findings-eng.pdf> accessed 26 May 2021.

purposefully, and contextual case-by-case factors. The ICJ, despite being premised on state-centrism, offers a great degree of flexibility in dealing incidentally with questions pertaining to NSAs and DFINSTEs through its advisory role to the United Nations, which unlike contentious cases does not require direct engagement with any state party, non-party, or NSA. The ICC is also based on a treaty and as such may face general questions of international law that pertain to statehood and related functions before being able to pursue its mandate of individual criminal responsibility for international crimes. Thus, how ICs engage with contested states within their respective mandates is a matter of international treaty law, and not necessarily the law of statehood under general international law.

In dealing with Palestine, both courts balance the substance of their mandates as set out in the ICJ Statute and the Rome Statute with the requirements of the state-centric international legal order based on contractualism and related jurisdictional questions. So far, the ICJ in its advisory capacity and the ICC at pre-trial confirmation of jurisdiction have not needed to resolve the question of Palestinian statehood under general international law in order to exercise their jurisdiction. Given the nature of the proceedings thus far and the specific mandates of both courts, neither court was tasked with that question. The ICJ advisory opinion (*Wall*) did not address the issue of Palestinian statehood under general international law because it was not asked to do so – but reaffirmed that IHL and IHRL applies there. The contentious case before it (*Palestine v USA*) is (at the time of writing) pending on the preliminary issue of jurisdiction: this will likely test whether and how the ICJ might deal with the problem of statehood in contentious proceedings. Meanwhile, the ICC has adopted an explicitly functional approach in confirming its territorial jurisdiction in Palestine, and the Prosecutor has opened her investigations. So far, therefore, both courts have displayed pragmatism within the context of their mandates, in light of the requests, and on the facts before them in attempting to enforce international law in relation to entities which might be considered NSAs or DFINSTEs under general international law.

6 Greening the Economy of Armed Conflict

Natural Resource Exploitation by Armed Groups and Their Engagement with Environmental Protection

Daniëlla Dam-de Jong [*]

Abstract

The exploitation of natural resources, and notably extractives, to fund armed conflict has been identified as one of the six principal pathways for direct environmental damage resulting from armed conflict. Armed groups, including those fighting in a non-international armed groups and *de facto* independent non-state territorial entities (DFINSTE), are often involved in these practices. Yet, they sometimes also play a valuable role in protecting the environment in territories under their control. This article explores the normative foundations for the vast practice by armed groups with respect to natural resource exploitation and examines the engagement of these actors with the core standards for environmental protection under international law across three different settings. It concludes that a clear legal basis for natural resource exploitation by armed groups is currently lacking, but that recognition of some rights to exploit natural resources is necessary for the purpose of protecting the inhabitants of territories under control of these groups. It further finds that it is essential that the international community clearly sets out its expectations with respect to environmental protection by armed groups more generally and, where possible, engages with these groups to green their practices.

Keywords

Environment – natural resources – usufruct – peace agreements

---

[*] Grotius Centre for International Legal Studies, Leiden University. The author is grateful to Joëlle Zonjee for her research assistance. She would also like to thank Jure Vidmar and Amrei Müller for thoughtful comments on previous drafts of this paper. Any remaining mistakes are the author's sole responsibility.

© KONINKLIJKE BRILL NV, LEIDEN, 2021 | DOI:10.1163/9789004507975_007

1 Introduction

It is often contended that the environment is a silent casualty of armed conflict.[1] Indeed, the infliction of harm to the environment is a common feature of armed conflicts. The use of chemical defoliation techniques employed by the United States in Vietnam during the 1960s, for instance, resulted in massive deforestation, which took decades to regenerate.[2] The lighting of oil wells by Iraqi troops upon their retreat from Kuwaiti territory is another example. The toxic smoke released as a consequence caused severe air and marine pollution.[3] These examples of scorched earth techniques are however not a thing from the past. Similar techniques are employed in contemporary armed conflicts, both in international and non-international armed conflicts. For instance, defoliation techniques were used by the government of Colombia against the Fuerzas Armadas Revolucionarias de Colombia (FARC) in an effort to eradicate coca cultivation by this armed group.[4] Furthermore, in the fight against Islamic State (IS) in the Middle East, oil infrastructure in Iraq was targeted by both the coalition fighting IS and by IS itself.[5] The harm that this type of attack causes to the environment and to human health may be severe and long-lasting, including serious disruption of ecosystems, pollution of drinking water and significant reduction of air quality.

The conduct of hostilities is however not the sole cause of environmental harm during armed conflicts, especially when considering internal armed conflicts. According to the UN Environment Programme (UNEP), around 40% of internal armed conflicts over the past 60 years

---

1 See eg. the UN Secretary-General's message for the International day for Preventing the Exploitation of the Environment in War and Armed Conflict, 6 November 2014.

2 See United Nations Environment Programme, *'Protecting the Environment during Armed Conflict: An Inventory and Analysis of International law'* (2009) 8.

3 *Ibid.*

4 This aerial spraying campaign prompted Ecuador to institute proceedings at the ICJ, because of the harm caused to fragile ecosystems within the territory of Ecuador. The parties reached an agreement before the Court could pronounce on the matter. See *Aerial Herbicide Spraying (Ecuador v. Colombia)* case documents <www.icj-cij.org/en/case/138> accessed 25 March 2021.

5 UNEP, 'Environmental issues in areas retaken from ISIL Mosul, Iraq - Technical Note', Rapid Scoping Mission July-August 2017, 1 September 2017 <www.unep. org/resources/publication/environmental-issues-areas-retaken-isil-mosul-iraq-technical-note> accessed 28 November 2019; Wim Zwijnenburg and Foeke Postma, 'Living Under a Black Sky: Conflict Pollution and Environmental Health Concerns in Iraq' (PAX, 5 December 2017) <www.paxforpeace.nl/publications/all-publications/living-under-a-black-sky> accessed 28 November 2019.

GREENING THE ECONOMY OF ARMED CONFLICT   177

have been linked to natural resources.[6] Whereas this includes situations in which natural resources are at the root of armed conflicts, such resources are also important drivers of armed conflict.[7] More specifically, revenues from natural resource exploitation constitute a primary means for belligerents to finance their military campaign and/or to maintain an administration in territory under their control.[8] Focusing exclusively on armed groups, relevant examples include coca cultivation by the FARC during the past armed conflict in Colombia, the exploitation of minerals and gold by various armed groups in the ongoing armed conflict in the east of the DR Congo, diamond production by União Nacional para. a Independência Total de Angola (UNITA) in Angola, by Revolutionary United Front (RUF) and Armed Forces Revolutionary Council (AFRC) in Sierra Leone, and by Forces Nouvelles (FN) in Côte d'Ivoire around the turn of the century as well as oil production by both IS and the Syrian Democratic Forces in Syria over the past years.

The exploitation of natural resources, and notably extractives, to fund armed conflict has been identified as one of the six principal pathways for direct environmental damage resulting from armed conflict.[9] The diamond exploitation by the RUF in Sierra Leone provides a relevant example of how such natural resource exploitation causes harm to the environment. A post-conflict environmental assessment carried out by UNEP in 2009 concluded that this exploitation resulted in pollution of waterways and degraded land.[10] This in turn threatens the health and

---

6   United Nations Security Council Verbatim Record, 'Maintenance of International Peace and Security: Root Causes of Conflict – the Role of Natural Resources' (16 October 2018) UN Doc S/PV.8372, 2.

7   Michael L Ross, 'What Do We Know About Natural Resources and Civil War?' (2004) 41 (3) *Journal of Peace Research* 337.

8   Karen Ballentine and Heiko Nitzschke (eds), *Profiting from Peace: Managing the Resource Dimensions of Civil War* (Lynne Rienner Publishers 2005); Michael Renner, *The Anatomy of Resource Wars*, Worldwatch paper 162 (2002).

9   David Jensen and Stephen Lonergan, 'Natural Resources and Post-conflict Assessment, Remediation, Restoration and Reconstruction: Lessons and Emerging Issues' in David Jensen and Steven Lonergan (eds), *Assessing and Restoring Natural Resources in Post-conflict Peacebuilding* (Earthscan 2012), 414. The other pathways are toxic hazards from the bombardment of industrial sites and urban infrastructure; a legacy of weapons, landmines, unexploded ordnance, and depleted uranium munitions; human displacement; the loss of water supply, sanitation, and waste disposal infrastructure; and direct targeting of natural resources, particularly as part of scorched-earth military tactics.

10   UNEP, 'Sierra Leone: Environment, Conflict and Peacebuilding Assessment, Technical Report' February 2010 45.

livelihood of local populations and seriously hampers efforts of post-conflict reconstruction. The UNEP assessment concluded, for instance, that 'mining sites that were expanded were not rehabilitated in any way, leaving effluent, degraded sites and lost arable land'.[11] Likewise, a 2017 UNEP rapid assessment regarding oil pollution in Iraq observed that 'makeshift refineries [operated by IS] use rudimentary practices creating a localized but a potentially significant pollution footprint'.[12] These practices can also have dramatic consequences for the protection of world heritage. The UN Panel of Experts on the Illegal Exploitation of Natural Resources and Other Forms of Wealth of the Democratic Republic of the Congo, for instance, concluded in its 2002 interim report that highly organized and systematic exploitation activities within and around UNESCO World Heritage sites in the DR Congo posed a significant threat to the integrity of these sites.[13]

At the same time, armed groups sometimes engage with environmental conservation in the areas under their control. An example concerns the FARC in Colombia. Although this armed group engaged in some highly damaging practices (such as clearing large swathes of land for illegal coca cultivation and polluting the soil and groundwater with toxic chemicals needed to produce cocaine), it also prohibited slash and burn practices to clear land in the Amazon beyond designated points, thereby contributing to the conservation of the forest.[14] Engagement with environmental conservation can also be a mere consequence of an armed group's presence. The military presence of the Sudan People's Liberation Movement (SPLM) in South Sudan during the armed conflict between Sudan and South Sudan, for instance, ensured a basic level of protection for nature reserves, although poaching was rampant.[15]

In light of these divergent practices, the current article aims to explore the international legal framework for natural resource exploitation by armed groups and resulting obligations to protect the environment.

---

11   *Ibid.*

12   UNEP, Iraq (n 5) 2.

13   UNSC, Interim Report of the Panel of Experts on the Illegal Exploitation of Natural Resources and Other Forms of Wealth of the Democratic Republic of the Congo (2002) UN Doc S/2002/565 [50], [52].

14   Lorenzo Morales, 'Peace and Environmental Protection in Colombia: Proposals for Sustainable Rural Development' *Interamerican Dialogue* (January 2017); Gena Steffens, 'In the Colombian Amazon, Peace has Environmental Consequences' *Global Post* (3 May 2018).

15   UNEP, 'Sudan Post-Conflict Environmental Assessment' June 2007 88-95 and 250-273.

Some of these obligations are directly applicable to armed groups, while others are self-imposed. Examples in the first category concern rules in the field of international humanitarian law that provide protection to natural resources. These rules are considered to be directly applicable to armed groups, as these have been specifically designed to impose obligations on such groups. Examples in the second category include rules in the field of international environmental law that apply to the management of natural resources. These rules do not impose direct obligations on armed groups and are considered not binding on them as a matter of law.[16]

This article focuses on the three most common settings for natural resource exploitation by armed groups. The first concerns exploitation of natural resources in territory under the control of armed groups as part of a non-international armed conflict (NIAC); the second concerns exploitation of natural resources by *de facto* independent non-state territorial entities (DFINSTE) and the third concerns exploitation by armed groups within a framework agreed upon as part of a peace process. The question that can be raised is, first, whether these political differences have legal ramifications and, second, whether the differences have an impact on armed groups' engagement with environmental standards.

The article is organized as follows. Section 2 inquires into normative foundations for the vast practice by armed groups and DFINSTE with respect to natural resource exploitation. It sets out to explore the relevant international legal rules that determine whether and under what circumstances these groups are entitled to exploit natural resources. Section 3 subsequently examines the core standards for environmental protection under international law and explores armed groups' and DFINSTE's engagement with these standards. In this way, the article aims to establish how armed groups view their environmental obligations under international law. Finally, section 4 provides recommendations on greening the practices of armed groups, based on the outcomes of the analysis.

---

16   One may however argue that some of these rules indirectly bind armed groups, in so far as they exercise authority over territory. This is discussed in more detail in section 3 of this article.

2 The International Legal Framework Governing Natural Resource Exploitation by Armed Groups

This section explores the normative foundations for natural resource exploitation by armed groups and DFINSTE, focusing on the identification of circumstances in which these groups may be entitled to exploit natural resources. It argues that international law does not recognize a right for armed groups or DFINSTE to exploit natural resources, except in certain defined circumstances. Section 2.1 discusses natural resource exploitation by armed groups in territory under their control as part of a NIAC; section 2.2 focuses on exploitation of natural resources by DFINSTE; and section 2.3 examines consent by the central authorities as a legal basis for natural resource exploitation.

2.1 Exploitation of Natural Resources by Armed Groups in Territory under Their Control as Part of a NIAC

An enquiry into the applicable legal framework for the exploitation of natural resources by armed groups should start with an exploration of international humanitarian law, as this is generally considered to be the *lex specialis* in situations of armed conflict and also the only field of international law that formulates direct obligations for armed groups. Yet, international humanitarian law contains few rules that have a bearing on natural resource exploitation and none of these is relevant for determining the authority of armed groups to exploit natural resources.

More specifically, Article 55 of the 1907 Hague Regulations, which contains the rule that is most pertinent for natural resource exploitation in situations of armed conflict, is only applicable to situations of occupation. This provision, which recognizes the position of occupying powers as *de facto* authorities entitled to exploit the natural resources in occupied territory within carefully defined circumstances, does not have a counterpart regulating the position of armed groups that exercise effective control over territory.[17] Furthermore, the only rule under international humanitarian law that does apply to natural resource exploita-

---

17   For a more detailed analysis of the position of occupying powers with respect to natural resources, see Eyal Benvenisti, *The International Law of Occupation* (Second edition, Oxford University Press 2012) 81-83; International Law Commission, Marja Lehto 'First Report on Protection of the Environment in Relation to Armed Conflicts, (30 April 2018) UN Doc A/CN.4/720; Daniella A Dam-de Jong, *International Law and Governance of Natural Resources in Conflict and Post-Conflict Situations* (CUP 2015) 226-233.

GREENING THE ECONOMY OF ARMED CONFLICT

tion by armed groups is prohibitive in nature and indirectly refers back to international law that regulates ownership over natural resources. The relevant rule is the prohibition of pillage, as contained in Article 4(2)(g) of Additional Protocol II and customary international law. [18] This prohibition has been interpreted broadly to apply to all forms of theft in the context of an armed conflict, whether perpetrated in organized form or by individuals.[19] It has also been confirmed to apply to the looting and plundering of a State's natural resources by another State in the context of an international armed conflict.[20] Its application to public natural resources in NIACs however raises distinct problems. Since the prohibition of pillage seeks to prevent acts of theft, it has to be determined who can claim ownership over public natural resources. The logic is that a violation of the prohibition of pillage is intrinsically linked to the question of legal entitlement to exploit those resources.[21] Whether armed groups are

---

18 The prohibition applies to all types of armed conflicts. Similar provisions exist for international armed conflicts. Furthermore, the prohibition is considered to be part of customary international law. The Appeals Chambers of the ICTY and the SCSL have expressly held the prohibition to be part of customary law applicable to non-international armed conflict. See *Hadzihasanovic, Alagic and Kubura* (Decision On Joint Defence Interlocutory Appeal) ICTY-IT-01-47-AR72 (11 March 2005) [37]; *The Prosecutor v Moinina Fofana and Allieu Kondewa* (Appeal Chamber Judgment) SCSL-04-14-A (28 May 2008) [390]; See also Rule 52 of the ICRC Customary International Humanitarian Law Study, <https://ihl-databases.icrc.org/customary -ihl/eng/docs/v1_rul_rule52> accessed 25 March 2021.

19 Compare the judgments of various courts with respect to pillage, listed in the ICRC IHL study. See <https://ihl-databases.icrc.org/customary-ihl/eng/docs/v2_rul _rule52> under X.

20 See eg. the judgment of the International Court of Justice in the Armed Activities on the Territory of the Congo case, where the Court applied the prohibition of pillage to the looting and plundering of the DR Congo's mineral resources by members of the Ugandan army. See *Armed Activities on the Territory of the Congo (Democratic Republic of the Congo v. Uganda)* (Judgment) [2005] ICJ Rep 168 [245]. The Court built on relevant judgments by the Nuremberg Tribunal and related tribunals acting under Control Council Law No. 10. See eg. the *I.G. Farben case, Trials of War Criminals before the Nuremberg Military Tribunals under Control Council Law No. 10* VIII (Washington DC: US GPO 1952) 1134.

21 It should be noted that even if there is *prima facie* a right to exploit natural resources, international law can impose limitations on that right. This is for instance the case for occupying powers, which have a responsibility to administer natural resources in occupied territory according to the rules of *usufruct*. See Convention IV Respecting the Laws and Customs of War on Land and its Annex: *Regulations Concerning the Laws and Customs of War on Land*, The Hague, 18 October 1907, Art 55. Likewise, a *prima facie* right can be withdrawn in cases of clear abuse, eg. through the imposition of sanctions by the UN Security Council.

entitled to exploit natural resources must therefore be answered through recourse to international law regulating ownership over natural resources.

Yet, international law in this field is not particularly helpful in determining this question either. Ownership of natural resources in international law is regulated by the principle of permanent sovereignty over natural resources (PSNR), which appeared in the post WWII era within the context of the decolonization movement.[22] At the core of the principle of PSNR is a right for States and peoples to freely dispose of their natural resources.[23] This principle is also reflected in human rights law. A right for peoples to freely dispose of their natural resources was included in identical Article 1(2) of the International Covenant on Economic, Social and Cultural Rights (ICESCR) and the International Covenant on Civil and Political Rights (ICCPR) as a component of the right of peoples to self-determination.[24] The drafting history of this identical Article 1(2) of the ICESCR and the ICCPR demonstrates that these provisions were strongly connected to the principle of PSNR as an aspect of the sovereignty of newly independent States.[25] Today, this connotation is still visible in the obligations that States have pursuant to Article 1(2) of the ICCPR. The Human Rights Committee stated in its General Comment No. 12 on the right to self-determination that the right to freely dispose of natural resources 'entails corresponding duties for all States and the international community'.[26] It further noted that 'States should indicate any factors or difficulties which prevent the free disposal of *their* natural wealth and resources contrary to the provisions of this paragraph and

---

22 See Nico Schrijver, *Sovereignty over Natural Resources: Balancing Rights and Duties* (CUP 1997).

23 UNGA Declaration on Permanent Sovereignty over Natural Resources (14 December 1962) Res 1803 (XVII).

24 See identical Article 1(2) of the ICESCR and the ICCPR, which states as follows: 'All peoples may, for their own ends, freely dispose of their natural wealth and resources without prejudice to any obligations arising out of international economic co-operation, based upon the principle of mutual benefit, and international law. In no case may a people be deprived of its own means of subsistence.' International Covenant on Civil and Political Rights (adopted 16 December 1966, entered into force 23 March 1976) 999 UNTS 171 (ICCPR).

25 Schrijver, (n 22) 36-76.

26 UN Human Rights Committee (HRC), *CCPR General Comment No. 12: Article 1 (Right to Self-determination), The Right to Self-determination of Peoples* (13 March 1984) [5].

GREENING THE ECONOMY OF ARMED CONFLICT

to what extent that affects the enjoyment of other rights set forth in the Covenant'.[27]

Nevertheless, it can be argued that the right to freely dispose of natural resources, by virtue of being a human right, also applies to the relationship between the State authorities and the people living in that State. In this context, the right for peoples to freely exploit their natural resources translates first and foremost into an obligation for State authorities, when they exercise control of public natural resources, to act on behalf of the people of the State and to exercise the related rights in the interest of the people.[28] Furthermore, as a corollary of the right to political self-determination enshrined in Article 1(1) of the ICESCR and ICCPR, the peoples' right to freely dispose of natural resources must be made effective through forms of public participation in decision-making over natural resources use.[29] The right to freely dispose of natural resources and the right to political self determination therefore create obligations for the government vis-à-vis the people of the State, impacting on the modalities and permissible objectives of natural resource exploitation. In contrast, these rights do not seem to provide a legal basis for the exercise of control over natural resources by other factions within a State purportedly acting on behalf of the people.[30]

---

27   *Ibid.*

28   This is most aptly described by the late Antonio Cassese, who argued that 'Article 1(2) [...] provides that the right to control and benefit from a territory's natural resources lies with the inhabitants of that territory. This right, and the corresponding duty of the central government to use the resources in a manner which coincides with the interests of the people, is the natural consequence of the right to political self-determination'. See Antonio Cassese, *Self-Determination of Peoples: A Legal Appraisal (CUP 1995) 55;* See also Ginevra Le Moli, *'President of the Republic at al v. Ali Ayyoub et al'* (2019) 113 (4) *The American Journal of International Law* 791.

29   This obligation has been articulated by the Human Rights Committee, which noted that the relevant obligations in Article 1 of the ICCPR include first of all the establishment of constitutional and political processes 'which in practice allow the exercise of th[e] right [to self-determination]'. See General Comment No. 12: The right to self-determination of peoples (Art. 1), adopted by the Human Rights Committee at its twenty-first session, 13 March 1984, Office of the High Commissioner for Human Rights [3] and Guidelines for the treaty-specific document to be submitted by states parties under Art. 40 of the International Covenant on Civil and Political Rights, (22 November 2010) UN Doc CCPR/C/2009/1 Art 1.

30   See eg MJ Peterson, 'Recognition of Governments', in Gësim Visoka, John Doyle and Edward Newman (eds), *Routledge Handbook of State Recognition* (Routledge 2019) 205-219; Stefan Talmon, *Recognition of Governments in International Law: With Particular Reference to Governments in Exile* (Clarendon Press 1998); See also

Does this imply that natural resource exploitation by armed groups in NIACs without a valid legal title is by definition illegal and violates the prohibition of pillage? Arguably, an exception can be envisaged for small-scale natural resource exploitation that would enable armed groups to ensure the continuation of daily life in the territories that are under their control. As the *de jure* government has lost control over these territories and is therefore not in a position to perform its obligations towards the local population, one could argue that an armed group that is capable of performing basic administrative functions would be entitled to exploit natural resources to generate revenues to sustain its own civilian administration of the territory and to cover the basic needs of the local population. There is no express legal basis for this right, but it follows from the rationale underlying the right of peoples to freely dispose of their natural resources, which aims to ensure that peoples actually benefit from their natural resources. It also follows from the pragmatism that is inherent in international law regulating other situations in which an authority has effective control over territory without a valid legal title, most notably international occupation law.

As mentioned at the start of this section, international occupation law recognizes that the occupying power – as *de facto* authority – is entitled to administer immovable public property, including mines, rivers and forests, in accordance with the rules on *usufruct*. These rules prescribe that the occupying power safeguards the capital of the property that it administers, which implies an obligation to use natural resources in a sustainable way, and that it acts in the interest of the population living in occupied territory.[31] Although formally not applicable to administration by armed groups, it is important to look at the rationale behind the normative framework underlying the international law of occupation. More specifically, it recognizes that the exercise of some public authority is es-

---

International Law Association, Final Report of the Committee on Recognition/ Non-Recognition in International Law (2018); DA Dam-de Jong, 'Armed Opposition Groups and the Right to Exercise Control over Public Natural Resources: A Legal Analysis of the Cases of Libya and Syria' (2015) 62 (1) *Netherlands International Law Review* 3.

31   See Lehto, (n 17). It should be noted that occupying powers who do not respect these limitations violate the prohibition of pillage; See *Armed Activities on the Territory of the Congo (Democratic Republic of the Congo v. Uganda)* (Judgment) [2005] ICJ Rep 168 [245]; Benvenisti, (n 17) 81-82.

GREENING THE ECONOMY OF ARMED CONFLICT

sential for the continuation of daily life in the occupied territory, overriding the need for a valid legal title.[32]

This same rationale underlies the so-called 'Namibia principle', referring to an often-quoted statement by the International Court of Justice in its advisory opinion regarding *Legal Consequences for States of the Continued Presence of South Africa in Namibia*.[33] There the Court accepted that the welfare of the local population should be taken into consideration when deciding on questions of whether or not to recognize the effects of legal acts undertaken by an illegal regime.[34] In other words, if recognition of particular acts would directly benefit the population, then their *prima facie* illegality should not bar such recognition. Under-Secretary General Hans Corell recommended the same approach when requested by the UN Security Council to assess the legality of exploration contracts issued by Morocco for Western Sahara. Corell concluded that '[a]n analysis of the relevant provisions of the Charter of the United Nations, General Assembly resolutions, the case law of the International Court of Justice and the practice of States supports the [...] conclusion [that] mineral resource activities in a Non-Self-Governing Territory by an administering Power are [not] illegal, as such, [but] only if conducted in disregard of the needs and interests of the people of that Territory'.[35]

Based on this reasoning and in analogy, it can be argued that natural resource exploitation by armed groups in territories under their control would be legal in so far as the proceeds contribute directly to the well-being of the population. There is also some State practice supporting this view. Yet, it is difficult to determine whether this practice confirms the relevant States' *opinio juris* with respect to the legality of natural resource

---

32   See eg. René Provost, 'FARC Justice: Rebel Rule of Law' (2008) 8 *UC Irvine Law Review* 227, 264; Sandesh Sivakumaran, *The Law of Non-International Armed Conflict* (OUP 2012) 530.

33   See Anthony Cullen and Steven Wheatley, 'The Human Rights of Individuals in De Facto Regimes under the European Convention on Human Rights' (2013) 14 (4) *Human Rights Law Review* 691.

34   *Legal Consequences for States of the Continued Presence of South Africa in Namibia (South West Africa) notwithstanding Security Council Resolution 276* (1970) (Advisory Opinion) [1971] ICJ Rep 16 [118], [125]. For an argument in favour of applying the Namibia principle to *de facto* regimes, see Cullen and Wheatley (n 33) 691-728; See also T De Waal, 'Uncertain Ground: Engaging with Europe's De Facto States and Breakaway Territories' (Carnegie Endowment for International Peace 2018) 31-33.

35   Letter dated 29 January 2002 from the Under-Secretary-General for Legal Affairs, the Legal Counsel, addressed to the President of the Security Council, (12 February 2002) UN Doc S/2002/161 [21].

exploitation by armed groups or whether these instances should be treated as violations of the principle of non-intervention. Most notably, the European Union adopted a Regulation in 2013 which exempted oil and petroleum products originating from territories controlled by the Syrian opposition from its sanctions against Syrian oil and petroleum products, provided it was 'reasonable to conclude that: (i) the activities concerned are for the purpose of providing assistance to the Syrian civilian population, in particular in view of meeting humanitarian concerns, assisting in the provision of basic services, reconstruction or restoring economic activity, or other civilian purposes'.[36] Another example concerns the decision by the US government in October 2019 to defend Syrian oil fields against the Syrian government and its allies. Defense Secretary Mark Esperin defended this decision by appealing to the need to secure continued access to the oil fields for the Syrian Democratic Forces that relied on them to fund the fighters guarding the prisons holding captured IS fighters.[37] However, as signalled, whether these instances of State practice should be considered as reflecting the *opinio juris* of these States with respect to the legality of natural resource exploitation by armed groups in territories under their control more broadly is open to question. More generally, the existing State practice is rare and inconclusive.

When it comes to armed groups themselves, little is known with respect to how they perceive their legal position regarding public natural resources in territories under their control, either in terms of rights (e.g. to exploit natural resources) or in terms of obligations (e.g. to administer natural resources for the well-being of the population). Most studies focus on the abuses and do not go beyond the role of natural resources in financing armed conflict.[38] Other studies focus on governance struc-

---

36 See Council Regulation (EU) No 697/2013 of 22 July 2013 amending Regulation (EU) No 36/2012 concerning restrictive measures in view of the situation in Syria, under Article 6a.

37 Phil Stewart, 'U.S. military envisions broad defense of Syrian Oilfields' (Reuters 28 October 2019) <www.reuters.com/article/us-mideast-crisis-syria-usa-oil/u-s-military-envisions-broad-defense-of-syrian-oilfields-idUSKBN1X72BH> accessed 14 March 2020.

38 See the systematic literature review conducted by Cuvelier, Vlassenroot and Olin in 2013, which concluded that '[l]imited information exists on the governance capacity and performance of non-state armed groups. [...] Evidence exists on rebels' income-generating strategies, but this evidence is mainly used to support claims that armed groups are guided by predatory behaviour, and that control over resources is needed to finance war efforts. Less is known about the functioning of rebel-controlled tax regimes to regulate commercial activities, racketeer practices,

GREENING THE ECONOMY OF ARMED CONFLICT 187

tures established by armed groups and their motivations for introducing particular types of governance. These studies conclude for instance that armed groups exercising effective and sustained control over territory tend to establish governance structures in the territory under their control.[39] They further show that whether or not armed groups are willing to provide basic services to the population depends on the extent to which they rely on the population for food, shelter and intelligence, overriding ideology as an explanatory factor.[40] Thirdly, this dependence on the civilian population seems to determine to some extent whether the availability of natural resources incentivises or disincentivises armed groups from establishing governance structures. Weinstein's study, for instance, shows that another factor explaining why armed groups establish or refrain from establishing participatory governance structures benefitting the population may be found in the extent to which armed groups rely

---

or rebel provision of security in return for resources.' See J. Cuvelier, K. Vlassenroot and N. Olin, 'Resources, Conflict and Governance: a critical review of the evidence', Justice and Security Research Programme Paper No. 9, October 2013, 17.

39 See eg J Weinstein, *Inside Rebellion: The Politics of Insurgent Violence* (CUP 2006) 163-197; Z Mampilly, *Rebel Rulers: Insurgent Governance and Civilian Life during War* (Cornell University Press 2011); A Arjona and others (eds), *Rebel Governance in Civil War* (CUP 2015).

40 J. Weinstein, *Inside Rebellion: The Politics of Insurgent Violence* (CUP 2006), 163-197. This does not necessarily rule out ideology as a significant factor; See eg. W Reno, 'Predatory Rebellions and Governance: The National Patriotic Front of Liberia, 1989–1992', in A Arjona and others (eds), *Rebel Governance in Civil War* (CUP 2015) 265-285, who distinguishes between predatory and justice-seeking armed groups. He argues that '[t]he leaders of Africa's anti-colonial rebel groups and those who fought Ethiopia's government through the 1970s and 1980s devoted valuable personnel and resources to manage economic activities and provide goods and services to non-combatants. Predatory groups, on the other hand, were primarily interested in their personal and group fortunes, with little or no sustained attention to pursuing a broader political project among people living in areas they controlled. Non-combatants were important for the rent- seeking opportunities that they provided, mostly as sources of loot and targets for extortion' (274). He further notes that both types of groups may create elaborate governance structures, yet 'predatory rebels [...] create façades and either ignore them – aside from trying to attract international recognition – or selectively enforce administrative rules to extract bribes' (279). Interestingly, Reno's chapter focuses on the National Patriotic Front, which was active in Liberia in the 1990s. This predatory rebel group, under the leadership of Charles Taylor, relied mainly on the exploitation of timber and rubber, for which it attracted rogue foreign companies. As such, the NPFL did not depend on the population for its basic needs.

188   6 – DAM-DE JONG

on the civilian population as labour forces for the exploitation of natural resources.[41]

These studies contribute to our general understanding of armed groups' practice with respect to the governance of territories under their control as well as their motivations for introducing forms of participatory governance and for providing basic services to the civilian population. They show that the establishment of governance structures is fairly common in territories under the control of armed groups. Yet, they also show that these structures may serve a myriad of purposes and are not necessarily beneficial for the civilian population. If these findings are translated to the legal domain, a tentative conclusion which may be drawn from these studies is that there is no uniform and consistent practice among armed groups to provide basic services to the population. Furthermore, the decision to provide basic services to the population does not seem to be inspired by a sense of legal obligation, but seems instead primarily driven by the needs and motivations of the armed group itself. Based on this assessment and the absence of consistent practice and *opinio juris* on the part of States with respect to natural resource exploitation by armed groups, there appears to be no solid legal basis for a right for armed groups to exploit the natural resources under their control.

2.2   *Exploitation of Natural Resources by* de Facto *Independent Non-state Territorial Entities*

The previous section examined situations in which an opposition movement exercises effective control over territory as part of an active NIAC, sometimes even of longer duration. It was argued that natural resource exploitation by these groups is to be considered illegal, except arguably where such exploitation contributes directly to the well-being of the population. The current section explores whether a more solid legal basis for natural resource exploitation can be found with respect to situations of *de facto* secession. This concerns situations in which a segment of the general population, often identifying itself as a people and having a distinct relationship with the territory concerned, declares its independence from the territorial State without the consent of the latter's government.[42] Examples include Northern Cyprus, Abkhazia, Nagorno-

---

41   *Ibid.*

42   Cullen and Wheatley define *de facto* regimes as 'territories that have achieved de facto independence in the face of opposition from the territorial State, but

Karabakh, Kosovo, and Crimea. These situations should be distinguished from classical power struggles between competing political factions in a State, although admittedly, this distinction cannot always easily be made, especially in situations where the power struggle is fought along territorial lines. For the purposes of this study, the determining factor for distinguishing between prolonged NIACs on the one hand and *de facto* secession on the other is whether the armed group has actually claimed a political future separate from the territorial State.[43] The assumption is that such claims are made effective through establishing State-like governance structures that encompass all aspects of public policy,[44] including with respect to the exercise of authority over the territory's natural resources.

The question can therefore be raised whether the establishment of State-like governance structures by DFINSTE affects their legal position with respect to the territory's natural resources. This requires an inquiry into whether DFINSTE indeed establish such governance structures and how these are treated by States. DFINSTE do indeed often articulate their position with respect to the territory's natural resources in their constitutive instruments. The constitutions of Abkhazia and Somaliland constitute good examples. Both constitutions base the authority of the State and its representatives on the 'sovereignty' of its people, thereby transpiring the idea that the authority of the State and its government rely on the consent of the people and that the government acts on behalf of and in the interest of the people.[45] With respect to natural resources, the

---

have not been accepted as 'States' by the international community'. Cullen and Wheatley (n 33) 694; See also M. Weller, 'Settling Self-determination conflicts: Recent Developments' (2009) 20 *European Journal of International Law* 111.

43   See also A Florea, 'Rebel governance in de facto states' (2020) 26 (4) *European Journal of International Relations* 1004, 1008, who mentions two key characteristics that set DFINSTE apart from other types of armed groups, namely a monopoly on violence/territorial control on the one hand and the goal of independence on the other.

44   *Ibid.*, who argues that there is an expectation that de facto states 'would display a complex governance architecture' as a means to ensure being accepted as the rightful authority of the territory.

45   See Article 2 of the Constitution of Abkhazia, which states that 'The sovereignty of the people shall be the basis for the State authority in the Republic of Abkhazia. The sovereignty bearer and sole source of authority in the Republic of Abkhazia shall be its people, i.e., the citizens of the Republic of Abkhazia. The people shall exercise their authority directly or through their representatives.' See The City of Sukhum, 'Abkhazia: The Constitution of Abkhazia (UNPO, 26 November 1994) <https://unpo.org/article/697> accessed 3 December 2020. Article 1(2) of the Con-

constitution of Abkhazia determines in its Article 5 that 'Land and other natural resources shall be property of the people and shall be used and protected in the Republic of Abkhazia as a basis of life and activities of its citizens'.[46] Likewise, Article 12.4 of the Constitution of the Republic of Somaliland states that '[t]he central state (government) is responsible for the natural resources of the country, and shall take all possible steps to explore and exploit all these resources which are available in the nation's land or sea....'.[47]

Various DFINSTE furthermore enact legislation regulating aspects of the management of natural resources, which is overseen by State-like institutions. Abkhazia, for instance, has enacted a law on investment activity, which applies to natural resources.[48] The management of its natural resources, including coal, various stones (marble, granite, limestone), water, agricultural land and timber, is furthermore overseen by its Ministry of Economy. Likewise, Somaliland's investment law, which regulates all foreign investment, refers to agriculture, livestock, fishing and mineral resources as priority areas for such investment.[49] An advanced system of governmental institutions has been set up to develop policies regarding key natural resources, most importantly water resources, land, livestock and fisheries and energy and minerals.[50]

---

stitution of the Republic of Somaliland determines that '[s]overeignty resides in the people who shall exercise it in accordance with the Constitution and other laws'. See 'The Constitution of the Republic of Somaliland' <www.somalilandlaw. com/somaliland_constitution.htm#Chapter1> accessed 3 December 2020. For a more in-depth analysis of the human rights implications, see Amrei Müller's contribution in this volume.

46 See Constitution of Abkhazia (n 45)

47 See Constitution of Somaliland (n 45).

48 Law of the Republic of Abkhazia on Investment Activity <http://investinabkhazia .org/upload/iblock/9ce/Law%20On%20Investment%20Activity.pdf> accessed 3 December 2020. Article 1 of the law determines that 'Investment means any objects of civil rights that have not been withdrawn from circulation and have monetary value, are invested by an investor in objects of investment activity in order to earn profit (income) and/or to obtain other useful deliverables or for any other purposes not related to the satisfaction of own (personal) needs of the investor, in particular: [...] 5) natural resources licence in cases when the legislation allows for the transfer of such rights'.

49 Promotion, Protection and Guarantees of the Foreign Investment law Article 4 <www.extractiveshub.org/servefile/getFile/id/2628> accessed 3 December 2020.

50 See Government of Somaliland Departments <https://www.govsomaliland.org/ article/departments> accessed 3 December 2020.

GREENING THE ECONOMY OF ARMED CONFLICT   191

It is however difficult to get a good sense of how these governance structures function and whether they are used for the distribution of basic services to the population. A recent study by Florea on governance institutions across all DFINSTE between 1945 and 2016 presents some interesting insights in this respect. He shows first that the type of natural resources found within a territory has an impact on the establishment of governance structures. The presence of mineral resources in a territory, for instance, has a negative effect on the establishment by DFINSTE of governance structures.[51] These findings are not surprising in light of existing scholarship on the resource curse, which shows that regimes that gain their revenues from natural resources are less reliant on their constituencies and are therefore less likely to provide public goods.[52] His second finding is however more surprising. Whereas he shows that dependence on taxation of labour-intensive natural resources, most importantly agricultural products, has a positive effect on the establishment of governance structures (as expected), he notes that the establishment of such structures does not seem to contribute significantly to the establishment of institutions for the provision of public goods.[53] This suggests that the establishment of governance structures on the one hand and the question of how natural resources revenues are spent on the other are two separate matters.

Looking at State practice specifically, it is important to note that States tend to avoid economic relations with DFINSTE, except when they have formally recognized their claim for statehood. Abkhazia again provides a relevant example. Abkhazia is heavily reliant on Russia, which is its main sponsoring State.[54] It has furthermore established some economic relations with the EU through the latter's 'non-recognition without engage-

---

51   A Florea, (n 43) 1024.

52   Collier and A Hoeffler, 'High-value Natural Resources, Development, and Conflict: Channels of Causation' in Lujala and S.A. Rustad (eds), *High-Value Natural Resources and Peacebuilding* (Earthscan, 2012) especially 303.

53   A Florea, (n 43) 1024. Florea suggests that this indicates that 'the revenues accrued through productive economic activities tend to be channelled towards the distribution of club, rather than public, goods.'

54   See for instance the Agreement on the Goods Trade Regime between the Government of the Republic of Abkhazia and the Government of the Russian Federation: <http://investinabkhazia.org/upload/iblock/ced/AGREEMENT%20on%20the%20Goods%20Trade%20Regime%20between%20the%20Government%20of%20the%20Republic%20of%20Abkhazia%20and%20the%20Government%20of%20the%20Russian%20Federation.pdf> accessed 3 December 2020; See also De Waal, (n 34) 12-13.

ment' policy, but these are exclusively of a humanitarian nature, consisting of an aid program for the rehabilitation of essential infrastructure.[55] Where more active trade relations have been established with DFINSTE, these are usually tied to an ongoing peace process. This is the case for Transdniestria and Northern Cyprus.[56] There are however no indications suggesting that States would be prepared to have trade relations with DFINSTE outside such peace processes.

2.3 *Exploitation of Natural Resources Pursuant to Transitional Arrangements in Peace Processes*

Whereas international law therefore does not bestow a right to exploit natural resources on armed groups or DFINSTE, except arguably when it is to satisfy the basic needs of the civilian population, such a right can be accorded to them by agreement. It is especially within the context of peace processes that such rights are sometimes granted to armed groups.[57] These arrangements can use either a political or a territorial model.

Political arrangements focus on integrating armed groups into State institutions, for example by establishing a transitional government in which the opposition is represented and which is often based on a fixed distribution of strategic political, administrative, and economic positions. This was, for instance, the case for Sierra Leone. The 1999 Lomé Agreement concluded between the Government of Sierra Leone and the Revolutionary United Front (RUF) grants full control of the exploitation of gold, diamonds and other natural resources to the transitional government, composed of members of the (former) Government of Sierra

---

55 See De Waal (n 34) 25-26.

56 For Transdniestria, see *ibid.* 35-47 and the PA-X peace agreement database for an overview of the agreements that guide the peace process, available at <https://www.peaceagreements.org/>.

57 For a critical appraisal of power-sharing arrangements, see J Levitt, *Illegal Peace in Africa: An Inquiry into the Legality of Power-sharing with African Warlords, Rebels, and Junta* (CUP 2012). It is important to note that the legal status of peace agreements concluded between States and armed groups is subject to debate. Some of these agreements qualify as treaties, but the majority is best regarded as internal arrangements within the domestic system. These agreements are relevant from an international legal perspective to the extent that they engage with international law. For a more extensive discussion, see C Bell, *On the Law of Peace : Peace Agreements and the Lex Pacificatoria* (OUP, 2008) and M Weller, M Retter and A Varga, *International Law and Peace Settlements* (CUP 2021).

GREENING THE ECONOMY OF ARMED CONFLICT   193

Leone and the RUF.[58] Furthermore, a Commission on the Management of Strategic Resources, National Reconstruction and Development, with mixed membership and chaired by the leader of the RUF, obtained exclusive competence to secure and monitor the exploitation of these natural resources on behalf of the government.[59]

Alternatively, power-sharing or wealth-sharing arrangements can also be territorial, granting an armed group administrative control over specific parts of the territory. These arrangements can be introduced as interim measures to gain confidence, leading ultimately to demobilization and effective integration of the opposition in the political structures of the State. This was for instance the purpose of the arrangement between the government of Angola and UNITA, which gave UNITA control over the economy of territory over which it exercised public authority, including the power to attract foreign investment.[60] Yet, territorial arrangements can also be introduced to give effect to calls for autonomy, as in secessionist armed conflicts. The 2005 Comprehensive Peace Agreement concluded between the government of Sudan and the Sudan People's Liberation Movement (SPLM), for instance, established separate spheres of responsibility for the national government, the South Sudanese government and local authorities. At the same time, it established a commission composed of representatives of these authorities to jointly manage and develop the petroleum sector.[61] This commission was established as part of a transitory arrangement pending the decision of the South Sudanese people regarding their self-determination. Another example of a territorial arrangement aimed at giving effect to calls for autonomy regards Cyprus. In 2004, a peace agreement providing for a federal structure was unsuccessfully negotiated between the Greek and Turkish Cypriots. This agreement would have granted a large degree of autonomy to the Turkish

---

58   Peace Agreement between the Government of Sierra Leone and the RUF (Lomé Peace Agreement), 7 July 1999, Articles V and VII.

59   Peace Agreement between the Government of Sierra Leone and the RUF (Lomé Peace Agreement), 7 July 1999, Article VII.

60   Lusaka Protocol (People's Movement for the Liberation of Angola-UNITA) (15 November 1994) Annex 6 Articles I (4)(c)-(d) and II (5).

61   Comprehensive Peace Agreement between the Government of The Republic of The Sudan and the Sudan People's Liberation Movement/Sudan's Liberation Army (9 January 2005) Chapter III art 3, 45. <https://peacemaker.un.org/sites/peacemaker. un.org/files/SD_060000_The%20Comprehensive%20Peace%20Agreement.pdf> accessed 28 March 2021.

Cypriot Constituent State. It also provided for benefit-sharing between the two communities with respect to offshore natural resources.[62]

The structures established by these agreements have, arguably, the effect of transforming armed groups into representatives of the State, whether as members of the national government or of local authorities. As such, they are under the same obligation as the government to act in the interest of the people. Furthermore, depending on the specific arrangements made with the central authorities, they are entitled to exercise authority over the exploitation of natural resources, as long as they do not renege on their commitments pursuant to the agreement.[63] This also implies that these groups, when acting in their capacity as State representatives, are under an obligation to respect the international environmental obligations that ensue from relevant treaties to which the State is a party and from customary international law, in any case in so far as these have been implemented in domestic law.

3 Environmental Obligations for Armed Groups: An Inquiry into Law and Practice

The previous section explored the normative foundations for natural resource exploitation by armed groups and DFINSTE, focusing on the identification of circumstances in which these groups may be entitled to exploit natural resources and under what conditions. It argued that

---

62   See UNSC UN Comprehensive Settlement Plan of the Cyprus Question 31 March 2004 <https://peacemaker.un.org/sites/peacemaker.un.org/files/Annan_Plan_MAR CH_30_2004.pdf> accessed 27 March 2021. The plan was rejected by the Greek Cypriots and a successor agreement has not been concluded as of yet. The question of who is entitled to decide on the island's natural resources has however become particularly acute due to a dispute between the Greek Cypriots and Turkey over offshore oil and gas drilling; See T Carney, 'The Legal Issues Regarding Drilling Off the Northeast Coast of Cyprus ', (*Opinio Juris*, 23 September 2019) <http://opiniojuris .org/2019/09/23/the-legal-issues-regarding-drilling-off-the-northeast-coast-of-cyprus/> accessed 3 December 2020.

63   In practice, there have been several instances in which armed groups did renege on their commitments. This has resulted in the government turning to the UN Security Council with the request to adopt sanctions under Chapter VII of the UN Charter. This happened, for instance, with respect to Angola and Sierra Leone. For Angola, see UN Security Council Resolution 864 (1993) imposing arms and petroleum sanctions for obstruction of the peace process and Resolution 1173 (1998) for diamonds specifically. For Sierra Leone, see Resolutions 1132 (1997) and 1306 (2000).

international law does not provide a solid legal basis for natural resource exploitation by armed groups or DFINSTE. Instead, such groups may obtain a derived right through a negotiated settlement. Furthermore, the principal condition underlying any exploitation by armed groups or DFINSTE would be that such exploitation contributes to the well-being of the population living in the territory under their control. The current section focuses on armed groups' and DFINSTE's engagement with environmental standards. Section 3.1 first briefly sets out the principal international legal standards for the protection of the environment related to exploitation of natural resources, while section 3.2 explores relevant statements by armed groups and DFINSTE themselves.

3.1 *International Legal Standards for the Protection of the Environment*

Relevant international legal standards relating to the protection of the environment against harm ensuing from the exploitation of natural resources stem from the notion of sustainable development and related principles, many of which have a firm foundation in international law.[64] The concept of sustainable development has been defined as 'development that meets the needs of the present without compromising the ability of future generations to meet their own needs.'[65] Balancing the interests of the present with those of future generations is key to sustainable development and is therefore reflected in several of its principles. First, the principle of inter-generational equity formulates a responsibility for the present generation to safeguard the opportunities of future generations to use the natural wealth and resources for their needs and aspirations.[66] This principle is however rarely translated into concrete obligations. It primarily serves to provide general guidance to States.

The interests of future generations are furthermore reflected in the principle of conservation and sustainable use of natural resources, which has arguably achieved customary status. This principle has been incor-

---

64 An overview and analysis of the principles of sustainable development can be found in the ILA New Delhi Declaration of Principles of International Law Relating to Sustainable Development (adopted on 2 April 2002) (31 August 2002) *UN Doc A/57/329*. This declaration is generally considered as an authoritative statement of the principles of sustainable development.

65 World Commission on Environment and Development, *Our Common Future* (OUP 1987) 8.

66 See E Brown-Weiss, *In Fairness to Future Generations: International law, Common Patrimony, and Intergenerational Equity* (United Nations University 1989).

porated in one way or the other in numerous conventions, including the Convention on Biological Diversity, the UN Convention on the Law of the Sea and the WTO Agreement.[67] It imposes limits on the use of natural resources for the purpose of preventing their decline and to ensure long-term development.[68] The principle of sustainable use therefore impacts on the direct use of the natural resources that are being exploited. It seeks to ensure that renewable natural resources are used in a way and at a rate that allows them to regenerate and that non-renewable natural resources are used with restraint to safeguard the opportunities of future generations.

The principle of sustainable use also seeks to prevent collateral harm ensuing from natural resource exploitation, such as caused by the release of chemical substances in the environment. This obligation to prevent collateral harm is addressed through the customary obligation to prevent significant harm to the environment of other States and to areas beyond national jurisdiction, derived from the 1941 Trail Smelter Arbitration and confirmed in several judgments thereafter, including by the International Court of Justice in two landmark judgments.[69] The principle of prevention entails a duty of care incumbent on States to take appropriate measures to prevent transboundary damage to the environment, including conducting environmental impact assessments when there is a foreseeable risk that significant environmental harm will occur.[70]

The principle of prevention however does not prohibit a State from polluting its own environment. It only seeks to avoid that such pollution has a transboundary impact. Does this mean that States have full discretion to pollute their own environment? Surely not, but relevant obligations stem mostly from treaty law. Article 14 of the Convention

---

67   Convention on Biological Diversity (opened for signature 5 June 1992, entered into force 29 December 1993) 1760 UNTS 79 art 2; UN Convention on the Law of the Sea (adopted 10 December 1982, entered into force 16 November 1194) 1833 UNTS 397 art 61; Agreement Establishing the World Trade Organization (adopted on 15 April 1994) 1867 UNTS 154 preamble.

68   See New Delhi Declaration (n 64) Principle 1 on the duty of States to ensure sustainable use of natural resources.

69   *Case Concerning Pulp Mills on the River Uruguay (Argentina v. Uruguay)* (Judgment) [2010] ICJ Rep 14 [101]; *Certain Activities Carried Out by Nicaragua in the Border Area (Costa Rica v. Nicaragua) and Construction of a Road in Costa Rica along the San Juan River (Nicaragua v. Costa Rica)* (Judgment) [2015] ICJ Rep 665 [118].

70   Draft articles on Prevention of Transboundary Harm from Hazardous Activities, with commentaries (2001) II Part Two *Yearbook of the International Law Commission* 148, 152; Pulp Mills (n 69) [101].

GREENING THE ECONOMY OF ARMED CONFLICT

on Biological Diversity, for instance, provides that each party shall '[i]ntroduce appropriate procedures requiring environmental impact assessment of its proposed projects that are likely to have significant adverse effects on biological diversity'. Furthermore, conventions such as the Ramsar Convention on wetlands and the UNESCO World Heritage Convention, require State parties to take measures to protect the nature reserves covered by the conventions.

It is important to observe that the concept of sustainable development and its related principles apply primarily to States. This is certainly true for the underlying obligations, which are all addressed to States. Nonetheless, it is argued that the principles are also relevant for natural resource exploitation by armed groups, as they formulate standards for exploitation of natural resources that apply regardless of the identity of the entity involved in such exploitation. This does not imply that these standards apply to armed groups as a matter of legal obligations. However, at the very least, they formulate expectations which any armed group with the aspiration to be recognized as a legitimate political actor should respect.

Furthermore, whereas international environmental law does not formulate obligations that directly bind armed groups, international humanitarian law does. General protection to the environment in NIACs flows from the fundamental principles of international humanitarian law, most importantly the principles of distinction, military necessity, proportionality and precautions in attack. Furthermore, principle 13(2) of the ILC draft principles on the protection of the environment in relation to armed conflict recognizes an obligation for combatants to take care 'to protect the natural environment against widespread, long-term and severe damage'.[71] This obligation is based on Article 55 of Additional Protocol I, which determines that '[c]are shall be taken in warfare to protect the natural environment against widespread, long- term and severe damage', but is argued to extend to non-international armed conflicts.[72]

---

71   See ILC, 'Report of the International Law Commission on the Work of Its Seventy-first Session' (29 April - 7 June and 8 July - 9 August 2019) UN Doc A/74/10 250-254.

72   *Ibid.* 252 under (7); See also rule 45 of the ICRC customary international law study, which is phrased differently but is based on the same treaty provision. The ICRC argued in 2005 that 'even if this rule is not yet customary, present trends towards further protection of the environment and towards establishing rules applicable in non-international armed conflicts mean that it is likely to become customary in due course.' See <https://ihl-databases.icrc.org/customary-ihl/eng/docs/v1_rul_rule45> accessed 29 June 2020.

These principles and rules impose constraints on combatants' freedom to employ the means and methods of warfare of their choice. However, some of these constraints are more theoretical than practical. This is the case for the prohibition to cause widespread, long-term and severe damage to the environment due to the insurmountable cumulative threshold of widespread, long- term *and* severe damage.[73] Furthermore, their relevance for other acts besides the conduct of hostilities that cause damage to the environment during armed conflict, such as the exploitation of natural resources, is less clear.

More generally, international humanitarian law contains very few rules that apply to natural resource exploitation in the first place, let alone that these impose limitations for the purpose of protecting the environment. The principle of *usufruct* from occupation law, which has been referred to in section 2, provides an exception. Based on this principle, an occupying power can only enjoy the proceeds of the properties it administers as long as it safeguards their capital. The interpretation of this principle is greatly influenced by contemporary scientific insights underlying the notion of sustainable use of natural resources.[74] However, as indicated in section 2, the principle of *usufruct* does not formally apply to situations in which territory is under the effective control of armed groups.

Other provisions that may impose limitations on natural resource exploitation for the purpose of protecting the environment include Articles 14 and 17(2) of Additional Protocol II. Article 14 formulates a prohibition to use starvation as a method of combat.[75] It aims to ensure that the local population retains access to the basic needs for survival, which may include objects located in or near natural resource exploitation sites. The provision is relevant for preventing some forms of environmental harm,

---

73 See for a critical approach towards this threshold, K Hulme, *War Torn Environment: Interpreting the Legal Threshold* (Brill 2004); Phoebe Okowa, 'Natural Resources in Situations of Armed Conflict: Is there a Coherent Framework for Protection?' (2007) 9 *International Community Law Review* 237,250. For an actual assessment of whether particular hostilities had met the threshold, see Final Report to the Prosecutor by the Committee Established to Review the NATO Bombing Campaign Against the Federal Republic of Yugoslavia 14 June 2000 at <http://www.icty.org/x/file/Press/nato061300.pdf> [14-25].

74 See ILC Seventy-first Session Report (n 71) 276-278; See also Dam-de Jong, (n 17) 228-229.

75 Starvation has furthermore been recognized as a war crime under the ICC Statute, both in international and – more recently – in internal armed conflicts. See Article 8(2)(b)(xxv) of the Rome Statue of the International Criminal Court (entered into force 1 July 2002) 2187 UNTS 90.

GREENING THE ECONOMY OF ARMED CONFLICT

most notably where this harm is inflicted with the specific purpose of starving the civilian population. Examples include destroying croplands to deprive the population of food or poisoning of rivers or water wells for the purpose of depriving the population of access to water. Such practices have been documented in various armed conflicts, including in Sierra Leone and Darfur (Sudan).[76] In this sense, the provision provides basic protection to the environment. Whether the prohibition also applies to environmental harm that incidentally results in starvation of the population, such as caused by massive pollution related to natural resource exploitation by belligerents, is however less evident. There is an ongoing debate as to whether the prohibition applies only to those instances in which indispensable objects are destroyed or removed for the specific purpose of starving the population or whether it also applies to situations in which starvation is incidental.[77] Based on the current understanding of the prohibition of starvation within the context of NIACs, the provision would not apply to situations in which starvation is incidental, thereby reducing the relevance of the provision for preventing serious environmental harm resulting from natural resource exploitation by armed groups.

Another potentially relevant provision is Article 17(2) of Additional Protocol II. This provision prohibits parties to an armed conflict to compel civilians 'to leave their own territory for reasons connected with the conflict'. This prohibition clearly applies to situations in which armed groups drive local communities out of areas to gain access to natural resource exploitation sites for the purpose of obtaining revenues to finance their armed struggle. The question can however be raised whether it also applies to situations in which local communities are indirectly forced to move, such as when natural resource exploitation by armed groups results in such serious harm to the environment that the population is no longer able to provide in its livelihood. In other words, does the provision only cover situations in which parties to an armed conflict actively compel local communities to move away or does it also apply to situations in which the displacement is incidental? The ICRC Commentary to the

---

76   For Sierra Leone, see UNEP, (n 10) 45; for Darfur, see Summary of Prosecutor's Application under Article 58, *ICC-02/05-152* (14 July 2008) 5-6.

77   See eg M Lattimer, 'Can Incidental Starvation of Civilians be Lawful under IHL?' (*EJIL: Talk!* 26 March 2019) <www.ejiltalk.org/can-incidental-starvation-of-civilians-be-lawful-under-ihl/> accessed 5 December 2019; See also F D'Alessandra and M Gillett, 'The War Crime of Starvation in Non-international Armed Conflict' (2019) 17 (4) *Journal of International Criminal Justice* 815.

provision remains silent on this question.[78] Yet, it can be inferred from the general context and from relevant practice that it is not sufficient that the circumstances in themselves are such as to compel the population to move away; any displacement has to be the consequence of a strategy on the part of the armed group exercising control over the territory.[79]

To conclude, the existing rules of international humanitarian law applicable to NIACs have some relevance for environmental protection, but primarily when harm to the environment is the result of the conduct of hostilities or when it is used as a method intended to inflict harm on the population. These rules do not contain any standards for the sustainability of natural resource exploitation by armed groups. This implies that we are left with standards related to the concept of sustainable development. In light of this, it is all the more interesting to explore how armed groups perceive their own obligations – or at the very least, how they frame their commitments – pursuant to international law.

3.2 Armed Groups' Adherence to Environmental Standards

In light of the ambiguities surrounding the international legal frame-work governing natural resource exploitation by armed groups, it is not surprising that public statements by armed groups regarding their environmental commitments with respect to natural resource exploitation are scarce. This is especially true for armed groups partaking in NIACs. There are some statements that refer to environmental protection, but either in a very generic manner or in relation to military operations. It is furthermore interesting to note that some of these statements build on standards contained in international humanitarian law, most notably Articles 14 and 17 of Additional Protocol II. The Sierra Leonean RUF's code of conduct, for instance, prohibited members to damage crops, yet it did not provide further specification.[80] Furthermore, a 2010 unilateral statement by the Kurdish People's Defence Forces stated in relevant part that

---

78   See Y Sandoz, C Swinarski and B Zimmermann (eds), *Commentary on the Additional Protocols of 8 June 1977 to the Geneva Conventions of 12 August 1949* (Martinus Nijhoff Publishers 1987) Art 17 1471.

79   See eg E Mooney, 'Displacement and the Protection of Civilians under International Law' in H Willmot, R Mamiya, S Sheeran and M Weller, *Protection of Civilians* (OUP 2016) 177-204, 189; and M Jacques, *Armed Conflict and Displacement: The Protection of Refugees and Displaced Persons under International Humanitarian Law* (CUP 2012) 49-76.

80   Revolutionary United Front, Eight Codes of Conduct <http://theirwords.org/> accessed 28 March 2021.

GREENING THE ECONOMY OF ARMED CONFLICT

'[c]ivilians will not be uprooted and will not be prevented from accessing fields, summer grounds and pastures. Means that are necessary for civilians to sustain their lives will not be attacked, food embargoes will not be applied and food stocks will not be destroyed.'[81] It is important to note that, while this provision expands the protection provided by Articles 14 and 17 of Additional Protocol II to include general protection to objects that are necessary for sustaining the livelihoods of civilians, it is only indirectly relevant for natural resource exploitation.

Some armed groups also engage with standards from international environmental law, although it is often difficult to ascertain whether or not this engagement rests on a genuine desire to abide by international environmental law proper. The Lord Resistance Army operating in the African Great Lakes Region, for instance, declared in 2006 that it would act as the curator of endangered species in the DR Congo's Garamba nature reserve where the group was operational at the time. It further declared that it would do 'everything possible to see that they are not harmed for posterity', implying a commitment to species conservation and to the principle of inter-generational equity.[82] This statement is particularly relevant, as the LRA derived a significant part of its revenues from poaching elephants and rhinoceros for their ivory.[83] Yet, as the LRA has continued its poaching activities since then,[84] it also signals that such statements are not necessarily reflected in practice.

Of a very different nature is the constitution adopted by the Sudan People's Liberation Movement (SPLM) in 2008 to mark its transformation from an armed opposition group to a political party. This document contains several references to sustainability. It notes, for instance, that the SPLM as a political party shall be guided by '[e]nvironment friendliness and sustainability of the utilization of natural resources'.[85] It further determines that the aims and objectives of the SPLM include advanc-

---

81 Document concerning the rules to be obeyed by HPG forces in war (Their Words 2010) art 5 <http://theirwords.org/media/transfer/doc/ut_tt_pkk_hpg_2010_15_0000 8142b5729731202a63103eba1a9a.pdf> accessed 28 March 2021.

82 'LRA Rebels Vow to Protect Rare Wildlife' (Independent Online South Africa) 21 August 2006 quoted in S Sivakumaran, *The Law of Non-International Armed Conflict* (OUP 2012) 528.

83 See eg Report of the Secretary-General on the Activities of the United Nations Regional Office for Central Africa and on the Lord's Resistance Army-Affected Areas (20 May 2013) *UN Doc S/2013/297* [7].

84 *Ibid.*

85 The Constitution of the Sudan People's Liberation Movement SPLM (Their Words May 2008) available at <http://theirwords.org/> accessed 28 March 2021.

ing environmental sustainability as well as protecting and preserving the environment and ensuring sustainable utilization of natural resources. These commitments to sustainability need to be read in the context of the ongoing peace process between Sudan and South Sudan at the time. As referred to in section 2.3, the 2005 Comprehensive Peace Agreement concluded between the government of Sudan and the Sudan People's Liberation Movement (SPLM), which predates this constitution, includes arrangements on oil exploitation. In this context, the 2005 agreement determines in its chapter on wealth-sharing that 'sustainable utilization of oil as a non-renewable natural resource [should be] consistent with... national environmental policies, biodiversity conservation guidelines, and cultural heritage protection principles'.[86] The SPLM's commitments to sustainable use of natural resources therefore confirm the commitments set out in this agreement and are based on an explicit grant of authority to engage in natural resource exploitation.

Peace agreements regularly contain references to sustainability. While those in the 2005 Comprehensive Agreement on Sudan are fairly specific, other agreements contain more generic references to sustainability. The 1996 Abidjan Peace Agreement between the government of Sierra Leone and the RUF, for instance, states that the principles guiding the socio-economic policy of Sierra Leone include '[p]rotect[ing] the environment and regulat[ing] the exploitation of natural resources in the interest of the people'.[87] Likewise, the government of the Philippines and the Moro Islamic Liberation Front agree in a 2012 agreement - through which they establish the autonomous region Bangsamoro - that sustainable development is crucial for the protection of the quality of life of the people of Bangsamoro and that the latter will therefore 'develop a comprehensive framework for sustainable development through the proper conservation, utilization and development of natural resources'.[88] Lastly, environmental protection, both generally and related to natural resource exploitation, has been a recurring issue on the agenda of the peace talks between the Colombian government and the FARC and is a prominent

---

86   Comprehensive Peace Agreement Sudan (n 61).

87   Peace Agreement between the Government of the Republic of Sierra Leone and the Revolutionary United Front of Sierra Leone (Abidjan Peace Agreement) (30 November 1996) art 26 (h) <https://peacemaker.un.org/sierraleone-peace -agreement-RUF96> accessed 28 March 2021.

88   Framework Agreement on the Bangsamoro (15 October 2012) Chapter IV art 8 <https://peacemaker.un.org/sites/peacemaker.un.org/files/PH_121015_Frame workAgreementBangsamoro.pdf> accessed 28 March 2021.

GREENING THE ECONOMY OF ARMED CONFLICT

feature of the 2016 final agreement.[89] This shows that both parties have recognized the need to protect the environment throughout the conflict, notwithstanding the fact that they have not always acted on this.

The importance of the commitments included in these agreements should not be underestimated, even though they are often indirect and their implementation is sometimes faulty. Since armed groups are parties to these agreements, the commitments included therein are based on their explicit approval. The agreements thereby reflect the intention of those armed groups to be bound by relevant norms regarding sustainability of natural resource exploitation. At the same time, it is important not to lose sight of the context in which they were concluded. These agreements aim to pave the way for a transition from armed conflict to peace. This also implies that the armed groups signing those agreements are willing to take on commitments which they do not necessarily perceive as binding on them beyond the confines of the peace process. Furthermore, the majority of these commitments is too generic to draw meaningful conclusions regarding armed groups' adherence to environmental standards.

Whereas statements by armed groups regarding their environmental commitments are generally scarce and primarily made as part of peace agreements setting out power- and wealth sharing arrangements, DFIN-STE more readily formulate their intention to protect the environment. Many of these entities have included environmental provisions in their constitutive instruments. Article 5 of the constitution of Abkhazia, for instance, referred to in section 2.2, determines that 'Land and other natural resources [...] shall be used and protected in the Republic of Abkhazia as a basis of life and activities of its citizens'.[90] It further determines

---

89   See eg Agenda Común por el Cambio hacia una Nueva Colombia (Government of Colombia-FARC) (6 May 1999) <https://peacemaker.un.org/colombia-agenda nuevacolombia99> accessed 28 March 2021 which sets out the agenda for the renewed peace talks between the government and the FARC. This agenda includes an item 4 called 'Exploitation and conservation of natural resources', with 'Protection of the Environment on the basis of Sustainable Development' listed as item 4.3; See also Acuerdo de los Pozos (Government of Colombia-FARC)(9 February 2001) <https://peacemaker.un.org/colombia-acuerdopozos2001> accessed 28 March 2021 [10], in which the parties emphasize the strategic importance of working on the protection and rehabilitation of the environment; See also Final Agreement for Ending the Conflict and Building a Stable and Lasting Peace (24 November 2016) *UN Doc S/2017/272*, Annex II. There are many references to sustainability and environmental protection throughout the agreement.

90   See <https://unpo.org/article/697> accessed on 11 March 2020.

that 'issues of ownership, use and disposal of natural resources shall be governed by the laws of the Republic of Abkhazia', while Article 53(10) formulates an obligation for the President to pursue policy in the field of environmental protection and to ensure the integrity of relevant legislation.[91] There is however little information available on how Abkhazia has given effect to environmental protection in its legislation and policy.[92]

Some *de facto* entities have not only included references to environmental protection in their constitutions, but have also developed institutional mechanisms for environmental protection that are modelled after those of States. The Republic of Artsakh (Nagorno-Karabakh), for instance, determines in Article 12 of its Constitution that '[t]he State shall promote the preservation, improvement and restoration of the environment, the rational utilization of natural resources guided by the principle of sustainable development and taking into account the responsibility towards future generations.' This provision engages both with the principle of sustainable development and with intergenerational equity. The self-proclaimed republic has a Ministry of Nature Protection and Natural Resources in order to give effect to these principles by enacting relevant legislation. It can furthermore be derived from various sources that Artsakh has actually enacted relevant legislation for the protection of the environment and that this legislation is clearly designed to implement international norms and standards on environmental protection. Its most recent voluntary report to the UN General Assembly on its progress towards implementation of the Sustainable Development Goals, for instance, mentions that Artsakh is in the process of defining and establishing specially protected areas for the conservation of biological diversity,[93]

---

91   *Ibid.*

92   A report issued by the Swedish Palmecenter provides some indications of environmental protection measures being taken. It notes that '[i]n spite of resource limitations, some measures have been taken to protect the environment. Controls have been introduced over timber as well as mining.' It however also notes that there are 'strong concerns about the degradation of Abkhazia's unique environment' due to Abkhazia's waste water treatment and waste management systems being seriously outdated. See T Hammarberg and M Grono, 'Human Rights in Abkhazia Today' (Palmecenter July 2017)<www.palmecenter.se/wp-content/uploads/2017/07/Human-Rights-in-Abkhazia-Today-report-by-Thomas-Hammarberg-and-Magdalena-Grono.pdf> accessed 28 March 2021 75.

93   Mher Margaryan, National Review on Implementation of the Sustainable Development Goals, Republic of Artsakh (Nagorno-Karabakh): Transformation towards Sustainable and Resilient Societies, Annex to the Letter from the Permanent Representative of Armenia to the United Nations addressed to the

GREENING THE ECONOMY OF ARMED CONFLICT

as required by Articles 7 and 8 of the 1992 Biodiversity Convention.[94] It furthermore has enacted specific environmental legislation regarding the management of water, land and the protection of endangered species.[95]

Somaliland constitutes another example of a DFINSTE that actively engages with international environmental norms and standards. Article 12.4 of the Constitution of the Republic of Somaliland states that '[t]he protection and the best means of the exploitation of [the country's] natural resources shall be determined by law'.[96] Although this provision does not automatically demonstrate engagement with international standards with respect to environmental protection, it should be noted that Somaliland has in fact signed several multilateral environmental agreements and adopted specific environmental legislation, establishing dedicated institutional mechanisms to promote sustainable development, setting up procedures regarding environmental impact assessments as well as forestry and wildlife protection.[97]

These examples clearly demonstrate that DFINSTE more readily communicate their environmental policies. This does not necessarily imply that their environmental governance is well developed. The institutional structures and normative frameworks that DFINSTE have developed vary greatly. Furthermore, some of the more sophisticated legal frameworks and institutions developed by DFINSTE can in reality be empty facades to convince the international community that these entities function as 'normal' States.[98] Nevertheless, even if primarily facades, the establish-

---

Secretary-General (7 August 2019) *UN Doc A/74/282* 27. It should however be noted that progress is slow, since a Law on Specially Protected Natural Areas was adopted already in 2007. See Initial voluntary report – The Republic of Artsakh (Nagorno Karabakh Republic), Annex to the note verbale dated 14 February 2019 from the Permanent Mission of Armenia to the United Nations Office at Geneva addressed to the Office of the United Nations High Commissioner for Human Rights (2 April 2019) *UN Doc A/HRC/40/G/3* [43].

94 Convention on Biological Diversity (n 67)

95 See The Republic of Artsakh Annex to the note verbale (n 93) [23 47]. It is interesting to note that Artsakh reports on environmental measures as part of the implementation of the right to self determination.

96 See <http://www.somalilandlaw.com/environmental_laws.html> accessed 11 March 2020.

97 *Ibid.*

98 Olga Shashkina, 'Exploring Environmental Governance in Eastern Ukraine, (Conflict and Environment Observatory (21 May 2020) <https://ceobs.org/exploring -environmental-governance-in-eastern-ukraine/> accessed 6 July 2020. There can however also be very legitimate reasons for explaining why environmental legislation is not effectively implemented. A 2011 report by the UN Secretary-General on

206   6 – DAM-DE JONG

ment of dedicated institutions for environmental protection does show the first signs of awareness of the need for environmental conservation.

4   Greening Armed Groups

This article set out to explore the international legal framework for natural resource exploitation by armed groups and resulting obligations to protect the environment, whether directly binding on armed groups under international law or self-imposed. A first conclusion which can be drawn is that the international legal regime applicable to natural resource exploitation is ambivalent. Whereas this article argued that armed groups are precluded from claiming a right to freely dispose of natural resources based on the general rules of State representation and the human right to self-determination, it is precisely the protection of the inhabitants of territories under control of armed groups that necessitates the recognition of some rights for armed groups to exploit natural resources. Such rights can be based on an analogous application of the law of occupation. This would allow armed groups to exploit natural resources for the purpose of maintaining a civilian administration. The need to protect the civilian population furthermore underpins the international legal regime applicable to NIACs, as included in Article 3 of the 1949 Geneva Conventions and in Additional Protocol II. More specifically, the Martens clause provides that 'in cases not covered by the law in force, the human person remains under the protection of the principles of humanity and the dictates of the public conscience'.[99] This clause indicates that the well-being of the civilian population is paramount and should therefore always be taken into consideration in interpreting and applying the law.

---

the protection of Somali natural resources and waters, for instance, observed that '[t]he levels of competency of Somali institutions responsible for environmental affairs and natural resources differ widely depending on their history and experience. Attempts to establish new environmental policies and legislation, together with the respective institutions, have been made in the regional administrations of Somaliland and Puntland. The relevant ministries in those regional administrations have limited human resources, and there is very limited capacity to implement programmes at the regional and district level.' See 'Report of the Secretary-General on the Protection of Somali natural resources and waters', (25 October 2011) UN Doc S/2011/661 [24].

99   Protocol Additional to the Geneva Conventions of 12 August 1949, and Relating to the Protection of Victims of Non-International Armed Conflicts (Protocol II) (8 June 1977), preamble.

A second conclusion that can be drawn from this article is that the legal position of armed groups is not determinative of its engagement with international environmental standards, yet its political status does seem to make a difference. Whereas armed groups participating in a NIAC rarely publicly state their intention to protect the environment, except in the context of peace agreements concluded with the *de jure* authorities, the authorities of DFINSTE more readily formulate environmental policies. This difference may be a consequence of the aspirations of DFINSTE to be recognized as a State, yet armed groups fighting in a NIAC for the purpose of overthrowing the government may likewise have an interest in adhering to environmental standards, to achieve international recognition and/or to win the hearts and minds of the people. A more convincing explanation for the difference is that it is a matter of prioritization. Armed groups fighting in an active NIAC may simply have other priorities than groups that have been able to secure stable control over territory. If this assumption is correct, one way to 'green' natural resource exploitation by armed groups is to raise their awareness of the long-term effects on the environment and the health of the population caused by the use of toxic chemicals. Furthermore, as most of these groups aspire some form of international recognition, whether this be as the government of a (new) State or – at the very least – as belligerents, it is important that the international community clearly sets out its expectations with respect to environmental protection by armed groups more generally and, where possible, engages with these groups to green their practices. This approach may be counter-intuitive, but in the long-run it is nevertheless imperative for safeguarding the right of peoples to freely dispose of their natural resources.

7 Armed Groups and Emergent States

Legal and Pragmatic Approaches to Filling the Gaps in International Law

Tom Hadden[*]

Abstract

Much of international law is focused on the legal relations between established states. It has less to say about the rules governing the emergence of new states, whether as a result of exercises of self-determination, of internal armed conflict, or the status of those involved in campaigns by popular movements or armed groups as they pursue their objectives of boundary changes, autonomy or independence. And yet, as a study of political maps from decade to decade shows, changes of this kind are quite common and the absence of legal regulation or guidance and the insistence on the territorial integrity of established states often leads to sustained conflict. The purpose of this article is to suggest ways in which these gaps in international law can and should be filled by the development of more practical international guidance on a wide range of disputed issues: the way in which the exercise of the right of self-determination should be exercised; whether it should result in internal autonomy, external independence or other forms of statehood; and the legitimacy of violence in pursuit of remedial self-determination in response to repression and communal discrimination. More generally there is a need for greater focus in international law on the processes of transition in state formation rather than the protection of currently established states.

Keywords

Internal and external self-determination – negotiated and remedial self-determination – territorial integrity and boundary change – legitimacy of violence – status of armed groups – recognition of emerging states

---

[*] Professor of Law, Queen's University Belfast and Kent Law School.

1 Introduction

The well-known claim that 'one man's freedom fighter is another man's terrorist' encapsulates some significant and important fractures in international law. One set of legal rules under international human rights and humanitarian law encourages national peoples to assert, and in some limited cases discussed below, permits them to fight for self-determination and independence; another under the traditional international law of nations is focused on the rights of states to preserve their established territories and to deal exclusively with other states on that basis. But history tells us that states and their boundaries are neither permanent nor fixed and that political maps and boundaries change significantly over long periods as a result of wars, revolutions and peaceful break-ups.

This contribution is designed to highlight these fractures: (a) by illustrating the regularity of changes in state formation and dissolution and in their boundaries; (b) by highlighting the inconsistencies and deficiencies in international law in dealing with these developments; and (c) by suggesting how more realistic and less counter-productive principles and rules might be developed.

2 The Normality of Change in State Formation, Dissolution and Boundaries

The main branch of international law tends to operate on the basis that states are fixed and stable entities and that international law is primarily concerned with legal relations between them.[1] In reality many states are relatively short-lived, and their boundaries often change over the years. A comparison of historical maps of political entities in the eighteenth, nineteenth, twentieth and twenty-first centuries shows that while some states are stable within fixed boundaries, many others are not.[2] The question for international law and lawyers is how to respond to changes in state formation and their boundaries.

---

1   This focus can be traced back to Emerich de Vattel, *La Loi des Gens* [*The Law of Nations*] (first published in 1758); for a current leading exposition see James Crawford, *Brownlie's Principles of Public International Law* (OUP, 9th edn 2019).

2   A useful source is Geoffrey Barraclough (ed), *The Times Concise Atlas of World History* (Times Books 1982) with detailed maps of state boundaries from century to century.

ARMED GROUPS AND EMERGENT STATES

There are many reasons for these changes: wars, colonial land-grabs, ethnic conflicts, the exercise of the right of self-determination by minorities and other divided peoples and perhaps least often negotiated agreements on boundary changes. A few comments on each of these and the response of international law and lawyers may be appropriate.

2.1   *European Wars and Peace Settlements*

In Europe the primary cause of state dissolution and formation has been war and the ensuing peace settlements. The foundation of modern international law in respect of state-based treaties and territorial integrity is often, perhaps wrongly, attributed to the Westphalian carve-up of Europe following the Thirty Years' War in 1648.[3] There was a similar carve-up after the Napoleonic wars at the Congress of Vienna in 1814 resulting in the creation of Belgium and Luxembourg and the absorption of Norway by Sweden and of Finland by Russia.[4] At the Versailles Conference in 1919 after the Great War of 1914-18 large numbers of new states were created in the Baltic and the Balkans.[5] In these and other peace deals Poland has been divided, abolished and reconstituted on numerous occasions, all following military campaigns.[6] The redrawing of boundaries, the restoration of old kingdoms and the establishment of new ones was not for the most part carried out in accord with any formal legal principles or procedures, but as a result of great or victorious power politics. In the years after Versailles a number of plebiscites were carried out under the authority of the newly constituted League of Nations in an attempt to apply the principle of self-determination promoted by President Wilson in 1919. But this was not a call for national self-determination but for taking account of the interests of the populations affected by governmental decisions:

---

3   The so-called Westphalian settlement often quoted by international lawyers as the foundation of state-centred international law was not in fact such a simplistic operation but a multi-layered set of agreements between multi-national empires, individual rulers and independent cities; Andrias Osiander, 'Sovereignty, International Relations, and the Westphalian Myth' (2001) 55 *International Organization* 251.

4   For a readable account of these negotiations and the objectives of the victorious 'great powers' see Tim Chapman, *The Congress of Vienna 1814-1815* (Routledge 1998).

5   For a readable account see Alan Sharp, *The Versailles Settlement: Peacemaking after the First World War, 1919–1923* (Red Globe Press, 2nd ed 2008).

6   For a simple summary of the troubled history and delineation of Poland see Jerzy Lukowski and Hubert Zawadzki, *A Concise History of Poland* (CUP 2019).

> A free, open-minded, and absolutely impartial adjustment of all co-
> lonial claims, based upon a strict observance of the principle that
> in determining all such questions of sovereignty the interests of the
> populations concerned must have equal weight with the equitable
> claims of the government whose title is to be determined.[7]

These plebiscites resulted only in marginal adjustments to previously imposed settlements.[8]

The settlements imposed after the war of 1939-46 followed a similar
pattern. Some previous states were reconstituted, though most of these
were soon absorbed into the Soviet Union until its collapse in 1991 when
most regained effective independence. Since then, the process of state
boundary adjustment in Europe has continued following serious armed
conflicts in the Balkans, the Caucasus and Ukraine, resulting in the emergence of a number of new, though formally disputed states and territories
in Kosovo, Transnistria, Abkhazia and South Ossetia and Nagorno Karabakh.[9]

The role of international law and lawyers in these conflicts and
settlements has usually been limited to drawing up treaties to reflect
the outcome of wars and insurgencies and the ensuing political deals.
International law, as will be seen in section 3 below, forbids the changing
of established boundaries by force. The newer but contested doctrine
of humanitarian intervention and the desire of some states to regain
historical territory, however, has led to international interventions that
have often turned out to be unsustainable or the cause of further wars
and new settlements. The legal status of the resulting facts on the ground
is usually left to an unregulated political process of recognition or non-
recognition by other states.

2.2   *Colonial Carve-up and Independence*

In Africa, the Middle East and parts of South-east and South Asia states
and state boundaries were for the most part established by European colonial powers. In many cases, especially in Africa, these often cut across

---

7   Point V of the 'Fourteen Points' speech given by President Woodrow Wilson on 8
    January 1918, accessible at < https://www.ourdocuments.gov/doc.php?flash=false&
    doc=62&page=transcript> accessed 17 June 2021.

8   For a more detailed account see Patrick Thornberry, *International Law and the
    Rights of Minorities* (OUP 1991).

9   Some details and analysis of the constantly changing factual situation in these
    areas are discussed in sub section 3.2 below.

ARMED GROUPS AND EMERGENT STATES

existing governmental and ethnic territories. But when decolonisation became the new norm in the 1950s, self-determination and independent statehood were pursued under the United Nations Charter within those colonial boundaries, whether by agreement or following armed insurgencies by 'national' freedom fighters. There were few attempts to seek the consent to this approach of the 'peoples' who had been granted the right of self-determination under the Charter[10] and subsequently in 1966 in common article 1(1) of the International Covenants on Civil and Political and Economic, Social and Cultural Rights.[11] In 1970 the UN General Assembly passed a resolution specifying that self-determination could be achieved by full independence or by integration in or association with another territory.[12] But this was assumed to be an issue for the whole colonial territory and no procedures were provided for making such a choice.

During the same time-period there was pressure from newly independent third world states to legitimise the armed campaigns of 'freedom fighters' under international humanitarian law. This was eventually agreed in 1977 under Additional Protocol I to the four Geneva Conventions, accepting that peoples 'fighting against colonial domination and alien occupation and against racist regimes in the exercise of their right of self-determination' were entitled to status as legitimate combatants and thus to be treated as prisoners of war rather than as criminals when captured.[13] This was not explicitly restricted to armed groups representing colonial territories as a whole, but a General Assembly Resolution of

---

10   One of the purposes of the United Nations set out in article 1.2 of the UN Charter is 'to develop friendly relations among nations based on respect for the principle of equal rights and self-determination of peoples': Charter of the United Nations (1945) 1 UNTS XVI.

11   International Covenant on Civil and Political Rights (adopted 16 December 1966, entered into force 23 March 1976) 999 UNTS 171 (ICCPR), art 1(1); International Covenant on Economic, Social and Cultural Rights (adopted 16 December 1966, entered into force 3 January 1976) 993 UNTS 03 (ICESCR), art 1(1). 'All peoples have the right of self-determination. By virtue of that right they freely determine their political status and freely pursue their economic, social and cultural development'.

12   Declaration on Principles of International Law Concerning Friendly Relations and Co-operation among States in Accordance with the Charter of the United Nations, UNGA Res 2625 (24 October 1970): 'The establishment of a sovereign and independent State, the free association or integration with an independent State or the emergence into any other political status freely determined by a people constitute modes of implementing the right of self-determination by that people.'

13   Protocol I Additional to the four Geneva Conventions (adopted 8 June 1977, entered into force 7 December 1978) 1125 UNTS 3, (Protocol I), art 1(4).

1960 ruled out any action that would disrupt the national unity or territorial integrity of 'a country'.[14] This was amended in the General Assembly Resolution of 1970 to rule out any action that would 'dismember or impair, totally or in part, the territorial integrity or political unity of sovereign and independent states conducting themselves in compliance with the principle of equal rights and self-determination of peoples and thus possessed of a government representing the whole people belonging to the territory without distinction of any kind'.[15] This wording was repeated word for word in the Declaration and Programme of Action at the Vienna World Conference in 1993.[16] This attempt by repeated assemblies of established states to reconcile the right of self-determination with the principle of the territorial integrity of established states has not of course resolved the inherent difficulties and contradictions in this area of international law. The prevailing approach within the United Nations to the protection of minorities, as will be seen, is to favour the development of regional autonomy or national power-sharing within established state boundaries. The concept of what is now generally referred to as 'remedial self-determination' or 'remedial secession' in cases where the terms of the 1970 Resolution and the Vienna World Conference are not complied with has not been seriously addressed or developed at an international level, though it has been widely discussed and analysed.[17]

2.3   Ethnic Conflict, Separatist Self-determination Struggles and Annexations

Serious ethnic divisions in countries in which different communities have been thrown together by international actors in pursuit of their own interests have led to boundary changes and state partitions long before the right of self-determination was recognised in international law, as for

---

14   Declaration on the Granting of Independence to Colonial Countries and Peoples, UNGA Res 1514 (14 December 1960), para. 6.

15   UNGA Res 2625 (1970) (n 12).

16   Adopted by the World Conference on Human Rights in Vienna, 25 June 1993, para.2.

17   In its Advisory Opinion on Kosovo's Declaration of Independence on 22 July 2010, at para. 84, the International Court of Justice held explicitly that it was not necessary to rule or comment on the issue of remedial secession. There is a huge literature on legal and political approaches to this issue; for a general account from a conflict resolution perspective see Marc Weller, 'Settling Self-Determination Conflicts' (2009) 20 *European Journal of International Law* 111; for a comprehensive up-to-date review of the literature see Noe Cornago, 'Beyond Self-determination: Norms Contestation, Constituent Diplomacies and the Co-production of Sovereignty' (2017) 6 *Global Constitutionalism* 327.

ARMED GROUPS AND EMERGENT STATES   215

instance in the Netherlands in the 1830s, Greece and Turkey in the 1920s, Ireland in 1921, India in 1947 and Palestine in 1948.[18] It has also led to the annexation of territory inhabited by kin populations in order to unite them with their mother countries, as in Schleswig/Holstein in 1866.[19] The preferred approach in international law where boundary changes were not acceptable was to negotiate bilateral or international treaties under which states would agree to grant special rights and treatment to ethnic or linguistic minorities which the international community would guarantee, as for example in the Balkans in the 1880s and under the newly formed League of Nations in the 1920s in respect of Poland, Greece and Albania.[20] But these treaties proved insufficient to satisfy demands for ethnic consolidation, notably in the German annexation of parts of Czechoslovakia and Poland in 1938-39.

The formal adoption of self-determination as a fundamental human right, however, has encouraged members of ethnic minorities to break away from the states in which they have found themselves and to seek independence or integration or association with neighbouring kin states. This has led to prolonged internal armed conflict in cases where the dominant political or military community has resisted all attempts to create separate autonomous regions or break-away states. In Kashmir the territory has been divided between India and Pakistan, each claiming the whole territory, resisting any proposal for any form of joint or linked referendums and engaging in sporadic armed conflict on the issues.[21] In Biafra and Katanga the newly independent national governments of Ni-

---

18   Basic details of these events can be found in *The Times Concise Atlas of World History*, Barraclough (n 2).

19   German forces took control of the territory from Denmark, *ibid*.

20   For a detailed account of these treaties and the role of the League of Nations see Patrick Thornberry, *International Law and the Rights of Minorities* (Oxford University Press 1991).

21   During the partition of India in 1947 the ruling Maharaja of Jammu (majority-Hindu) and Kashmir (majority-Muslim) had to decide whether his territory should join India or Pakistan; as conflict developed the United Nations ruled that a referendum should be held on the issue, but India refused to allow this and there was serious armed conflict between Indian and Pakistani forces and local irregulars. Control of parts of the territory has since been divided between India and Pakistan and the United Nations still maintains a monitoring force along the 'line of control' established by the warring parties. Despite continuing demands for self-determination, sporadic unrest and a series of peace initiatives the Indian government has maintained effective control of most of the territory and resists the holding of a referendum. For an up-to-date account see Victoria Schofield, *Kashmir in Conflict* (I B Tauris 2021).

geria and Congo brutally suppressed attempts by resource-rich provinces to break away and establish their own independence.[22] In Sri Lanka the attempt by Tamils in the north and east to establish their own state led to twenty years of armed conflict and the eventual triumph of state forces in an equally brutal final assault on the insurgent Liberation Forces of Tamil Elim (LTTE) in their final area of control.[23]

In other cases, kin states have continued to intervene to annex or control territories in which 'their people' live. Massive Turkish forces intervened to block any form of unification with Greece, following a Greek Cypriot coup and established the Turkish Republic of Northern Cyprus.[24] Russian forces intervened in the Caucasus to secure control by pro-Russian Abkhazians and Ossetians of Abkhazia and South Ossetia from newly independent Georgia[25] and to assist dissident forces in establishing the break-away territory of Transnistria from Moldova.[26] More recently Russian forces have allegedly intervened in parts of Ukraine to support local pro-Russian populations in breaking away from national Ukrainian control.

Hardly any of these cases involved any attempt to consult the people of the territory concerned. In the case of Russian intervention in Crimea there was a hastily organised referendum though it has been alleged not to have been either free or fairly conducted.[27] Similar objections have been raised to a referendum in the Kurdish province of Iraq in 2017, not least as the territory claimed included oil-rich areas outside its established boundaries.[28] And the referendum in 2018 over independence for

---

22   Joshua, Castellino, 'The UN Principle of Self-Determination and Secession from Decolonized States: Katanga and Biafra' in Peter Radan and Aleksandar Pavkovic (eds) *The Ashgate Research Companion to Secession* (Routledge 2011).

23   For an overall account see Kallie Szczepanski, The Sri Lankan Civil War. available at <https://www.thoughtco.com/the-sri-lankan-civil-war-195086> accessed 2 February 2021.

24   The details of this invasion and the legal consequences are set out in *Cyprus v Turkey* 131 (2014), App no 25781/94 (ECHR, 12 May 2014).

25   The events are summarised in *Georgia v Russia* App no 38263/08 (ECHR, 21 January 2021).

26   The events are summarised in *Ilascu & others v Moldova & Russia* App no 48787/99 (ECHR, 8 July 2004).

27   Steven Pifer, 'Crimea Six Years after Illegal Annexation', available at <https://www .brookings.edu/blog/order-from-chaos/2020/03/17/crimea-six-years-after-illegal -annexation/> accessed on 2 February 2021.

28   Katie Klain and Lisel Hintz, The Kurdish referendum and its fall-out, available at <https://reliefweb.int/report/iraq/series-miscalculations-kurdish-referendum -and-its-fallout> accessed on 2 February 2021.

ARMED GROUPS AND EMERGENT STATES

Catalonia was declared unconstitutional in the Spanish courts and partially obstructed by Spanish police.[29]

International law and lawyers are rarely called on or listened to either in cases of attempts by politicians or armed groups to assert independence or in cases where some kind of referendum is proposed or held. The prevailing approach seems to await the outcome of the conflict before eventually accepting what has emerged. This is partly because the causes and outcomes in terms of state formation and recognition are determined by political and military forces rather than legal rules. But it is nonetheless unsatisfactory, as will be argued below, that the only firm rule of international law appears to be a ban on the use of force to secure change, a ban that is so widely ignored; and also, that there are no rules to regulate or influence the process of state formation or boundary change. The part of international law that governs relations between states – the law of nations appears to be more like a club where access is governed by established members rather than any more usual understanding of the rule of law.

2.4 Peaceful Exercise of Self-determination and Negotiated Boundary Changes

Peaceful transitions following political negotiation or legal adjudications fit much better with established international law, especially if two or more states enter into a treaty. But they are very much the exception rather than the rule.

In Ireland in the 1920s an attempt was made to assess the balance of assumed local preferences – though not to ask those concerned – in respect of the British government's decision to exclude six northern counties from the agreement with the newly constituted Irish Free State comprising the other twenty-six counties; but the findings of the internationally Boundary Commission were suppressed and ignored.[30] Another rare example was a regional referendum in northwest Cameroon resulting in the transfer of an English-speaking – in colonial parlance – area into neighbouring Nigeria.[31] The break-up of the Soviet Union and of Czechoslova-

---

29 Constitutional Court Judgment No. 31/2010, of June 28, 2010; Judgment 114/2017 of 17 October 2017 - translation available at <www.tribunalconstitucional.es.en/jurisprudencia> accessed 22 May 2021.

30 *Report of the Irish Boundary Commission 1925*, with an introduction by Geoffrey J Hand (Irish University Press 1969).

31 For a detailed account of this and related cases see Thomas D Musgrave, *Self-Determination and National Minorities* (Oxford University Press 2000).

kia into the Czech Republic and Slovakia was achieved by peaceful political negotiation rather than popular voting.[32] There have also been some governmentally agreed referendums, notably in Quebec and Scotland, though in neither case was a majority for change achieved.[33] Attempts to dictate outcomes or secure effective rulings in the International Court of Justice, as in Western Sahara, Palestine and Kosovo, as will be seen, have usually been unsuccessful. In contrast to national courts which can adjudicate under written constitutions, international courts have generally preferred not to lay down rules of international law on such difficult issues.

3 The Inadequacies of International Law

Why are international law and international lawyers reluctant to develop formal principles and rules to deal with changes in state boundaries, state dissolution and the formation of new states? And why do international courts avoid the related issues of how the right of self-determination can legitimately be implemented and how insurgent armed groups seeking to break away from established states and thus to determine their political status and freely pursue their economic, social and cultural development should be treated? These are difficult issues to which there are no easy answers. But some discussion of the underlying problems and of the way in which more helpful principles and rules might be developed is clearly needed.

3.1 *Undue Focus on the Law Governing Established States*

One primary reason is perhaps the commitment of international law to the preservation or restoration of the status quo for established states as the only proper subjects of this branch of law. Much of traditional international law – the law of nations – is focused on the creation and interpretation of bilateral and multi-lateral treaties between established states

---

32   R H Cox & E G Frankland, 'The Federal State and the Breakup of Czechoslovakia: An Institutional Analysis' (1995) 25(1) *Publius* 71-88.

33   The 1998 referendum in Quebec was challenged but upheld by the Canadian Supreme Court, on the basis of an eventual duty to negotiate in good faith, in *Reference re Secession of Quebec* (1998) 2 Supreme Court Reports 217; the Scottish referendum in 2014 was authorised with the consent of the United Kingdom government by the Scottish Parliament under the Scottish Independence Referendum Act 2013.

and on the adjudication of disputes between them. The Vienna Convention on the Law of Treaties of 1969 makes it clear that it applies only to states, 'The present Convention applies to treaties between States.'[34] It adds the formal definition that '"treaty" means an international agreement concluded between States "in written form and governed by international law ...'.[35] Agreements with armed groups or emergent states are not included, though peace and related agreements are regularly made between states and international bodies and insurgent groups.[36] Non-state bodies are also excluded from initiating or participating in cases at the International Court of Justice. Its statute and rules of procedure are based on the principle that only recognised states are entitled to seek its judgement or opinion on matters of dispute between them: 'only states may be parties'.[37] Signatory states have automatic status, as do others if they have deposited a declaration accepting the court's rulings and the obligations of UN Member States.[38] Many of the ICJ's cases are focused on these issues of status and procedure as those involved seek to achieve or avoid a substantive judgement.[39]

Emerging states and other aspiring armed groups are thus generally excluded from seeking adjudications of their rights under the rules of international law. A good example is the conclusion of the International Law Commission in 2001 in respect of responsibility for internationally wrongful acts, asserting that liability for such acts by an 'insurrectional movement that becomes the new Government of a State' prior to its recognition only becomes operative after recognition.[40] Nor are they able to rely on their potential status as freedom fighters exercising their right of self-determination under Protocol I of the Geneva Conventions since

---

34   Vienna Convention on the Law of Treaties (1969) 1155 UNTS 332, art 1.

35   *Ibid.* art 2(1)(a).

36   For a general account of their development and status see Christine Bell, *On the Law of Peace: Peace Agreements and the Lex Pacificatoria* (Oxford University Press 2008).

37   Statute of the International Court of Justice (1946) UKTS 67, art 34.

38   *Ibid.* art 35.

39   For a detailed account of these procedural disputes see Robert Kolb, *The International Court of Justice*, Ch VII (Hart Publishing 2014).

40   Draft Articles on Responsibility for Internationally Wrongful Acts, (adopted by the International Law Commission at its 63rd session, in 2011, and submitted to the UNGA as part of the Commission's report covering the work of that session (A/66/10)), art 10.

there is no specific international body with jurisdiction to make rulings on the application of the rules of international humanitarian law.[41]

On the other hand, though international lawyers are reluctant to hold non-state groups liable for human rights violations on the grounds that they are not permitted to become parties to international human rights conventions,[42] individual members of insurgent groups and leaders of emergent states are in practice more at risk than representatives of established states of being held to account for violations of international humanitarian law. Individual members of armed groups are also liable to severe sanctions as terrorists under most national criminal laws. They are also more likely to be charged and convicted in cases at international criminal courts since members of state forces are typically protected by their governments.[43]

There are, however, some potential openings for development. The International Court of Justice can be asked by the General Assembly to give advisory opinions on issues that include the rights and liabilities of non-state bodies.[44] A good example is the advisory opinion on *The Wall* in respect of the self-determination rights of Palestinians.[45] There have also been some recent expert reports to the Human Rights Council, for example in respect of the continuing conflict in Yemen, stating that both state and non-state forces are responsible for human rights violations within the area of their control as well as for breaches of international humani-

---

41   It is the policy of the International Committee of the Red Cross not to make rulings on the issue and neither the Protecting Powers under the main Geneva Conventions nor the Independent Humanitarian Fact-Finding Commission under Protocol I (n 13) art 90 have ever done so.

42   The leading human rights NGOs, Amnesty International and Human Rights Watch, adopted this view in holding that armed groups could only be accountable under the law of armed conflict. The European Court of Human Rights has also adopted this view in a series of recent cases in which human rights violations by armed groups have been attributed to neighbouring states that have been held to have been in a dominant position in the territories concerned, as in *Ilascu v Moldova & Russia*, (n 26).

43   Under the Statute of the International Criminal Court, governments can protect their own forces by instituting their own inquiries and decisions on prosecutions (art 17) and can also refer cases of alleged violations by non-state forces to the ICC Prosecutor (arts 13-14): Rome Statute of the International Criminal Court (1998) 2187 UNTS 38544.

44   Statute of the International Court of Justice (n 37) art 65.

45   Legal Consequences of the Construction of a Wall in the Occupied Palestinian Territory (Advisory Opinion) [2004] ICJ Rep 136.

ARMED GROUPS AND EMERGENT STATES

tarian law under the Geneva Conventions and Protocols.[46] And national courts are beginning to reflect the rules of international humanitarian law on the status of allegedly terrorist organisations in their counter-terrorism policies.[47]

3.2 *No Clear Rules for the Recognition of Newly Emerging States*

A further related problem is that there are no binding rules for the recognition of newly emerging or aspiring states. The 1933 Montevideo Convention on the Rights and Duties of States (Montevideo Convention) sets out some basic criteria:

> The state as a person of international law should possess the following qualifications: (a) a permanent population; (b) a defined territory; (c) government; and (d) capacity to enter into relations with the other states.[48]

The Convention also rules out the recognition of any forcible change in the territorial integrity of an established state:

> The contracting states definitely establish as the rule of their conduct the precise obligation not to recognize territorial acquisitions or special advantages which have been obtained by force whether this consists in the employment of arms, in threatening diplomatic representations, or in any other effective coercive measure. The territory of a state is inviolable and may not be the object of military occupation nor of other measures of force imposed by another state directly or indirectly or for any motive whatever even temporarily.[49]

These provisions clearly place recognition of any change in the hands of established states. In practice the criterion for acceptance as a new

---

46 Report of the Group of Eminent International and Regional Experts on Yemen to the Human Rights Council, 17th August 2018, UN Doc. A/HRC/39/43.

47 A prosecution against Kurdish PKK suspects in Belgium was suspended on the ground that it had not been shown that the PKK was operating as terrorists in breach of the provisions of Protocol I to the Geneva Conventions: Belgian Court of Cassation on 28 January 2020.

48 Montevideo Convention on Rights and Duties of States (adopted 26 December 1933, entered into force 26 December 1934) 165 LNTS 19; it should be noted that the Convention is not widely ratified and that its provisions may not all be regarded as customary international law.

49 *Ibid.* art 11.

member of the international legal order is formal or *de facto* recognition by other established states. It is unclear whether there is any minimum requirement for general acceptance as a state or whether international law applies only between mutually recognising states.

The rules for acceptance as a Member State of the United Nations illustrate this lack of clarity, not least as acceptance as a Member State may not constitute recognition by all other Members. The Charter provides that membership is 'open to all ... peace-loving states which accept the obligations contained in the present Charter, and in the judgement of the Organization, are able and willing to carry out these obligations'.[50] But the decision on admission is granted to the General Assembly only 'upon the recommendation of the Security Council'.[51] This means that any Permanent Member can block acceptance indefinitely: for example, Palestine which is recognised by 137 Member States was finally admitted to 'non-member observer status' by the General Assembly in 2012 but was rejected by the Security Council for full membership;[52] Transnistria which declared independence in 1990 and is recognised by only three other unrecognised entities and no current UN Members, has no status within the UN; and Kosovo which declared independence in 2012, is currently recognised by 102 UN Members but is treated by the UN as a territory under UN administration (UNMIK).[53]

3.3 *No Clear Rules for the Legitimacy or Otherwise of Self-determination*

Nor are there any rules to govern the legitimacy or otherwise of the exercise of the right of peoples to self-determination. Despite the high profile of the concept in the UN Charter, in the International Bill of Rights,[54] and in other UN documents the international law bodies have sought to avoid making any binding or clear decisions on how it is to be applied in particular circumstances. All that has been stated in the context of de-colonisation, as has been seen, is that self-determination may be exercised by creating a new state, integrating with another state or emerging into any other political status, but must not dismember or impair the territorial

---

50   *Ibid.* Art 4.1.

51   *Ibid.* Art. 4.2.

52   UNGA Res 67/19 (29 November 2012).

53   The United Nations Interim Administration Mission in Kosovo (UNMIK) was initially authorised by UNSC Res 1244 (1999) and its mandate has since been regularly renewed.

54   Art 1.2 UN Charter (n 10) & art 1.1 ICCPR (n 11).

ARMED GROUPS AND EMERGENT STATES

integrity of any established democratic and non-discriminatory state.[55] The Human Rights Committee in the *Lubicon Lake Band* case concerning a claim by a first nation people in Canada refused to rule on the issue on the ground that the Optional Protocol under the ICCPR provided only for individual rather than group applications.[56] The International Court of Justice in the *Western Sahara* case also failed to reach any precise or binding decision on how the right should be applied and who would be entitled to vote in the circumstances of the case; the basic issue remains unresolved in the hands of a succession of international working groups.[57] And in its advisory opinion on Kosovo the International Court of Justice decided that there was nothing in international law that prevented an emerging state from declaring its independence.[58] But it found it convenient not to address the issue of 'remedial self-determination' in cases where the established state is not possessed of a government representing the whole people of the territory without discrimination of any kind. The legitimacy of the use of violence by those 'fighting against colonial domination or racist regimes in pursuit of their right to self-determination' under international humanitarian law has also been avoided by the Court and international lawyers continue to argue about the status of this provision in non-colonial situations.[59]

As a result, it is left to those claiming to exercise the right of self-determination to adopt their own procedures and for other states to decide whether to accept or reject their validity. In the growing number of disputed territories, such as Kashmir, Transnistria, Nagorno Karabakh, Kurdish Iraq, Crimea and eastern Ukraine, international law is notable by its absence, other than of course support for the principle of territorial integrity.

---

55   UNGA Res 2625 (1970) (n 12).

56   *Ominayak (on behalf of Lubicon Lake Band) v Canada*, Merits, Communication No 167/1984, UN Doc CCPR/C/38/D/167/1984.

57   Western Sahara (Advisory Opinion) [1975] ICJ Rep 12.

58   *Accordance with International Law of the Unilateral Declaration of Independence of Kosovo (Advisory Opinion)* [2010] ICJ Rep 403; in the more recent *Legal Consequences of the Separation of the Chagos Archipelago From Mauritius in 1965 (Advisory Opinion)* [2019] ICJ Rep 169, however, the ICJ focused almost exclusively on the law and procedures for de-colonisation rather than any concern for the rights of the islanders to self-determination.

59   Additional Protocol I to the Geneva Conventions 1977 (n 13), art 1.

3.4   *No Procedures for Transition*

Finally, there are no formal principles or procedures to guide those seeking self-determination on how to gain international support for an orderly transition from their current to possible future structures or for affected states on how to respond. There is huge emphasis in human rights courts and institutions and in academic writing on transitional justice.[60] There is no equivalent focus or interest in transitional legitimacy. As so often in legal thinking, there has been an undue focus on maintaining or restoring the status quo or compensating those affected by forced changes rather than accommodating and regulating the processes of justifiable changes in the status quo.

4   Filling the Gaps in International Law

The argument thus far has been that international law in focusing so heavily on the stabilisation of post-war and post-colonial settlements and the protection of the interests of a self-recognising and self-interested club of established states has failed to recognise or provide for more peaceful and legitimate modes of transition in state boundaries and state creation. This will involve a difficult choice between different ways of achieving the best outcome for all the peoples affected. In what might be termed the human rights and equality model it is the duty of every state, whatever its territorial boundary and population mix, to provide a structure within which every individual and every ethnic, religious or linguistic community enjoys the same rights and the same proportional and effective involvement in the processes of governance. One approach to this choice, which might be thought of as the established view in international law, is to seek to achieve this outcome within the boundaries of every currently established state. This is may be achieved by general good governance, including the grant of various forms of internal self-government. The other, which might be thought of as the remedial approach, is based on what is sometimes the more pragmatic and perhaps realistic view that in many established states the dominant community has failed to achieve the human rights ideal in its treatment of non-dominant communities and that those populations, if they qualify as a people, should therefore be entitled to break away and create

---

60   For an overall historical and current assessment see Cheryl Lawther, Luke Moffett and Dov Jacobs (eds), *Research Handbook on Transitional Justice* (Elgar 2017).

their own autonomous or independent structures which will better deliver human rights to all their people. This may be achieved by various forms of external self-determination, whether by peaceful negotiation, by negotiation during or after violent protests or insurrection or by the acceptance of a declaration of independence or the loss of control over break-away territory. This is a difficult choice because, also in reality, those who succeed in breaking free from abusive regimes often treat their own minorities badly and thus also fail to comply with their human rights duties.

If the remedial approach is accepted as valid in even a small number of cases, what is now required is some internationally accepted guidance on appropriate procedures for the valid exercise of the right to external self-determination and the progressive recognition of emergent states. These should include: (i) guidance on how to define the territory concerned; (ii) guidance on whether internal or external self-determination is potentially legitimate; (iii) guidance on the circumstances in which external remedial self-determination is legitimate; (iv) some minimum standards for an acceptable majority of voters, given that a simple majority in what is often a divided community may generate further conflict; (v) some rules for international supervision or monitoring of the campaign and voting arrangements; (vi) guidance on the legitimacy of violence; (vii) guidance on state engagement with armed groups; (viii) guidance on the rights and responsibilities of armed groups and emerging states; and (ix) some rules on the extent to which and at what stages in the evolution of emergent states other established states and international organisations should be expected or required to recognise them. These are issues that need to be considered in a sequential order since each stage in the assessment is important to any overall conclusion on the legitimacy of any claim and of action in pursuing it. It must be remembered, however, that none of the overlapping and interrelated concepts involved can be precisely defined. That is why what is required is a set of flexible guidelines on the factors to be taken into account in dealing with them all.

4.1 Guidance on Territorial Issues

In so far as there are any established principles or practice on the implementation of self-determination it is that it should be in respect of the population or people of a historically defined territory, whether a previ-

226   7 – HADDEN

ous state or a current administrative area.[61] The difficulty with this is that the concept of a 'people' or the closely related concept of a minority is not territorially determined.[62] The widely adopted Capotorti definition of a minority is:

> a group which is numerically inferior to the rest of the population of a State and in a non-dominant position, whose members possess ethnic, religious or linguistic characteristics which differ from those of the rest of the population and who, if only implicitly, maintain a sense of solidarity, directed towards preserving their culture, traditions, religion or language.[63]

The main additional element likely to be required to qualify as a 'people' seeking a right of self-determination by secession is some kind of territorial concentration, if only because the option of creating a new independent state or joining with another seems to require a defined territory. But this will often not correspond with internal historical or administrative boundaries, which in some cases may have been created in order to make secession difficult. In respect of Kashmir, for example, the Muslim dominated area of the Vale of Kashmir is joined both historically and administratively with Jammu which has a Hindu majority, thus making claims for self-determination in Kashmir alone more problematic.[64] In other cases, such as the Kurdish dominated areas of Turkey, Syria, Iraq and Iran, the members of a 'people' are divided between different established states none of which are willing to allow them to join together in any form of self-determination.[65]

The guidance on these issues that would be most useful would be the relevance of the degree of concentration in a particular area, the extent to

---

61   This is not formally laid down but can be deduced from the way in which decisions on referendums on independence or autonomy have been formulated; for a general account see Marc Weller (ed), *Universal Minority Rights, A Commentary on the Jurisprudence of International Court and Treaty Bodies* (Oxford University Press 2007).

62   It was this issue that caused difficulty for the International Court of Justice in its Advisory Opinion on the claim of the Sahari people (n 57).

63   Francesco Capotorti, Study on the rights of persons belonging to ethnic, religious and linguistic minorities, UN ref. ST/HR(05)/H852/no.5 (1991).

64   Schofield (n 21).

65   The demands for Kurdish self-determination are complicated as a result of the undertakings which appeared to have been granted in the aftermath of the war of 1914-18.

ARMED GROUPS AND EMERGENT STATES

which the distinctive ethnic or linguistic or possibly religious population in the area dominates all other components and whether the territory can be easily differentiated or separated from the rest of the state territory; it might also be helpful to include some account of the historical basis of that concentration and its likely maintenance.

4.2 Guidance on the Choice between Internal and External Self-determination

A closely related issue is whether a people – or a minority – is to be granted a right to secede or a measure of internal self-government. The extent of territorial concentration and the physical location of that concentration is important for both purposes.

There is a general preference in state practice and in international documents for internal self-determination, if only as it is likely to be less contentious and more easily reconciled with territorial integrity.[66] The extensive set of internationally agreed declarations and conventions on the treatment of minorities point towards a choice between general provisions on non-discrimination, fair participation and the encouragement of integration and at the furthest extreme the creation of autonomous regions within state boundaries. Though there is no mention of minority rights in the Universal Declaration of Human Rights, since the 1960s there has been a progressive development of international instruments on the issues. The International Covenant on Civil and Political Rights states only that of *member*s of ethnic, religious, or linguistic minorities 'shall not be denied the right, in community with other members of their group to enjoy their own culture, to profess and practise their own religion or to use their own language.[67] By the 1990s international concern over the risks of violence stemming from the denial by states of the rights and interests of minorities led in Europe to the Helsinki Final Act and the Copenhagen Document within the Organisation for Security and Cooperation in Europe[68] and then to the UN Minorities Declaration of 1992, all of which focused on the duty of states to protect the existence of minorities and to promote their cultures and languages. The UN Declaration

---

66   This is the approach of the OSCE High Commissioner on National Minorities in a series of recommendations on dealing with internal ethnic tensions, available at <www.osce-hcnm.org> accessed 22 May 2021.

67   ICCPR (n 11) art 27.

68   Final act of the 1st CSCE Summit of Heads of State or Government 1975; Document of the Copenhagen Meeting of the Conference on the Human Dimension of the CSCE, 1990.

specifically provided that persons belonging to minorities shall have 'the right to participate effectively in decisions on the national and, where appropriate, regional level concerning the minority to which they belong or the regions in which they live, in a manner not incompatible with national legislation'.[69] Similar provisions were developed for indigenous peoples to have extensive rights on their cultures, their land and their environments and some form of communal decision-making on a communal rather than a purely territorial basis on matters that have a direct impact on their lifestyles: 'Indigenous peoples, in exercising their right to self-determination, have the right to autonomy or self-government in matters relating to their internal and local affairs, as well as ways and means for financing their autonomous functions'.[70] Though indigenous peoples had campaigned successfully for the inclusion of a reference to self-determination, however, established states insisted on a restatement of the principle of territorial integrity.[71]

It should be noted that territorial concentration is not essential for other forms of internal self-determination. In Belgium, for example, internal functional self-determination has been granted to linguistic communities on a non-territorial basis along with a structure for three main self-governing territories: Flanders, Wallonia and Brussels.[72]

The criteria on which some more detailed guidance would be helpful are those which differentiate a right to external self-determination from those which would justify various forms of internal self-determination. These would include, in addition to those identified in the Capotorti definition, the numerical strength, the degree of concentration and the extent of predominance of the aspirant population in a particular area; the location of the area and whether there are historical or geographic

---

69 Declaration on the Rights of Persons Belonging to National or Ethnic, Religious and Linguistic Minorities, Adopted by General Assembly Resolution 47/135 (18 December 1992), art 2.3.

70 United Nations Declaration on the Rights of Indigenous Peoples (13 September 2007) UN Doc A/Res/61/295, art 3.

71 *Ibid.*, art 46.1: Nothing in this Declaration may be interpreted as implying for any State, people, group or person any right to engage in any activity or to perform any act contrary to the Charter of the United Nations or construed as authorizing or encouraging any action which would dismember or impair, totally or in part, the territorial integrity or political unity of sovereign and independent States.

72 For a simple account see Tom Hadden & Elizabeth Craig, *Integration and Separation: Rights in Divided Societies* (Fortnight Educational Trust 2000) 8-11; for a general survey see Colin Harvey and Alex Swartz, (eds), *Rights in Divided Societies* (Hart Publishing 2012).

ARMED GROUPS AND EMERGENT STATES

circumstances that would make it feasible to draw coherent boundaries; and the presence in the immediate area of kin populations with which the seceding territory might be joined.[73]

4.3   Guidance on Remedial Self-determination

Any preference among established states for various forms of internal self-determination or autonomy, however, can be outweighed by the extent of discrimination, ill-treatment or exclusion of either a minority or a people under the concept of so-called remedial self-determination, in cases where internal self-determination is denied and some, though perhaps not all, the criteria for negotiated external self-determination are met. As already indicated, the concept of a continuing right to self-determination separate from decolonisation was introduced in 1970 and reaffirmed in the Vienna Declaration in 1993 as an exception to the principle of territorial integrity in cases in which states are not 'conducting themselves in compliance with the principle of equal rights and self-determination of peoples and thus possessed of a government representing the whole people belonging to the territory without distinction of any kind'.[74]

This formulation would apply most directly to minority communities that have been effectively excluded from any participation in the processes of government or threatened with absorption or elimination. There are many examples of this in both historical and current times. Some of the most salient current cases are those of the Kurds in Turkey, the Rohingya in Myanmar and the Uighurs in Sinjiang, in all of which there have been sustained campaigns for remedial self-determination in response to state policies aimed at the suppression of their distinctive identity and culture, resort to public protest and ultimately armed action in response to state repression. The doctrine might also apply to those communities whose rights as minorities under the conventions and declarations adopted in recent years have been consistently rejected or ignored.

One of the conditions under which external remedial self-determination can be regarded as legitimate, however, is a commitment by those in control of the seceding territory to respect the human rights of all its inhabitants and in particular those of new minorities that may

---

73   Though it has not been developed on the basis of a right to self-determination, the recent discussions on the transfer to Serbia of the mainly Serbian North Mitrovica enclave within Kosovo is an example of a pragmatic approach to a change in established boundaries.

74   UNGA Res 2625 (1970) (n 15) and the World Conference on Human Rights, 1993 (n 16).

be created as a result. A useful example might be the insistence by the European Union to an equivalent principle in respect of states seeking to join the Union.

Continuing denial that the concept of remedial self-determination constitutes a principle of international law would in effect deny the validity of most other minority rights since they have been adopted by similar General Assembly resolutions and international affirmations. In most cases the grant of one or other of the many forms of internal self-determination or autonomy will be sufficient compliance. But where the criteria of minority status, territorial concentration and clear majority status in that territory are met but the grant of any form of internal self-determination or autonomy is refused, the validity of claims for external remedial self-determination by secession is difficult to dispute.

4.4 *Guidance on Voting and Required Majorities*

The idea that a simple majority of voters in a referendum on independence or other change of status for a given territory is sufficient is also problematic. The concept of a people with a territory and a shared aspiration for secession or autonomy, as already indicated, assumes that there is an overwhelming consensus or at least a very clear majority view within the territory. If the territory contains large numbers of others opposed to any such change or if the majority in favour may well be overturned in a subsequent election or referendum, it is not evident that the people as a whole have opted for such a major constitutional change. A marginal result either way may also result in increased communal tension and lead to demands for a rerun. This suggests that in any referendum a weighted majority of some kind, or at the very least a clear majority of the population entitled to vote, should be required to establish legitimacy. In many states a weighted majority is required for internal constitutional change. And in the 2006 referendum in Montenegro on secession from what was the former Yugoslavia – in practice from Serbia as the only other remaining component – and to allow an application for EU membership, the European Union required a majority of at least 55%.[75]

As stability in the longer term as well as immediate legitimacy should be a significant criterion for a newly emergent states or autonomous

---

75   The 55% requirement was set by the Montenegrin Parliament in coordination with the European Union: see <https://www.cfr.org/backgrounder/montenegros -referendum-independence> accessed 22 February 2021; the result in May 2006 was 55.5% in favour.

ARMED GROUPS AND EMERGENT STATES 231

territory, guidance on the kind of majority required in particular cases would be helpful.

4.5 Guidance on International Supervision or Monitoring

If the implementation of the principle of self-determination of peoples is to be regulated by international law, international supervision or monitoring of the process should be available. International monitoring of ordinary political elections is now expected and widely implemented by international bodies. It should be extended to all aspects of the organisation and implementation of self-determination including in particular the formal procedures for initiation, the designation and registration of eligible voters and the preparation for and actual conduct of any national or regional referendum.

4.6 Guidance on the Legitimacy of Violence

A different though related set of issues arise when peaceful claims for internal or external self-determination are rejected and communal violence and then freedom fighters emerge. As already noted, freedom fighters are granted a measure of legitimacy in Additional Protocol I to the four Geneva Conventions if they are fighting against alien domination and racist regimes in pursuit of their right to self-determination.[76] If the concepts of alien domination and racism are viewed as a reflection of those of the absence of representative government and the discrimination specified in respect of remedial self-determination, they are granted equal status to that of the state forces they are opposing under that part of international humanitarian law that governs the conduct of armed conflict, known as *ius in bello*. As such they are entitled to be treated as prisoners of war and cannot be held criminally liable for their mere participation in the fighting. It is clear under the Protocol, however, that freedom fighters must adhere to the principles of international humanitarian law in their choice of targets and proportionality in the impact of their operations.

This raises a difficult question under another branch of international law governing the resort by states to the use of force in pursuit of their legitimate objectives, known as *ius ad bellum*. The basic principle set out in the United Nations Charter is that states are not entitled to use force in their relations with other states unless specifically authorised by the

---

76   Additional Protocol I to the Geneva Conventions, 1977 (n 13).

Security Council.[77] But this is subject to the right of individual and collective self-defence against an armed attack by other states which is well established in customary international law and specifically guaranteed under article 51 of the United Nations Charter. If freedom fighters representing peoples whose right to self-determination has been denied and whose legitimate peaceful protests have been met with state force, they should similarly be entitled at least to a right of self-defence. And as already argued, the grant to them of equal status to state forces under international humanitarian law gives to them the right to engage in lawful acts of war, as is also indirectly recognised for state forces in international human rights law under the European Convention on Human Rights.[78] This position is recognised by the leading human rights NGOs, Human Rights Watch and Amnesty International, both of which routinely assess the actions of armed groups under international humanitarian law.[79]

The legitimacy of violent protest and armed struggle in situations that fall below the criteria of Protocol I and are governed by Common Article 3, customary IHL and/or and Protocol II is less clear and in need of further explanation. In principle the rights to resistance and self-defence in the face of state repression and violence should be upheld, subject to the general criteria of proportionality and minimum humanitarian standards. In international as opposed to national law, however, the main focus is likely to be initially on the legitimacy of state action in response to organised communal action in pursuit of legitimate claims to internal self-determination or if that is denied to external self-determination as outlined above. It may then shift to the legitimacy of international support for those engaged in such organised internal communal or armed resistance or assertions of external independence. But when peaceful resistance escalates into organised armed action and non-international armed conflicts, international law clearly shifts its focus again towards compliance with international humanitarian and armed conflict law, as for example in respect of the ANC in South Africa. And this focus clearly applies to all forms of non-international armed conflict whether

---

77   Art. 2.3-4 of the UN Charter (n 10).

78   European Convention on Human Rights (ECHR), art. 15.2, authorising a derogation in respect of lawful acts of war from the right to life under art 2 during a state or emergency.

79   Amnesty International, *Putting the Spotlight on Armed Opposition Groups*, AI Index ACT 3372/79; Human Rights Watch, Annual Report 2010: *Civilian Protection and Middle East Armed Groups* by Joe Stork, <https://www.hrw.org/node/259102> accessed on 10 March 2021.

ARMED GROUPS AND EMERGENT STATES

in the context of de-colonisation or claims for internal or external self-determination within or out of established states.

These are difficult issues but should not for that reason be regarded as beyond the scope of international law and of principled guidance. One of the reasons that peoples seeking remedial self-determination resort to violence is that there is no other way of achieving it, since there is currently no effective way of pursuing it by legal action. The starting point should be guidance on the legitimacy of the claim to remedial self-determination under international human rights law followed by guidance on the resort to violence under general international law, though it is largely silent on the legitimacy of the resort to violence within established states. Finally, guidance on the legitimacy of the methods of armed conflict adopted under the law of armed conflict is needed. As argued below, this guidance is likely to focus on the commitment and performance of organised armed groups to the applicable principles of both branches of international law.

4.7   Guidance on State Engagement with Armed Groups

A closely related issue is whether and in what circumstances state governments should be expected to engage with the representatives of armed groups. The formal position in international law, at least as currently formulated within the United Nations, is that any form of organised armed action in pursuit of political objectives is likely to be regarded as terrorism and that states should not engage with those responsible.[80] In practice, however, states regularly open unofficial channels of communication or negotiation with armed groups and this is widely regarded as a useful way of moving towards a peaceful political settlement.[81] There is some basis in international practice, both historically in terms of parlaying between opposing armies, for the grant of safe conduct to those involved and more recently, for example under the Mitchell Principles

---

80   As required under UNSC Res 1273 (1999) and regulated by the Counter-Terrorism Committee; for a critical account see the report of the UN Special Rapporteur of the Human Rights Council on the promotion and protection of human rights and fundamental freedoms while countering terrorism, UN Doc A/73/361 (3 September 2018).

81   For a survey of contacts and negotiations of this kind see Jonathan Powell, *Talking to Terrorists* (Bodley Hewad 2014).

in Northern Ireland, for requiring a cessation of hostilities while negotiations take place.[82]

The formal position under European human rights law is also unhelpful in focusing exclusively on State responsibility rather than that of armed groups in effective control of break-away territories, as in respect of the ruling that Moldova should have exercised greater diplomatic efforts to regain control of Transnistria while only Russia was held responsible for violations by the breakaway authorities.[83] In its latest decision in the interstate case of *Georgia v Russia* the European Court of Human Rights has reverted to a strict separation of the law of armed conflict in respect of active hostilities and human rights responsibilities when control by invading forces has been established without again any consideration of the responsibilities of emergent state authorities.[84]

Some initial guidance on all these issues would clearly be appropriate, at least until some more general rules of conduct could be formulated.

4.8 Guidance on the Rights and Responsibilities of Armed Groups and Emerging States

One of the key issues for discussion in this collection has been the extent to which armed groups and emergent states are or should be bound by international human rights law, environmental law and trade law in addition to international humanitarian law. They are clearly already bound by the laws of armed conflict as soon as their operations reach the level of intensity or territorial control to trigger Article 3 common to the four Geneva Conventions, Additional Protocol II or, in exceptional cases, all four Geneva Conventions and Protocol I thereto in line with Article 1(4) of the latter. There is also some support in expert reports to the UN Human Rights Council for the application of some socio-economic human rights in territories under effective control by armed groups.[85] The best general approach for human rights law would appear to be to tailor the extent of such obligations to the extent of practical control and deliverability,

---

82 A set of principles or conditions on which future peace negotiations in Northern Ireland should be based devised by US Senator George Mitchell, included in a January 1996 report on weapons decommissioning; available at <https://cain .ulster.ac.uk/events/peace/docs/gm24196.htm> accessed 19 Feb 2021.

83 *Ilascu and Others v Moldova and Russia* App no 48787/99 (ECHR, 3 July 2004).

84 *Georgia v Russian (II)* App no 38263/08 (ECHR, 21 Jan 2021).

85 Report of the Group of Eminent International and Regional Experts on Yemen to the Human Rights Council (n 46).

ARMED GROUPS AND EMERGENT STATES

on the principle that responsibility should follow functional control.[86] This could be accompanied by internationally organised monitoring, assistance and training in the delivery of essential rights. But it might be counter-productive to insist on complete adherence to all the provisions of relevant human rights conventions as a condition of any form of responsibility. The achievement of overall compliance should be regarded as a matter for progressive action, as with the general principle for all established states of the progressive realisation of social-economic rights in accordance with the available financial and other resources.

4.9   *Guidance on International Recognition*

When the governance of a breakaway territory has become more stable, and its borders are more clearly delineated, the related question of international recognition becomes more significant. There is a wide range of rights that armed groups and especially emerging states should in principle be granted, such as the right to join international organisations, the right to become parties to international conventions and the right to take legal action against other states. As suggested above, the starting point in this might be decisions by international agencies and bodies that are not wholly subject to veto by any of the existing membership. The issue of more general recognition by other states is likely to be more problematic. In current international law, as already indicated, this is left entirely to the diplomatic policies of individual established states. In principle a similar approach to that suggested above based on the functional capacity of an emerging state to meet the relevant obligations involved would appear to be appropriate. And if all the criteria and procedures set out above in respect of the processes of self-determination and the acceptance of human rights responsibilities are complied with, there should be an expectation of international recognition, if necessary through a UN General Assembly or Security Council resolution or requirement.

5   Conclusions

The absence of rules of this kind contributes to the tendency of marginalised ethnic communities, often in ethnic frontier zones at the borders of

---

86   This was suggested by Lea Raible in an unpublished outline in Belfast in 2019, entitled 'International Law's Authority and Non-State Actors' (on file with author); for a different view see Amrei Müller, in her contribution to this special issue.

established states, to resort to communal protests, other forms of political campaigning and various forms of violent action in order to achieve changes that need to happen and often eventually do happen in the aftermath of localised insurgency or international wars.[87] But international lawyers at the behest of established states continue to be wary of any move to encourage or legitimise the break-up of those established states on the ground that it would lead to even greater instability and conflict. That is a dispute that cannot be resolved by legal arguments alone. As the concept of self-determination is so well-established, however, and is already such an incentive for conflict and insurgency, a serious attempt to develop a comprehensive set of international principles or guidelines on how it should be handled in international law is long overdue and might help to discourage the resort to force or arms that is currently so common.

As customary international law is developed from state practice, the best basis for development is a focus on the ways in which states, armed groups and proto-states actually behave rather than how current international law expects or requires them to behave. But some state and non-state practices are good and potentially a basis for customary law while some are not. The traditional view in international law is that general good practice by states must be accompanied by *opinio juris* – an acceptance that it is followed because it is thought to be legally required. But this is not always the way in which good practice becomes law. More often than not the process of legal development is also driven by moral argument from independent writers and campaigning by their supporters. Some notable examples in international humanitarian and human rights law are the campaigning by Henri Dunant leading to the initial Geneva Conventions, the speeches of Woodrow Wilson on the right of self-determination and recent campaigns on the prohibition and clearing of land mines.[88] Other significant legal developments such as the substance of

---

87   The need to make special provision for these 'ethnic frontier zones' in which members of different nations or ethnic communities share territory was developed by Frank Wright in *Northern Ireland: A Comparative Analysis* (Rowman and Littlefield 1988).

88   Protocol V on Explosive Remnants of War to the Convention on the Restriction of Certain Conventional Weapons, adopted on 28 November 2003 available at <https://documents-dds-ny.un.org/doc/UNDOC/GEN/G03/653/61/PDF/G0365361 .pdf?OpenElement> accessed 22 May 2021.

ARMED GROUPS AND EMERGENT STATES

the Paris Principles on National Human Rights Institutions,[89] the Abo Declaration on Minimum Humanitarian Standards[90] and the Belfast Guidelines on Amnesty and Accountability[91] have been initiated by collective groups of academics and practitioners. In the present context this is likely to be the best way forward for the development of international law on the rights and responsibilities of armed groups and emerging states.

The starting point should be coordinated documentation and analysis of current practice in respect of disputed/unrecognised territories or areas controlled by armed groups. This should be complemented by an analysis of how the armed groups and their de facto governments as well as other bodies, such as trade negotiators, international agencies and NGOs and their field officers, deal with practical problems on the ground with armed groups that control territory.

Some of the contributions to this collection have identified some patterns and some specific examples of these practices. As already noted, there is a tendency to assert that non-state armed groups and those controlling or administering stable territories have human rights obligations which in effect replace those of established states that have lost that control. These groups have also been encouraged by both internationally established bodies and non-governmental organisations to commit to the standards of conduct and governance that are expected of established states.[92] There is also well-established practice in negotiating cease-fires and wider peace settlements with armed groups and their political representatives despite the fact that they have been categorised as terrorists and included in internationally agreed lists of bodies with which no

---

89   Principles relating to the Status of National Human Rights Institutions (The Paris Principles), adopted by UNGA Res 48/134 of 20 December 1993.

90   Declaration of Minimum Humanitarian Standards, adopted by an expert meeting convened by the Institute for Human Rights, Åbo Akademi University, in Turku/ Åbo Finland, 2 December 1990.

91   Produced by an international group of lawyers and practitioner in 2013 and published by the Transitional Justice Institute at the University of Ulster, available at <www. ulster.ac.uk/__data/assets/pdf_file/0005/57839/TheBelfastGuidelinesFINAL_000 .pdf.> accessed 22 May 2021.

92   See e.g. Ezequiel Heffes and Marcos Kotlik, 'Special Agreements as a Way of Enhancing Compliance with IHL in Non-international Armed Conflicts: An Inquiry into the Governing Legal Regime' (2014) 96 *International Review of the Red Cross* 1195.

dealings should be contemplated or accepted.[93] There is similarly some emerging practice among international trade bodies to recognise and assist in the negotiation of trade and tariff arrangements between established and formally unrecognised territories.[94] At a lower level vehicle registration plates have been recognised for a number of formally unrecognised territories.[95]

A comprehensive collection, tabulation and categorisation of these practices and patterns is an essential prerequisite to securing general acceptance of new rules of customary and eventually conventional law. This documentation and analysis can lay the foundation for a set of agreed guidelines or best practice which should and could in time become customary or conventional law. As with other independent initiatives of this kind it will be important to entrust the work to an internationally balanced team of experienced legal and political participants with sufficient credibility and reputation to ensure that their proposals are taken seriously. The underlying conclusion of this article is that this development work cannot be left to representatives of established states and their lawyers since their primary commitment is to the maintenance of the current regime rather than to provide legal principles for the recognition and regulation of realities on the ground.

---

93   See PA-X Peace Agreements Database, compiled at the University of Edinburgh and available at <www.peaceagreements.org.> accessed 22 May 2021.

94   See the contribution by Marios Iacovides, 'Ambiguities in World Trade: WTO membership and Pragmatic Solutions to Trading with De Facto Independent Regimes' in this volume.

95   Vehicle registration plates for some disputed territories have been negotiated outside the official international system (for example with OSCE support in respect of Transnistria), see <https://en.wikipedia.org/wiki/Vehicle_registration_plates_of _Europe#Dependencies_and_disputed_territories> accessed 22 May 2021.